My Inspirations

My Inspirations

Gabriel Bekö

My Inspirations

By Gabriel Bekö

This book first published 2024

Publisher: BoD · Books on Demand GmbH, In de Tarpen 42,
22848 Norderstedt

Print: Libri Plureos GmbH, Friedensallee 273,
22763 Hamburg

Copyright © Gabriel Bekö 2024

All rights reserved.

ISBN: 978-8-7430-6003-1

Cover design by Gabriel Bekö with the help of AI image generator

I dedicate this book to Dalia and Jonatan

CONTENTS

PREFACE

The power of personal stories is indescribable. When we are asked about the most influential elements that have shaped our lives, most of us begin to search among the experiences and individuals that have left a mark on our decisions and our understanding of the world and ourselves. We try to recall what others have told us, how they have treated us, what they have taught us. Perhaps we tell other people's stories that have moved us, and by that we might move others.

What is a better place to begin examining personal inspirations if not one's own insignificant life and the numerous catalysts that shape it, especially when it feels worthy of appreciation? I sympathize with those readers who question the value of an ordinary chronicle of an uncelebrated author. However, an abundance of stories of prominent individuals exists, and examples from relatively unexceptional lives can be just as inspirational as those from extraordinary ones, if not more. They reflect the plenitude of opportunities for profound stimulations in our common lives.

My intention with this book was certainly not to exemplify the practicability and reasonability of the reflections previously described in my first book *Reflections on the World of Human Inspirations: In Search of Authenticity*, a work that was born as an originally unintended byproduct of writing the one you are holding in your hand. Nor was it to provide a recipe for a journey to enlightenment, which I must yet discover. This book could be understood, however, as the description of my personal journey that has led to the convictions presented in my earlier work.

The main sources of my inspirations can be grouped into two categories: history and encounters. History is an extremely complicated science, but it is the greatest of teachers. It is the foundation of the path to wisdom. To quote the great Cicero, *"Historia est testis temporum, lux veritatis, vita memoriae, magistra vitae, nuntia vetustatis,"* or "History is truly the witness of times past, the light of truth, the life of memory, the teacher of life, the messenger of antiquity".

Events of the world, news related to the causes we deeply care about, much of the information we deliberately seek to increase our understanding and learn about what reaches us without effort, whether it is political, ecological, social, humanitarian, technological, or of any other sort, all of it is part of history. So are facts and tales, chronicles and anecdotes, hardships, successes, and failures. We are part of history. Human history is generated by people (at least beyond what concerns pure nature, if anything of that sort is still left out there), and it impacts people. Global history encompasses personal histories. But it is not only about the well-known ones, it is not only about statesmen, poets, celebrities, or kings. It is especially about all of us, about the everyday lives of everyday people. It is our own little history within the grand history of the world that makes us who we are. We can't understand ourselves without understanding our past. It is this recognition that can help us draw inspirations that will steer our future toward a history we can be proud of.

Encounters inspire through the wonderful and the

dreadful we see, hear, and live through, the joy and suffering we experience or observe directly in the lives of others, the treatment we receive, the moments we wish never to forget, the ones we wish never came, and the ones that spark sudden realizations. Encounters are related to history; today's encounters are tomorrow's history.

The significant elements that seem to repeatedly surface throughout the book like a common thread through my inspirations are war, oppression, poverty, and other hardships that I did not suffer but the impacts of which I observed and always remained conscious and compassionate about. Another is my fascination with people, their stories, skills, capacities, and wisdom. They make me want to share them with others and facilitate interactions between people I know but are unknown to each other. I often feel the urge to make my unconnected acquaintances, distant and near, meet each other and make new, lasting connections. To care for my networks of colleagues, family, and friends, and connect their members, not least across these domains and across borders. True networking is less virtual than it is real, and it is not only to stay connected within a cohort, generate ideas, or forge collaborations but to bring diverse people closer to each other.

Inviting my closest colleagues to travel in my home country in the company of my parents, so the people I admire most could meet one another and take part in unforgettable adventures made unique by the composition of the group, is among my most cherished memories. As time passes and the notion of aging sinks in, my appreciation for friendships and other much valued personal connections is reaching a new level. I reflect on past acquaintances, identify faded and long-disappeared fellowships, track down people not seen for many, many years, reestablish connections, and continue where these were left off. This is one of the activities I find most fulfilling.

Caring for people's inner world is what brings true joy and improves lives. It even makes work more enjoyable and can facilitate a more successful professional life. Our humanity can advance our profession perhaps more than the other way around. Positive human interactions can do wonders. Smiles can be more powerful than academic publications, lectures, or fame, and when they go hand in hand, the impact is amplified. Smile elicits smile, kindness returns kindness. I remember telling myself in my teens that I wanted to be a person who always smiles at others. Did I just sense at that point the power of smile and the energy naturally joyful people can radiate? I leave it to others to judge whether I have succeeded in becoming one of them, but it may well be that smiles have been guiding my strongest inspirations. Could it be that this trigger of perception of a person's inner good, in combination with a sensation of trust, respect, and perhaps emotional safety, has had a profound influence on me throughout?

This book is an attempt to put the first forty years of my own history under the magnifying glass, extract the most memorable and influential moments that have led to an ocean of positive inspirations, and let them form part of the history of those whose interest they awaken. Let them inspire. The driving force behind each moment that touches our heart, puts a desire in our mind, kicks off a passion, and urges us to act is unique and personal. You may find some of my inspirations analyzed here absorbing or directly inspiring, others may be uninteresting or even disagreeable. It's fine, this is *my* story. But this book will transcend its descriptive character if it makes you think about your own story. Seek therefore the big picture, the guiding patterns. You may recognize some of them in your own life, or you may have different, more fascinating ones. Because our daily inspirations strongly depend on us, on the lives we lead, the environments we live in, the people we know, and the new acquaintances we obtain. I remain hopeful that my story will help you find yours.

Let this book inspire first of all you, my dear Jonatan and Dalia. This book has been written especially for you. May it serve as the starting point as you examine your own past and continue to shape what will become your own history.

September 2024

MY INSPIRATIONS

1

A TWENTIETH CENTURY ANCESTRY

"We cannot always build the future for our youth, but we can build our youth for the future."

–Franklin D. Roosevelt

The lives of my grandparents and my parents up until my first memories of them is to me just as much history as anything learned in history class. But it is a very special history because it offers what no school or book can offer. What it offers is an unparalleled step towards the understanding of my own life and towards the appreciation of its gifts, blessings, opportunities, and challenges, provided by the first-hand stories of the generation whose lives had been marked by a World War and whose hopes had been shattered by the Iron Curtain. It is a generation that more often fantasized about running with a suitcase than had the strength and courage to do so, and which finally saw the glamour of another world but only on TV and only to realize that dreams would remain dreams.

This generation, which learned to extract the best of what fate slipped in its path, turn it into success and happiness, and remain hopeful and contented, taught me to realize how fortunate I am, that nothing comes without a price, and that nothing, not peace nor prosperity, should be taken for granted. There are no guarantees issued for anyone. History is rich in abrupt, unnatural, and detrimental changes caused by few whose decisions can lead to societal shock and unexpected misery all too suddenly for way too many people. And although this general nature of the past millennia has been rather recently broken by rapid progress in the luckiest parts of the world, nobody can predict with certainty if and how long it will last. These realizations of mine were later reinforced by learning the fascinating history of another family, that of my better half. But let's start from the beginning.

My grandparents were teenagers or in their early twenties when Hitler and the Nazis plunged the world into one of its darkest periods. They lived in two neighboring small villages about thirty kilometers from the second largest city of Czechoslovakia, Bratislava. It was a significant distance at that time. They only made the one-hour horse carriage ride to the nearest town of Šamorín six kilometers away for basic necessities two to three times a month. Schooling was of little importance, working on the family farm was inherent. Later in life, boys often joined their fathers in their vocation. Getting married and becoming caring and diligent mothers and wives was all that was expected of girls. Indeed, both my grandmothers bore the flag on the household front in support of their husbands' battle for economic survival.

My maternal grandmother Erzsébet (Elisabeth in Hungarian, often shortened to Erzsi) came from a poor family living in the small village of Bacsfa (today Báč in southern Slovakia), just a stone's throw away from the Danube River. Both her parents worked at the nearby manorial court. Her father was the lord's carriage rider. It was said that the lord loved riding his horse and he could depart in any direction and ride for hours without leaving his lands. My great-grandfather loved to clean and prepare the carriage for the Sunday rides across the endless estates. He was proud of his service, which he performed with dignity. His wife, my great-grandmother, was a housemaid in the castle. The family was well respected and fairly treated by its employer. It was given a lovely home near the castle, a large piece of land to cultivate to their own benefit, and a pay. My grandmother retold in her nineties with a glitter of happiness in her eyes the stories of her friendship with the lord's children and the joys of countless hours of play with them. The years at the court were the best ones she remembered.

Erzsi became a housemaid herself and was serving in Budapest when World War II broke out. Her father was a man who would do anything to protect his family from more hardship. He did not hesitate to go and bring her home amidst shooting on the streets of Budapest. Erzsi was not allowed to return until the end of the war. When the war ended, however, the Beneš decrees led to plans of massive deportation of Hungarians from Czechoslovakia. Due to the lacking support of the Allies, the expulsion was later termed "population exchange". A different term for the same misery. As the sick and weak were said to be spared from deportation for the time being, my great-grandfather decided to take his chances and make himself turn ill. Family recollections refer to drinking something that made him suffer from high fever for weeks. The family remained rooted in Bacsfa until this day.

For no girl in Erzsi's shoes was education beyond the basic eight-year elementary school of any priority. There was instead plenty of motherly inspiration from my great-grandmother, whom I remember visiting frequently with my grandmother before she passed away when I was about seven. It was that traditional thousands of years old inspiration to become nothing less and nothing more than a good wife and mother by the time a girl was ready to establish her own family.

Erzsi married a very honest, warmhearted man named Vili Domonkos. They both attended the same school class, the only one available in the village. Vili was from a richer family of peasantry. His father owned hectares of fields and forests. Peasants with large land possessions were respectable members of the village society. They were saluted as manors or gentlemen, as family letters recently found in the attic of my grandmother's house confirm. Family history also indicates that earlier generations of the Domonkos family belonged among the nobility.

Vili's father was remembered as an arrogant man always wearing a uniform similar to that of the hussars (medieval Hungarian cavalry). It is said that one day he slapped a man from anger so hard that he became deaf in one ear. He feared nobody when his family needed protection. As the Russian liberators crossed the country towards the end of World War II, they were infamous for their desire for local girls. The soldiers were going from house to house meticulously looking high and low. My great-grandfather hid his daughter Etus in the haystack in the barn. The soldiers approached the house. After not finding anyone inside, one Russian approached the barn. He opened the door, entered, looked around but saw nobody. He started walking toward the haystack, as if he sensed something unusual about it. My great-grandfather then grabbed the pitchfork standing in the hay and told the Russian, "If you make one more step, I'll kill you". The soldier turned around and left the barn.

After southern Slovakia was annexed to Hungary following the First Vienna Award in 1938, Vili was not spared from being drafted into the Hungarian army, which fought on the side of Nazi Germany. He was sent to the Russian front, where he was taken prisoner of war. It is not known where this occurred, but it is fair to assume it was somewhere on the Leningrad–Moscow–Stalingrad line (St. Petersburg–Moscow–Volgograd today), which was as far as the German war campaign reached on the Eastern Front.

Vili was released after the war and began the arduous walk home from wherever in the Soviet Union he may have been at the time of his release. Only a few survived the journey and reached their home in re-established Czechoslovakia. The long and grueling walk took months. Food was so scarce on the way that Vili often tried to dig up roots from the ground and feed himself with anything that resembled food. Weighing forty kilograms, he collapsed when he finally reached the gate of his father's house—the house where he and Erzsi lived for the rest of their lives. Erzsi passed away in this house in 2020.

Few years later, this part of my family too was standing on the platform waiting for the train that would deport them to Hungary. Nobody in the family knows what the reason was that at the last moment they were told not to board the train and return home. Vili and Erzsi got one more chance to fall in love with each other. But their love would be put to the test again and again. Vili's parents opposed the marriage on grounds of social and economic differences between the two families, but he never gave up on her. The following years brought further challenges caused by the unkindness of Vili's parents towards Erzsi. She soldiered on through decades, until she finally earned more respect from her mother-in-law than what her mother-in-law had for her own daughters.

My grandfather learned peasantry from his father. High education wasn't a priority even among those whose land ownership secured a certain social status. His peasant career was hindered by the war. Soon after the war the communists came to power and the family properties were lost to collectivization. Everything was confiscated apart from modest homes. Lands, forests, cattle, horses, agricultural equipment, all had to be turned in for the benefit of the state. The wealthy Kuchta family was moved out of the castle, most likely into one unit in a concrete block of state-built flats provided as compensation. Vili was given employment in the newly established, state-owned United Agricultural Cooperative. There he was very successful. He adapted to the circumstances, he set goals, loved his work and did it the best he could. He was skilled and talented, but, most of all, he was determined to succeed. Year after year he was decorated as the most productive employee of the union. He received thirteenth and fourteenth salary bonuses. Nobody could achieve bigger yields on the pig farm. Nobody could make a sow farrow more piglets than the ones in his care. He fostered his state-owned pigs with love.

Vili and Erzsi created a home of harmony, love, wisdom, strong moral values, and faith. They raised their two daughters in a happy family environment despite the challenges that politics, society, and its often outdated but changing traditions put in their way. Economic progress also followed. They were now able to enjoy modest vacations, and they were the first ones in the village to own a car and a black-and-white TV. Villagers used to gather in their house to watch the first broadcasts in the 1960s. And while Vili was the breadwinner, had authority and enjoyed respect in the house, Erzsi oversaw the economy. She was wise with money, she always asked her husband for approval of her spending, but she never got no for an answer.

Auntie Katica was a distant relative of Vili living in Bratislava. She remained unmarried and lived with her father in an elegant, old-fashioned house with a stylish antique interior. They were a typical example of what was left of the pre-war aristocracy, so-called *Prešporáci*, citizens of Prešporok. Prešporok was the name of Bratislava before 1919, which originated from its German name Pressburg from the times when most citizens of the "Beauty on the Danube" in the Austro-Hungarian Empire spoke both Hungarian and German.

Katica was always elegantly dressed, wore a brooch in her hair, had her favorite café in town and a brother in Vienna, behind the Iron Curtain. After her father died, she felt the house was too big for her. Vili encouraged her to sell it and move to the countryside. He built a one-room extension to the house for her, and Katica moved in with a few pieces of furniture and a sewing machine. She was a tailor, and she had a well-established clientele.

My mother used to sit by her sewing machine and watch her work. This was the time when her passion for fashion began to develop. The desire to create something as beautiful as a dress of the latest fashion, or perhaps even dictate what people call fashion, grew in her. She decided to study tailoring, a school that would not finish with a graduation certificate. Vili, a devoted reader of books about geography, history, and animals, demanded that both his daughters graduate from secondary school. But my mother had one dream in her mind only, and there was nothing that could deter her. She became an exceptionally good tailor. With passion for vocation inherited from her father, she was the best in class, and everyone quickly realized her talents. She followed the latest fashion at home and abroad and created whatever garment she wished to wear regardless of whether there was understanding for it or not in the countryside. Envious ladies in the village used to call her "the clown".

My mother felt that her profession was different from those of most other women around her, many of whom out there, away from the big cities, were trained sales assistants or waitresses. (These professions weren't reserved for students, but, unlike today, they were respected and required professional training). She sensed the element of creativity and art in her work. She decided to study fashion design at a boarding school in the remote town of Trenčín, the capital of the Czechoslovak textile industry and fashion. In the meantime, however, she fell in love and followed her heart and dream to establish a family instead of a career. After giving birth to my brother and me, she continued to feel the inspiration to address another dream of hers—teaching her profession. She desperately needed a high school graduation certificate to be able to study at a higher education institute. She pursued a distance learning program and left the family every Saturday for five years to study economy at high school level, which would guarantee her the much-needed graduation diploma and her father's ultimate satisfaction and pride. She would leave us subsequently every Saturday for another two years to obtain a pedagogical degree qualifying her to teach tailoring.

Mom's talent was best demonstrated by the way I dressed throughout my childhood. I was always the most modernly clothed kid in class. Sometimes scandalously modern. My mother used to sew clothes for the family based on the German fashion magazine *Burda*, which was a couple of years ahead of the Eastern Bloc fashion. It wasn't always fun though. I remember the elegant wide beige pants with green stripes, which earned me a mockery for going to school in what my classmates saw as "pajamas". But my brother and I had every stylish rag one could ever wish for, and it only cost my parents the price of the material.

My paternal grandmother Julianna (known to people as Juli) and her sister were orphans. Their mother died early, and their father remarried. The stepmother refused to accept the girls in her new household and demanded her husband to abandon them. As hideous as such a relation between a father and his daughters may sound nearly a century later, he agreed. The girls were adopted by their mother's family. Juli's sister was in Budapest during World War II. Lacking the kind of love and care of a father that my other grandmother enjoyed, there was no savior coming for Juli's sister. Her dream to become a nun never materialized. Juli lived the rest of her life with the knowledge that her sister was first raped then either killed or she committed suicide in Budapest.

Juli obtained her elementary school education before the war. She married my grandfather Jani in early 1946, soon after the war had ended and after having known him for a mere three months. They settled in the first house of the village twenty minutes' walk away from my mother's family. Juli began to carry out what was expected of a woman in the country at that time. To take care of the household and the small farm and raise their two sons and a daughter. The marriage wasn't a happy one. I never saw my grandparents sharing a bedroom or speaking particularly nicely to each other. Juli was submissive, Jani was rough. They were the antipodes of my maternal grandparents; their relation was stormy, their home untidy.

Jani, born in 1918, learned carpentry after completing elementary education. He was inclined to personal growth. He was a very skilled carpenter with a profound love for math, which he was proud of. He often flashed with unaided multiplication of two double-digit numbers. His friends liked to double-check him, but he failed rarely. His qualities were soon recognized, and he was promoted to group leader.

Jani had also fought in the Hungarian army and was captured by the Soviets. He was another of the very few fortunate ones who survived the thousands of kilometers long walk home across devastated land. After the war, he set up his own business. He was a carpentry master, and he trained apprentices. The communists, who had recently come to power, classified him for his initiative as a *slave owner*, *capitalist*, *bourgeois*, or something unwanted of that sort. It didn't take much those days, after the Vienna Award became void in 1947, to be jailed or killed if one was a Hungarian in the newly recreated Czechoslovakia. Jani was jailed in 1950 on a fabricated charge of exploiting his apprentices. At the time my father was born, Jani was in prison, and Juli had to handle my five-year old uncle and the birth of my father on her own. Jani was soon after bailed out. It took him several years to repay his benefactor, a distant relative.

From the late 1950s and early 1960s group leader positions held by Jani demanded appropriate secondary education. Vocational secondary schools with graduation and a diploma equivalent to a high school degree started to be common in the late 1950s. Jani realized that he could benefit from such a degree. After five years of distance learning, he graduated from a secondary school for civil engineering around the age of forty. He became the leader of the construction group for one of the agricultural cooperatives. Feeling the joy of all aspects of construction, he continued to design buildings and supervise their completion. He revised stress analysis exercises from school over the years to come, to make sure he wouldn't forget what he had learned in the field of statics.

Although Jani began working in the building construction business, and vaulted wooden roofs became increasingly uncommon with the new government program to conserve forests, he never gave up his original profession, carpentry. He has been recognized throughout his life as one of the best carpenters in the region. And one of the best singers of Hungarian folk songs, which men sang every evening in the local tavern after a few beers and *stampedli* (shots of spirits). It didn't happen often that he came home sober from the pub during those final years that I remember with him. He continued to work until a few weeks before his death from liver cancer at the age of seventy-five.

For decades after Jani's death, I occasionally met someone who proudly said that he had known my grandfather. The master barber in one of my hometown's barber shops used to recognize me immediately when I entered. He asked me if I was the son of Tibor or Zoltán since Jani's two sons resemble each other nearly indistinguishably. "Your grandfather was a great man," he used to say. "I am proud to have known him many years ago, that old master who knew what it takes to be a master in craftsmanship," he added. Jani was one of the very few who always saluted him with the distinguishing title *master*. The barber never let me go without adding that the region has not seen a man who could sing more folk songs than Jani, nor who could sing with the sentimentality only he could perform.

In their teens, my father and his brother routinely helped with various private carpentry and construction projects that Jani was hired to complete over the weekends. From sheds and barns to house roofs and church tower reparations, skilled hands were always in demand, and extra income was never to be refused. As the boys grew older, they weren't short of money. Jani shared the profit of the day equally.

By the time my parent's generation entered teenage years, it became inherent to continue to study after elementary school. My uncle Zoltán continued in his father's footsteps and studied civil engineering at a technical secondary school. My father Tibor often visited his five years older brother in the dormitory in Bratislava and listened in awe as Zoltán praised his school, its new premises, and all the excitement he experienced as a diligent student in the big city. Zoltán was a good student, and he later aspired to enroll at the technical university, although he would decide not to complete the program three years into his undergraduate studies.

Tibor naturally followed his brother and father in their endeavor to study civil engineering. After graduating from the civil engineering program of a technical secondary school in Bratislava, he was also enrolled in a university program, but at that time their sister Éva was about to start secondary school. The first intention was to make her become a civil engineer as well, but my grandmother rejected the idea. Éva attended a secondary boarding school of economics. Jani couldn't support both Tibor's college studies and his sister's boarding school. Éva graduated and worked as an administrator over the decades to come. My father never regretted not having a college degree.

My parents' and their siblings' education were in line with the average trends at the time. It was higher than that of their parents, but a university degree was still rare and highly regarded. Their education resulted from societal and family inspiration to climb to higher rungs of the then existing social ladder. It is noteworthy that nearly all grandchildren (nine out of ten) of my paternal and maternal grandparents have obtained a university degree. There are among us engineers, teachers, a linguist, a lawyer, an environmentalist, and a doctor. None of us feels special in any way for having a college or university degree in an age when not having one almost seems more awkward.

The Warsaw Pact invasion of Czechoslovakia on the night of 20–21 August 1968 was not a very dramatic event for my father. The tanks appeared one day standing on the squares of Bratislava, and they would remain there over the weeks following the invasion. Tibor and his friends found it amusing to talk to the uninterested soldiers. On the other hand, my mother was just twelve when a rumbling noise woke her and her sister in the middle of the night. Their house stood next to a major road leading to the Hungarian border. The parents were on vacation in Hungary, and Vili's sister Vinci (Vincencia) came from Budapest to look after the girls. When Vinci woke up, she immediately recognized the noise that was so clear in her memories from a quarter century earlier. "These are tanks," she said to the girls.

They were afraid to go out on the street, so they sneaked instead along the fence to the end of the backyard, from where the view of the road winding through the village was clear. "The Russians have invaded your country," Vinci added. Next morning the villagers went cheerfully out to the road and waved to the passing soldiers, not understanding the consequences of this historic day. What mattered to my family most was that Vili and Erzsi were unable to return from Hungary, and Vinci could not go back to Budapest for another two weeks.

Tibor was spending the summer of 1969 undertaking an internship in West Germany organized by the technical secondary school he was attending. The experience was an eye-opener. Observing technical progress, discipline, strict rules, and a culture of thrift taught him things he wouldn't see in Czechoslovakia for decades to come. He learned to respect his work and do it with utmost devotion and perfection. I've heard my father referring to that summer endless times. The items, values, lifestyle, attitudes that arrived in the East during the years after 1989 would strike him like *déjà vu*. When his colleagues later in his professional life protested the implementation of new company rules, when a new technology had to be adopted, or when he noticed a "Western solution" on a construction site while walking on the street, he noted, "I have seen this when I studied in West Germany in '69. It took a while for it to arrive."

One day after his return from West Germany, my father met a couple of friends in the local pub. Naturally, he described the experience and his impressions with enthusiasm. He talked about the technical advancements, about the lessons to be learned from the sense of responsibility and attitude he had never seen before, but also from the scrimping and saving he did not expect in his wildest dreams to see in the West, which he observed as being far beyond what he was used to back home. A few days later the secret police knocked on the door. He was taken to a long interrogation about his stay in the West and its effect on him. Eavesdropping ears were everywhere, and intimidation was a common method to deter from opposing the communist ideology. The 1969 experience was supposed to reoccur in 1970, but it was prevented by the consequences of Alexander Dubček's Prague Spring and the subsequent invasion of Czechoslovakia by the Soviet Union and the Warsaw Pact countries.

My father obtained many of his personal qualities during the mandatory two-year military service that followed his graduation. I never heard him speak of the service in negative terms. He always considered this period of Cold War era service during his late teens critical for his personal development. It was here that he tasted the power of compliance, diligence, and learning. He continues to be proud and thankful for the inspirational years that "turned boys into men and taught men discipline."

He climbed the ladder in the military quickly especially because of his sense of obedience and discipline. His superiors realized his organizational and communication skills and sent him to a military school. He became an officer within a few months and with that his military years turned into years of freedom, independence, and fun. He was gaining new skills with his responsibilities, which he learned to handle with ease. He learned to deal with those of both higher and lower ranks as he tried to please both and deliver what was required of him. He became one of the most trusted comrades for many of his superiors, who did not hesitate to share with him the most intimate challenges of professional military life. These insider views proved to be crucially important for resisting the convincing pressure towards a professional military career. The skills gained in the military happened to be essential especially later, when the political and societal situation took a hundred-eighty-degree turn in

1989. In the early 1990s, when state companies, including the one where my father worked as a construction project manager, were dismantled as a result of privatization shortly after the fall of communism, he established a private construction company, which would secure an economically comfortable life for our family.

>«

I enrolled in kindergarten at the age of five, one year before school. In that first and last year of kindergarten, we learned about the greatness of Lenin, evilness of the imperialist capitalist Western powers, and the honorability of our saviors, the Soviets. It was never too early to be engulfed in the communist brainwashing. We drew the Soviet flag next to the flag of the Czechoslovak Socialistic Republic, and we used to sketch Aurora, the battleship that signaled the beginning of the Great October Socialist Revolution of 1917, which actually took place in November, at least according to the Gregorian calendar.

In primary school, we held a two-day civil defense practice twice a year. We learned about air-raid precautions, gas masks, and first aid. Every child was infused with the dream to advance on the communist ladder, starting with becoming *iskra* at the age of six (meaning *spark*, an early childhood scout organization), then *pioneer* (communist boy scouts wearing red scarfs), then member of *Sväzarm* (union for cooperation with the army; a more advanced movement but still reminiscent of the boy scouts), and finally member of the Communist Party, the ultimate, well-deserved honor after all the precursors. We were provided with plenty of powerful inspiration necessary to have a bright future under the system that was never meant to fail.

This western part of the then Eastern Europe, in which I was growing up, was not exactly the bottom of the world during my life's first decade, which coincided with communism's last decade, before the region began its transition to become the eastern part of the Western world. Putting ideology aside, the rate of progress and the slowly but steadily increasing standard of living provided a comfortable life with an enjoyable, even if at times dishonest, culture to the majority. The years of westernization that followed were for most people many times more arduous and devastating. Many even today are nostalgic about the days of communism, as the abrupt changes are still in the memory of all but the youngest. But the transition has been far better than what many other nations, such as the former Yugoslavia, Romania, or those in the Caucasus or Central Asia, had to endure.

My parents created a safe and healthy environment to grow up in. My father secured the income and the necessary material needs we may have had. He demonstrated every day that honest hard work pays off in every society, even where it may seemingly be discouraged. He worked in a large state construction corporation during the day, and in the evenings and weekends he tended everything else that required attention or could raise our living standard. He fixed the house, cultivated peach, paprika, and watermelons for sale on lands of substantial size belonging to my grandparents, he produced hundreds of liters of wine, helped friends and family with their construction projects and manufactured everything that was needed but was difficult or too expensive to obtain. He studied to the very last detail, designed, and then built on his own or with the help of friends his trailers, furniture, kennel, paprika grinding machine, grill, smokehouse, sausage stuffer, grape destemmer, wine press, and nearly everything else around the household that was needed or required replacement.

He could not rest until what came to his mind was completed. He obtained the necessary knowledge from books and from the best experts he could find in the country, or sometimes beyond its borders, and then he performed the task for the first time. And then again and again, improving with every iteration. Until today he knows only one type of attitude to every challenge: perfectionism through knowledge and rigor. He demanded the same attitude from his children. When I wished for a dog, I first received books. One about the various breeds, another about dog training and care. Only after conquering the theory and understanding the responsibilities was I allowed to obtain a dog, which came with the obligation to put the knowledge into practice.

My father must be one of the most inspired people I ever knew. He becomes excited from everything he hears and sees. New ideas, goals, and solutions are constantly flooding his mind. He sets several new goals for himself every day, some being simple ones, others complicated long-lasting projects, but he burns for all of them equally. My brother Adrian and I used to be involved in many of his personal projects. Once our homework was ready after school, we were asked to help with everything we could help with and learn what we could not. We assisted in painting, farming, wine making, changing windows, mixing and casting concrete, building a terrace, a formwork, a roof, a summer house, and more.

My mother was the family's equal-load-bearing second backbone. She single-handedly managed, as a full-time engagement, the entire household and most of the everyday child-raising. She woke us up in the morning, prepared breakfast and the snack box for school, she awaited our arrival with the most incredible warm lunches every day, helped with the homework, played with us, talked to us, listened to our joys and worries, read us good night stories, and put us to bed. She drew posters of our favorite cartoon characters, spent days and nights designing and sewing the most wonderful pieces of garments and costumes for carnivals (as in my father's case, things were preferred to be made, not purchased), cared for us when we were sick. On Sundays, she drove us to church and to visit our grandparents. During the summer months, she took part in every moment of the family's intense land cultivation efforts.

Throughout my early years in elementary school, she meticulously checked every day if we learned everything we were supposed to know the next day in school. She skimmed through the last topic in my book, tested me orally, and called out every detail that I missed in my summary talk. If I had missed a considerable number of important facts, she asked me to read the chapter a few more times and try to summarize again a little later. Skipping school was hardly an option. Mom always objected when dad insisted that we join him on one of his enjoyable business trips. Coming home from school with a B for a test or a quiz was frowned upon. With her double- and triple-check technique the day before, getting a B was simply not fancy. Maybe she felt it reflected her imperfection as much as mine.

Both my parents were inspired by the benefits of the family arrangement (gender roles, as it is termed today) they grew up in, rather than by what became the norm in the meantime—the two working parents. My grandfathers were the breadwinners, they secured an income, which they then usually passed on to their wives. They had the authority and could have had the final word if they wanted to, but in the end things happened as their wives quietly wished for. My grandmothers took care of the children, their moral development, the household, yard with the livestock, the fruit and vegetable production, all the non-monetary income of equal importance. Their husbands brought the badly needed cash, but they ensured it lasted until the end of the month. Whenever they needed to buy something out of the ordinary, like new shoes for the children or a jacket for their husbands, they discussed it with their husbands, who first questioned the necessity but never really objected.

I grew up in a period of political indetermination when communist socialism was replaced by capitalism, via something anarchistic between the two. All these forms of society embraced the equality and liberation of women. Communism did so maybe even more vigorously than capitalism, at least in theory. Marxist feminism even accused capitalist economy with the oppression of women. In reality, gender equality in communism was something of an illusion. With whatever came after communism came undoubtedly more feminism, often in its radical form. Rather unsurprisingly, therefore, I don't remember feeling any inequality between men and women while growing up. Neither did I feel inequality between my parents and their roles even though my mother never had a real job. How could I feel any? It was their joint decision, and I only benefited from it as a child.

My father worked tirelessly to secure an income that covered the family's needs and wishes while my mother worked around the clock with everything else. The two completed one another. Their importance and respect towards each other's contribution was identical. The productive labor (financially compensated) and the reproductive labor (seemingly uncompensated) had equal weights, and they elicited equal hardships and pride. My father was proud of the house he had built and his extra diligence that secured a comfortable life for the family, while my mother was proud of a perfectly kept household, children performing well in school under her guidance, the neat record-yielding garden, clothing hand-made according to the latest fashion, always fresh food, and a larder of plenty. Significant income generation without a pay slip. A healthy diet never required attention, as its opposite wasn't known at home. It wasn't much that we needed to get from the grocery store, and the words *organic, ecological,* or *processed food* entered my vocabulary only in adulthood.

Although my father was the primary authority in the family, both parents appreciated each other's indispensable roles with a sense of respect. Despite their differences, occasional quarrels, and my father's wish to see my mother spend more time on self-education, I heard mom often speak highly of dad and dad describe mom innumerable times as the most wonderful wife anyone can wish for, one with qualities I may want to look for when searching one day for a spouse of my own. It wasn't rare that other men, colleagues or friends, asked dad where and how he managed to find such an admirable partner.

Accepting distinct gender roles did not give our family less financial freedom, and it took away a lot of the stress often caused when busy work schedules must be combined with children's school activities, daycare opening and closing times, sick leaves, caring for elderly parents, appointments with authorities, and all other private issues that must be taken care of. Planning days off and vacations was easier, unnecessary temptations were minimized. And there was time and consideration for the many aspects important for the maintenance of a harmonious family environment and a healthy relationship between children and parents, for openness, communication, play, spirituality, exercises of attentiveness, diligence, and responsibility. My parents set their priorities, and they never doubted them.

Most if not all my schoolmates' mothers were working and sharing the household duties with their husbands, just like most parents do today. When we had to fill in elementary school a form with our parents' occupation, I didn't feel proud to write next to my mother's name the word *housewife*. But I was proud of not having to eat in the school canteen most kids complained about or stay in after-school, and I loved being instead welcomed home by mom, who was waiting with freshly cooked meal right after classes. My case was enviable among the kids. And so was my mother's case among many of the mothers.

These were remnants of the past social structure, which people remembered from their childhood and which some were still able to identify with. But it was no longer the trend, it wasn't always affordable, and with increasing material wealth and expectations they often lacked the inspiration and drive to live by it and recognize its luxury. Both my parents believed that this division of duties would be the best for the togetherness and happiness of the family and for the prosperity of their children. It has paid off, and although it is far not the only factor that affects the integrity of a marriage (if it does at all), I value it even more when I realize that many of the families that used to be around us in my childhood are no longer functional, complete families.

Even at an advanced age, mom and dad continue to be as hard-working from early morning till late evening as one can only imagine, entirely for their own pleasure and for the benefit of the family. Dad builds, fixes what needs to be fixed (sometimes even what doesn't), and secures a more-than-enough income that he generously spends on his children and grandchildren, who are not in need of it. Mom prepares magical holidays and frequent family feasts, maintains the tidiest, wonderfully decorated residence and its ornamental garden, and cultivates a five-hundred-square-meters land, where she grows almost every kind of vegetable that can grow in the south Slovakian climate (and that is a lot) in an amount sufficient for the family during most of the year. More than a hundred jars of her pickled fruits and vegies stand in the larder at any time.

My grandparents worked sedulously not only until the day of retirement but until the day they could no longer move or take care of themselves. In their footsteps, my parents love to work all the time, try to get better at what they do, fulfil their duties, make new ones, and enjoy the products of their diligence. Tangible and intangible products. Wealth was never a topic or a lifestyle in our home. "Work ennobles man," used to be the motto.

Conversations involving money were mostly conducted in the spirit of saving regardless of sufficiency. Minimize expenses, avoid unnecessary spending. Mom sewed most of our clothes, which were more fashionable than anything available on the COMECON market. We were taught to switch off the lights when leaving a room in the house or pay a small fine into a common money saver. And when we wanted a new bike or came up with a wish of similar extent, we were given the chance to earn its price first.

There was always plenty of opportunity to help against a little payment. After dad came home from work, we used to go to our peach orchard, vineyard, paprika field, or watermelon rows, which provided the legally untaxable, generous second income and pocket money for my brother and me every time we walked to the roadside with a couple of boxes and a balance to sell the produce to the passersby. Later we were paid by square meter of paint job, by hour of construction work, by the number of completed festoons when stringing up paprika to air-dry, or by the number of bricks when cleaning them from mortar for reuse after a demolition. It was not child labor but learning the real value of money, the respect for the effort it takes to earn it, and towards everything it provides. On the other hand, one way or another, we always got everything we wished for. Either by saving up for it or by patiently waiting for a birthday or Christmas. Sometimes as a surprise on a completely ordinary day. We were never denied an optional school trip or an extracurricular activity of our choice, from occasional dance lessons in school to joining a fencing club over many years.

Our lives began to change when I entered the teenage years. Puberty wasn't the main reason though. Adrian and I got a little sister, and at about the same time our country embarked on a long journey from throwing away its Eastern legacy to becoming part of the new West, a journey from communism to capitalism. Soon after, Czechoslovakia split into two countries, and we were on the side believed to be more disadvantaged, poorer, and much less favored by the world around. State corporations slowly disappeared, and my father decided to establish his own construction company. There was a lot more insecurity, more stress, and longer working hours.

Dad usually worked around sixteen hours a day, six to seven days a week. He continued to enjoy his job but at a different level. Instead of leading large public building construction projects, he was now responsible for every aspect of his business that focused mainly on family house construction and renovation. Securing new projects, convincing the customers that what they desired was flawed and could be improved, preparing price offers, negotiating blueprints, obtaining materials and subcontractors, writing invoices, calculating employee salaries, hiring, and firing, arranging team building events, solving his employees' private problems and a myriad of technical details on site every day, everything was part of the job description.

His technical, intellectual, and leadership qualities, but especially his adaptability, were remarkable. He continued to learn by the minute. There is no other way when you live in a newly formed state that decides to change course by a hundred-eighty degrees and develop a new political and economic system while lacking the experience of doing so. Coping with constant changes in legislation and the economy and the sudden oversupply of the market with new and often dubious technologies and products was a challenge. Dad visited just about every civil engineering fair in Central Europe over the coming years, and every time he came home with hundreds of pamphlets and brochures about various products and unique solutions. He loved especially the ideas collected in Austria and Germany, which were not yet known in Slovakia.

No matter how tiring it was, dad loved the new challenge. The results of his everyday efforts were perceptible, and the satisfaction of the investors and future house owners kept him going. Honesty and fairness towards those who trusted him and towards his employees was extremely important to him. When generosity towards employees was generally being replaced with exploitation, he treated his employees with Christmas bonuses and free wine tours to Hungary. Already back when he was project manager in the state construction company, he raised the wages of his on-site team leaders above what company policy permitted, even if he had to regularly defend the necessity of the extra expenses in front of his bosses. He believed that the additional effort and responsibility deserved supplemental financial compensation, and he understood how much all of this meant for quality.

What mattered most to him was the unparalleled quality, which he demanded from everyone, especially himself. Service providers usually claim that they are satisfied when their customers are happy. My father was pleased only when he knew there wasn't the slightest possibility the customer could ever question anything he delivered, whether visible or hidden in the construction. This was true about the price as well. He believed that hard work, honesty, generosity, and humbleness in business can provide utmost quality at the most competitive price.

He refused to build what he saw regrettable, and his reputation entitled him to do so. When he saw the blueprints of a new project, he often advised the investors first to re-design the building from scratch, to make it habitable by his standards. Future building owners were eventually grateful for a much better product than they initially envisioned. When dad was happy with the job, there was nothing the customer could possibly complain about.

He was perhaps fortunate to live in an era and society in which young people had the opportunities to work their way up on the professional ladder by learning on the job, and certificates and diplomas didn't have the weight they have today. The experience and expertise he gained over the years became highly respected and envied by many engineers around him, despite his lack of a university degree. He did not receive a major claim for repair in the nearly twenty-five years he ran the company. Over the last decade, despite significant economic downturns brought about by the 2008 financial crisis, he had to turn down orders instead of chasing new ones.

Diligence, honesty, and quality prevail in an ideal world. But it was not so certain in the world we were living in. In the 1990s honesty began to be a unique feature in business, unqualified yet strong competition emerged, and longevity was in jeopardy without the use of corrupt methods. Many private company owners were visited by what people called the *mafia*. Dubious personal protection companies promised to ensure that nothing would happen to those entrepreneurs and their families if they paid a monthly fee or handed over a substantial share of the turnover, but they could not guarantee their safety otherwise. They could guarantee big problems though. Many small companies went out of business due to this practice. There was nothing one could do about it, with authorities, including the police, being corrupt or scared to act.

My father never liked to display success or act as a company owner and director. He did not use advertisements, the company cars had no company logo on them, he kept his office at home, and he did not put up the company name on the hardly noticeable commercial building, which he built in a small countryside village. He drove an old car, usually just as worn and dirty as the ones his employees drove to the construction sites. When he treated our family to a new car, he continued to use the old one for work, just to make his employees feel that he was one of them. He considered showing modesty and equality an important part of company morale.

Many changes were forced upon the family by the life the new post-communist age brought along. Farming, wine making, peach harvest, or pig slaughter were discontinued forever. The Club, an active union of friends from the days of their bachelorhood, which my father belonged to, ceased to exist. The Club used to meet regularly to discuss everything men love to talk about and to enjoy moments of high spirits. It also organized canoeing, goulash cooking, and pig roasting events for the members' families. But in the post–Cold War world of stress and work around the clock, time for such pleasures was no longer to be found. Human relations were changing, and they often disappeared as economic incentives moved to the forefront of priorities. Our family felt it firsthand. My father and his brother established the company together, but their fundamentally different work ethics and personalities made their relationship deteriorate. A decade passed after my uncle left the company before the brothers were able to talk to each other again.

Everybody in the family became involved in the business. Mom helped with the paperwork and other secretarial tasks. Adrian and I earned most of our pocket money working on the various construction sites during the summer. As soon as we obtained a driver license, dad asked us to drive employees, transport supplies, deliver documents. When our sister Valika became a teenager, she decided to try manual labor during a few summers too.

After Adrian and I embarked on our civil engineering studies at the university, we were gradually given more professional tasks like preparing technical drawings, calculating material needs, writing reports, or performing on-site checks. We studied civil engineering, and we lived civil engineering. We learned a great deal from each other. Dad profited from our access to experts at the university, and we benefited from his immense experience and the opportunity to see and try out in the field things we had heard in the classroom. The three of us often spent hours discussing blueprints, designs, and technical solutions, sometimes only because we enjoyed hearing each other's opinions and ideas.

Dad prided himself on the fact that he started the company "with two shovels and a hammer taken from home". But he worked incredible hours even as the business began to run more smoothly, as mom took over some of the paperwork, a bookkeeper the economics, and the new company building was packed with the necessary equipment, cars, truck, building materials, all collected little by little without any mortgage ever being considered. Dad only allowed himself as much as he could afford. Banks and financial institutions weren't to be trusted.

The extra work hours and the capital saved were not turned into expression of wealth and representation. Dad used to tell us that he could probably afford a big fat Mercedes, or two, or three, but what a stupid thing it would be to drive one. Instead, he invested in the company, in his children's future, in daily pleasures, primarily traveling, cultural events, and cherishing friendships, and of course in his passion—construction, construction, beloved construction. Work was his hobby. He renovated and re-renovated our house, refurbished the summer house, built another company building, and another one and another one, which he never really needed. Fabrication was a safer way to preserve the savings than dealing with the banks. And it meant a lot of fun too.

He did not wish the company to grow, and he wasn't dreaming that his children would one day take over the family business. He was hoping that we would choose an easier career, a more cultured one, which does not rely on daily work with people with relatively low intellectual qualities and a weak sense of responsibility, as, he felt, was often the case with his laborer employees. Since his departure from the managerial position in the ill-fated state firm, he considered that part of his new job the most challenging especially because he never allowed quality to be compromised. Dad often emphasized the fact that losing the daily contact with intellectuals he could continuously learn from and whose educated opinions he could always count on while working at the state firm came as the biggest blow when the political changes forced him to start his own company. Now he had to work much harder for information and knowledge, especially general, all-embracing knowledge and enlightening discussions unrelated to work, than when it was readily available and always present among colleagues.

In the 1990s dad enjoyed playing with the property restitutions. He didn't only look at the properties his parents and my mother's parents were now entitled to, almost half a century after the communists nationalized all private property, including horses, cattle, and farming equipment. He took great pleasure in looking in the archives and identifying the rightful owners of pieces of land around the town, some perhaps attractive but now being desolate no man's lands. When he set his mind to buying one, the delight was in tracking down those current owners who a generation or two after nationalization had no idea about the possessions they suddenly had the right to claim.

He commonly ran into the difficulty of having to find a whole family tree of descendants of the original owners from the middle of the twentieth century. This resulted in numerous emotional experiences, from announcing old and poor individuals that they were actually rich to wholeheartedly reuniting across the Slovak-Hungarian border siblings that had not known about each other's existence. Mom and dad eagerly described these fascinating incidents, which had so much power to teach and inspire.

I always found it hard to understand how dad could do so much with his time. As if he stretched the twenty-four-hour days to be twice so long. On top of the already overwhelming business-related duties came the tasks to please everyone who relied on his personal contacts and advice. Making phone calls to find out things on behalf of others, picking up a carful of homemade goodies from his butcher friend to distribute among his other friends, collecting the cassettes with the complete Beatles collection that he asked a music loving friend to prepare for me when he heard that I was becoming a fan, or making one of the frequent visits to friends, acquaintances, and relatives who asked him to come over, look at the house, and give recommendations regarding refurbishment. Needless to point out that it never crossed his mind to charge for such services.

The number of tasks he is still able to complete with unconditional élan, enthusiasm, and vigor on a daily basis continues to impress everyone, including me. Many are self-imposed tasks; he never hesitates to offer his assistance when he knows he could be helpful. He has always found the time and energy for every favor asked of him. He rarely says no and never forgets a request. Dozens of bullet points are on his to-do list every day. What gets on the list does not disappear until it is completed. Whatever isn't completed one day, is rewritten to the next day's list.

When asked what drove him to work sixteen hours a day for nearly five decades, my father gives a simple answer—family. His goal was not to accumulate wealth or establish a dynasty of successful civil engineers. He simply wished his family to enjoy a little more than the average citizens did, to maintain that quality of life, secure for his children an easier start on the journey into adult life regardless of the unforeseeable political and economic challenges and achieve all this while staying with his feet on the ground.

Seeing him working with the same engagement after turning seventy, when he enjoys a hard-earned and well-deserved financial security and his children have moved out of the nest and into that adulthood he's helped so much to start off, it must be said that another reason for his tireless diligence has probably been the passion for usefulness, accomplishment, fulfilment, and satisfaction of his endless inspirations. He constantly works especially because he loves to work, to be productive, to set goals, and he enjoys when those goals are achieved. Every time his family warns him of the effects of stress, he argues that he never knew what stress was and has never felt its effects. Perhaps this is the case after all because of his love and enthusiasm for everything he does, and because in much of it there is a good dose of challenge and learning and an element of giving and sharing.

»«

My father loved to spend quality time with his children. He played with us rough-and-tumble when we were little, kicked the ball, fooled around in the small unsophisticated swimming pool, started the outdoor fireplace in the weekends to roast bacon on sticks and capture on a fresh slice of bread its grease dripping as it began to sweat. He taught us skiing from a young age. But there was little time for such activities. He often asked us to drive with him when he had some business to attend to in the evenings or weekends so we could spend more time together. While he was working in the state firm, he let us skip school for a day a few times a year, despite mom's opposition, to join him for a business trip across the country. Apart from visiting the construction sites of future hospitals, factories, and other public buildings where we were fascinated by the trucks, cranes, and other heavy machinery, we always stopped at a historic site or a cozy town, where dad gave us a guided tour. He knew the country inside out. During the long drives we talked just about everything from the places we passed and the teachers we disliked in school to the girls we were interested in and the interests and dreams that were developing in our minds.

It was dad who inspired me to begin keeping a diary. One day when I was seven, he handed over to me a hardcover notebook and explained what a diary was. I learned to write a few months earlier and it sounded like fun. The first record is from 3 May 1987, and it describes a weekend spent with my extended family canoeing, playing football, and spotting deer in the woodland along the Danube River. When I recently opened the diary after many years, I realized to my surprise that I continued writing about major events until 1993. I consider it quite an achievement considering that children's attempts with new undertakings tend to be extremely short-lived.

My first authoring activities summarized especially family vacations, but it is a great joy and a source of inspiration today as a father to read about the moments of boyhood cheerfulness, amazement, jealousy, frustration, anger, or even desire to take revenge on my brother after a good load of teasing and mocking. It is fascinating to read about the joy I felt when I saw and touched Ayrton Senna's McLaren-Honda on display in Budapest after he won the Hungarian Grand Prix in 1991, the year of his third World Championship title, about a visit to the former communist presidential hunting lodge in the Tatra Mountains, or about my reflections on the fact that we no longer could pay with the Czechoslovak koruna after the country had split into two independent states. The diary also contains my first ski lift ticket, various tickets to museums, entertainments, and public transportation, postcards sent by mom and dad from their hard-earned trip to the forbidden West, and original autographs of famed Hungarian comedians, which I have obtained after knocking the door of their dressing room following their shows in our town's culture house. My handwriting seriously deteriorated during the six years that I kept the diary. The last record is from the Istrian peninsula in Croatia, my first trip to the seaside in July 1993.

Mom and dad were always prepared to give a piece of advice, no matter what the issue was. There were no secrets in the family. Dad used to regularly ask us since kindergarten about the girls we liked. Not to approve of our taste or disapprove of our choice. It was about staying open to each other and not missing any opportunity to give guidance when an emotionally developing child, a vulnerable one or just one in love, may need it most. Advice came from every angle all the time, whether my siblings and I thought we needed it or not.

We were taught to develop as many personal principles as possible, in every aspect of life, and stick to them strictly. "Life without principles isn't worth anything," dad used to say. We were constantly reminded that the noblest of arts in the world is learning to live life itself and that one of the most pivotal parts of that artwork is the selection of a spouse. We were encouraged to reason, always and about everything. "Whatever you do, do it well. You can't even clean your bottom properly without using your brain," we heard frequently. When we couldn't pass the right tool at the right time while we were helping fix something around the house, dad used to say with a strict voice: "My father used to slap me when this happened". I was glad my father never applied that technique, because I failed too often to hand him exactly what he needed without being reminded.

Mom was stricter concerning our performance in school. Bringing anything but an A for a quiz or an exam was followed by an expression of disappointment: "Why? You should have spent a little more time on it." Dad was more easy-going probably because he never was a strong student himself. He knew that good grades constitute a small fraction of what it takes to be happy and successful. But if we didn't behave to his liking, it was he who did not hesitate to demonstrate his parenting credo through fair punishment. Adrian and I were about twelve and ten when we broke the glass in our bedroom door after a Tom & Jerry-like pursuit of each other across the house. We were instructed to fix it: borrow a hand trailer, take off the door, drag it through the town to the glazier, pay for it, and take it home. It was a lesson in teamwork, responsibility, and consequences.

The only slap I ever got from my father, and one that followed from the wall right after, was at the age of fourteen, when I came home from a schoolmate's birthday event few streets away one hour later than promised, without calling home and asking for permission. It wasn't about my parents being worried and certainly not about their style of parenting, which flooded my life with love and care. It was a lesson about broken agreements. I tend to strongly dislike tardiness until this day, although that may have other reasons as well.

We paid a fine for forgetting to turn off the lights after leaving a room, and we were banned from the TV for a few days when we happened to disrespect our parents. On the other hand, crashing the car at a later point didn't have repercussions. Mom and dad had understanding for unintentional mistakes, and they knew the emotional roller-coaster we were going though in such moments even without words of rebuke. They understood that such events carried an inherent sense of penalty and had the power to inspire scrutiny of our conscience and evolution of prudence.

Dad believed that only punishment, his translation of "helping to understand the consequences", can turn a young man into a decent, sturdy, careful, and virtuous person. He often expressed his conviction that a child cannot be properly raised with love alone, only with strict rules and consequences of disobedience. As the two aren't mutually exclusive (even if he often presented them as such), reality on the ground was of course different. We received a lot of love from both parents, each conveying it in a different way. After dad had turned sixty, he admitted the wrongness of his rhetoric and agreed that love, although certainly not doting with no limits, is indeed the most powerful tool to raise a person or shape a relationship. Principles, authority, and discipline are just parts of it. They are some of the instruments that can be applied along with, and in the name of, love. He finally began to preach what he had been practicing all along.

Then there was the television, with seven available channels, most of them public. Dad most of the time hated that evil little idiot box. He was furious when he caught us watching non-educational, violent, shallow programs or anything that did not match his definition of spending time wisely. We were requested to underline in the printed TV guide a limited number of programs that we planned to watch the coming week and this way avoid viewing shows we never intended to watch in the first place. Dad also voiced his distaste for celebrities overrated by the entertainment industry and for the limited attention that TV channels, especially commercial ones, paid to education and to individuals who truly contribute a great deal to the advancement of society, like doctors, scientists, academicians, engineers, and the like.

I might have been about twelve or thirteen when a substitute teacher initiated one day in class a debate unrelated to the curriculum. She asked us about things like the music we liked and our thoughts on values, religion, and society. When the class extensively discussed various pop singers of the time, I conveyed the attitude I used to face at home and suggested that we talk less about people who might not deserve to be glorified as much as they are. I wasn't of course very popular. The true source of my frustration may have been the fact that my knowledge of contemporary pop music was far from up to date. But I knew instead about bands that meant nothing to my classmates.

I knew The Beatles, The Yardbirds, The Shadows, Steppenwolf, Creedence Clearwater Revival, Zager & Evans, Donovan, and many others that I heard among the hundreds of hours of recordings that my father had collected decades earlier on his Philips reel-to-reel tape recorder imported from West Germany during the summer training in 1969. Each tape had its index notebook with images of the mostly British and American bands and the exact counter numbers for each song, which he obtained from friends with contacts to Western sources or from Radio Free Europe whenever its jamming by the communists was ineffective.

My father considered learning to be the solution to every challenge, every problem. "The day when one learns nothing, is wasted," he said. Both our parents unconditionally supported our education and career plans. Adrian and I received private German lessons from the age of eight, when there was still little prospect of learning it in school. Nobody could foresee that by the time I would turn ten, the mandatory Russian classes would be replaced by German, which seemed incredibly easy with the head start I had.

When I became a teenager, dad often reasoned about the huge variety of jobs a society can offer. He supplied me with books on existing educational and career opportunities to tantalize my interests. He often talked about his friends and acquaintances he considered wiser or more educated than himself. People whose achievements impressed him and whose opinions he sought with trust. Academicians, specialized physicians, engineering experts, authors, and the like. He tried to infuse me with unorthodox ideas when considering my options for the future.

He came home one day and told me about a fellow working at the Soil Science and Conservation Research Institute. He believed choosing a career so uncommon, specialized, and beneficial to society must be fulfilling. He didn't mention a single word about whether it would be financially rewarding, he simply loved the idea of working with and for knowledge. As the public sector became increasingly underfunded, he began though to emphasize that passion alone might not be a sufficient criterion guiding the decision about career, especially if one doesn't want to remain relatively poor or resort to dishonest practices to secure higher income.

Once we were enrolled at university, our parents secured an environment in which there was nothing we had to prioritize higher than our studies. We were welcome to continue living with them, and they supported us with the necessary cash. Mom still prepared the daily sandwich as she used to do during the preceding twelve years, and she served a warm meal as soon as we arrived after an hour and a half long commute from the capital. It was clear to them that the benefits of full economic support facilitating our education outweighed the benefits of financial independence, if there were any, not to mention the pressures and risks maintaining that independence can put on one's performance in college. Adrian and I already understood the values of hard work and scrimping, and there was no need to jeopardize our studies by letting life teach us those again. But schooling was considered only a part of education.

We heard repeatedly that a degree is a starting point, a job at hand, while learning must occur beyond the teachings of the school, and it may never cease. We were urged to develop our attitude and cultivate ourselves. Set goals and toil to achieve them regardless of how small or big they may be. Educate ourselves in diverse crevices of life, especially those that schools won't ever reach. Self-reflect and be open to self-criticism because only so can we achieve self-awareness.

It could not have been emphasized enough that the choice of a career is important, but more important is how well we do it. Because in every profession, it is only a minority that performs the job really well. Belonging to the average, which is prone to making errors and lacks the vital sense for detail, was strongly discouraged. We were taught that the work of a skilled and knowledgeable plumber can be just as unique and impressive as that of a lawyer of a similar caliber. No need to admire all doctors just because of their medical degree. But admirable are the outstanding ones because everything becomes art when done with passion. We were often reminded that we could gain respect with any profession if we aimed for perfection. A shoemaker or a heart surgeon, a Tomáš Bat'a or a Christiaan Barnard. We could become anything through determination and hard work.

These weren't hollow theories, boring monologues. They reflected reality through concrete examples. Hearing a fascinating story, meeting an intriguing person, reading a quote, or experiencing an impressive moment, mom and dad wanted to share it all, they wanted to initiate debates. They awakened our interest in various directions every time they themselves felt captivated. It was their inspirations being directly fast-tracked to us.

For every topic raised, every issue faced, there were personal examples ready to drive the message home. They were no gossip but lessons to learn from. Stories of great many lives and destinies, from childhood anecdotes about the kids in the village who played dangerous games while tending the family herds out in the fields to the palette of stories about the struggles and joys in the lives of various friends and acquaintances.

Fascinating were dad's observations about the developments in the marriages and families of his secondary school classmates, updated every five years after their reunion. So were his recollections from his two-years-long compulsory military service in the 1970s, where he was obliged to deal with personal issues of those he supervised as well as of his superiors, with whom his personality helped him to build trustful relationships. He was regularly requested by higher-ranking officials to assist with organizing parties, cover for them, camouflage their secrets, but also to listen to their sorrows over their failing marriages and unhappy wives and children. He saw through the true face of communist military life and the toll it took on the families of military men. This experience turned out to be crucial.

His skills were recognized soon after he entered the program, and he was being shepherded toward a career as a professional military officer. He was sent to the academy, where he developed an attraction to the theories of Marxism and Leninism; it was a prefabricated path toward early party ideology. Only his signature was required to access the one-way road to communist military life. But he knew all too well that he had to avoid the pressure to sign those ill-famed papers and get out at the end of the compulsory service. He soon became disillusioned with the tasteless political system and its absurd formalities. The early faith in it and the enthusiasm, which initially secured him privileges in the company where he worked, were replaced with silent indignation and pretense. Because one could only concur or suffer.

It was one of dad's military stories that helped me to overcome the challenge when a long-lasting dislike developed between me and the Slovak language teacher in elementary school. I felt I had to work harder than others to prove myself. In high school, where I was the only Hungarian in the class, history repeated itself. I felt resentment at being picked for an oral exam every couple of days, far more frequently than most others. Oral tests on the topic we worked with in class the previous time used to be routinely performed. Teachers randomly selected a few pupils who were then asked to summarize, or rather recite, what was learned in that subject's previous session. The thoughts swirling in our heads before the class was like a nightmare. Will I be the "chosen one" this time? Am I well prepared? Will I remember everything in my monologue or recall when being asked about the facts I missed?

My distaste towards these two teachers was unfortunate because, with Slovak language being one of the major subjects, I was stuck with them over a period of four years in both cases. What helped me to re-classify my two teachers from a mighty beast to a human being, and eventually become one of their most beloved pupils, was the way dad overcame a similar situation when he was in the military.

He used to live through similar nervousness every time he had to report to one of his arrogant and pugnacious superiors. He had difficulties with handling the moment when he was about to enter the office. A friend had recommended him to evoke an image as soon as he entered: picture the chief sitting on a toilet, with pants down, eyes like ping-pong balls, face red like a lobster, trying to get the job done. Because in the end he is just a human being like everyone else. It worked. Dad had to use the trick a few times, but soon he was able to enter the chief's office with a smile and deliver his report without taking the unfairly coarse response personally.

>«

In our family, we discussed everything that any of us found interesting or important. It is probably the magic of boundless communication, the frequent discussions, and the countless personal stories shared between us that inspired me the most while living with my parents. The man-woman relationship was one of the most debated topics. We discussed John Gray's popular but controversial book *Men Are from Mars, Women Are from Venus* when I was barely fifteen. It was never too early for mom and dad to begin teaching us about the differences and the challenges that come with them. Live demonstrations of those differences were also quite frequent. They had their disagreements and arguments, which they rarely concealed from us when we were teenagers. When the emotions after a quarrel calmed down, they explained to us the cause of the dispute. The explanation was sometimes impartial, other times rather biased. But openness was considered an integral part of our preparation for life. As we grew older, Adrian and I, and later Valika as well, began to take sides in the arguments with our own developing opinions.

We discussed love, generational differences, human relationships, parenting, faith, politics, history, and virtually everything people discuss. We did it sometimes peacefully, other times fiercely. When we were teenagers, Adrian was the better debater. He was the older, more quick-witted, his opinions were met with more respect than mine. He could occasionally win a dispute with dad by making him run out of reasonable arguments. But swaying dad wasn't easy. When Adrian and I challenged the family rules, it rarely ended in our victory. When the exchange of opinions turned too untamed, the debate often ended with dad exclaiming, "As long as you live in this house, you follow my rules". He rarely admitted defeat. He was convinced about the correctness of his views and the accuracy of his judgment, which was generally sharp as a razor. He trusted his much broader experience than that of rebellious teenagers even when he was outright wrong about the deeper underlying connections relevant for the topic. It was rarely the case, but his outdated and unfounded views in some areas (particularly women, which he couldn't consider equal to man in anything, and capitalism, which he could blame for just about everything), which grew out of experience and observation rather than facts, were becoming more radical with time. (Perhaps dad was unlucky with the intellectuality of women and the nature of the relational problems he encountered among his friends and acquaintances during his life, or he just interpreted them, like society, in his own, biased way. Maybe he was insufficiently aware of explanatory theories and statistics. Observations and life experience can be powerful in forming opinions but not necessarily representative of the truth.)

Opposition and conflict, within certain boundaries, can be inspirational. Witnessing occasional arguments between parents and rough disputes between parents and children can inspire determination to avoid them later in life or courage to take up the fight for a better relationship in the long run. They are part of a process of mutual teaching and learning, a convergence, a maturation of relationships. It took mom decades to adopt some of what dad asked from her since the first day of their marriage, and it took dad about thirty years to understand and admit some of the mistakes he had made in marriage and parenthood. But they both reached that point of realization and continue to enjoy a more delightful union.

Family dustups are not pleasant. Yet, I appreciate having been part of them because of the great deal they have taught me. They were a kind of healthy disagreements that offered open discussions, explanations, realizations, and solutions. They were a form of communication (even if imperfect in their nature), which left strong impressions and have thus helped me to reach the maturity of views my parents had reached at a much later age. I believe it is also partly thanks to these early lessons that my brother, sister, and I continue to have a deep and conflict-free relationship with each other and largely with our parents too. We continue to openly share our joys, problems, stories, and opinions. We don't hesitate to ask for each other's advice, and we don't hesitate to advise one another, whether we are asked to or not. We were mentored by our parents while we lived with them, far beyond our eighteenth birthdays, and we receive guidance even now, whenever our parents judge it appropriate. Its acceptance or rejection is our own choice, but it is available whenever we might need it. Because the ultimate lesson is this: no matter how well-prepared we are, relational challenges do catch up, and they require us to constantly reflect, be reminded, learn, and compromise.

»«

It is with age that we begin to truly understand, appreciate, and perhaps emulate the role our parents have played in our lives. With time, we look back at our memories of not only events but personal qualities as well.

Mom did not talk much about deep personal philosophies the way dad did, but she reinforced dad's theories by living them. What made her role so incredibly powerful was living an exemplary moral and virtuous life of kindness, humility, simplicity, and love, which she radiated every minute. Her tender heart continues to be highly regarded among all who know her. She knows no envy, no spitefulness, no material competition. She returns occasional envy or meanness of those suffering from their own shallowness and unfounded pride with the respect and affection that she has always demonstrated towards everyone. It was also mom who guided us to faith—a pragmatic, rather moderate version of Catholicism. She taught us to pray and took us to church on some Sundays, but beyond that, she did not interfere with the way our spiritual inclinations were changing with age. She was there to listen when we had a conflict with dad. She never really took sides, but she tried both to understand our sorrow and to explain dad's standpoint.

Dad saw his primary purpose in providing for the family. He believed establishing and maintaining material security and comfort was a way to express love, and we often argued about the appropriateness of this approach. Adrian and I used to feel fortunate to have the kind of mother we had and for the spiritual and emotional traits we may have inherited from her besides the determination and endurance that dad raised us towards. Looking back, however, I realize what a great deal of non-materialistic values dad brought into the family.

He taught us to appreciate and love all the beauty the world has to offer. He talked about the splendor of the four seasons, the charm of the sunflower and poppy fields, he hiked with us in the mountains, taught us skiing, took us to spot hares. He visited with us beautiful cities and taught us to appreciate their history and architecture. He introduced to us the theater. The first major performance I saw was The Wizard of Oz in the Hungarian National Theater in Győr, when I was thirteen. It was the start of a passion. Over the next many years, we had a season-ticket, with which we annually enjoyed about eight performances of various genres.

My parents' generosity will continue to inspire me for the rest of my life. Time and effort were no limiting factors when someone asked for help or when an opportunity appeared to return a favor. When an acquaintance lost everything and had nowhere to stay, dad gave him work and furnished one of his construction site trailers to temporarily accommodate him. A lot of people asked for loans, some for small ones, others for more substantial amounts. Dad almost never refused and rarely requested any agreement to be signed. He was surprisingly unconcerned when in some cases he did not see the money back. He also sponsored our schools, my fencing club, and every other organization that approached him. He often complained that the town had never asked him to contribute when numerous deficiencies in it could have been fixed with relatively modest means.

When my close friends from high school needed to refurbish an old apartment after getting married, dad offered his non-profit construction services because he knew how hard the beginnings could be for newlyweds shortly after college. And when one of dad's former employees suddenly passed away years after his employment was terminated, mom and dad decided to support his daughter with a fixed amount of money every month until her graduation from university.

Mr. Múčka was dad's long-time mentor, friend, and

colleague in the state company in the 1980s. He was a skilled architect, who designed our house, and a devout nature lover and hiker, whose paintings of the picturesque Slovak landscape were decorating nearly every wall in our home. He was a very humble and kind man, who taught dad some of the simple joys of life. When I was about seven, he hiked the Fatra Mountains with us on our family trip. He built for us figures made of chestnut, and he insisted on riding the train home with my brother and me while our parents drove because he knew what an adventure it would be for us. During the splendid journey, he played cards with us, sang songs, and played his mouth harp, which he always carried in his breast pocket. Before every Christmas, he sent us through dad a box of Christmas wafers that he baked. A year after he passed away at an old age, dad visited his tomb in the cemetery and realized with astonishment that it still wasn't more than a pile of dirt and a wooden cross. He felt such a disgrace that he tracked down Mr. Múčka's neglectful middle-aged children and asked for permission to build a tomb over their father's grave.

Mr. Múčka was also the architect of my paternal grandparents' tomb. Mom and dad wanted to honor Juli and Jani one last time with a little more elegance than the conventional solution of a concrete frame filled with soil for flowers and a standard tombstone standing at the front of it. They felt deep respect towards them, despite the relatively run-of-the-mill relation they had. Once the blueprints and the 3D images of the memorial were ready, dad handed them over to his siblings and asked them to express their opinions or alternative ideas. After he hadn't heard back from them for months, despite repeated reminders, he built the tomb. The community praised the result, but my aunt and especially uncle were more comfortable ignoring the effort, let alone its costs, although they all inherited equally. (My aunt actually inherited more than her brothers, after they agreed to compensate her for providing my grandmother with housing and daily care during the last years of her life.) It was easier to argue against the project with dislike and lack of approval.

The manifestations of envy, greed, competition, and intrigue in my extended family would make up for another book. There was no shortage of putting wealth before family, questionable definitions of fairness in inheritance disputes and within-family land grabs, huge intellectual differences to the extent that made conversation impossible. What will remain an inspiration for me is the fact that I saw my parents always handle these situations with dignity and generosity, no matter how unjust they may have seemed. The notion of payback was unknown. Instead, they continued to support even relatives whose respect towards them was sometimes doubtful and who only called when they needed something.

The reverential attitude to friendship was another admirable quality I frequently encountered while growing up. Having many friends from all walks of life was always central in dad's life. He is blessed with the skill to get acquainted with people with incredible ease and befriend them within minutes. A casual chat at a fair in Moravia or a water bike rental in Hungary, and we were going for a family visit before long. Many of these friendships continued over years and decades, numerous never came to an end.

Language was not a barrier to friendship. My parents' friendship with Peter and Tonny from the Netherlands began when Peter rented our summerhouse, as he was starting his short-lived business with automotive parts in Slovakia. Especially the monthly evenings when the rent was to be paid became joyous nights of bonding. After more than thirty years, the friendship is going strong without a common language between them. I acted as interpreter when I was a teenager, but nowadays a pen and paper, a touch of receptive multilingualism, and a random interchange of words in German, English, Slovak, and Hungarian are sufficient for them to spend hours and days together and talk about almost anything.

I've seen nearly every corner of Hungary and much of Slovakia and the Czech Republic through the many short trips with which my parents treated Peter and Tonny every time they came to Slovakia. They used our summerhouse whenever they wanted (by then for free), we stayed in their house when we paid a visit to Holland. I had the pleasure of painting the houses they lived in over the years, which allowed me to visit the country and earn some pocket money. Peter used to be a top manager in the automotive business. I found his reflections on business leadership inspiring, and I loved to drive the many different cars he had over the course of time. And to Tonny, I could always confidently vent my anger when I battled my parents.

They remain the only couple, apart from relatives, that are routinely present at birthday celebrations, weddings, holidays, or other family events. Their love for Slovakia and friendship with our family resulted in a wild idea suggested by dad one day. To consider having a summerhouse in Slovakia, which he would be happy to build for them. A year later, a house bigger than their home in the Netherlands was standing without a single contract, financial agreement, or document concerning obligations and liabilities ever requested by either side.

Dad knew how quickly friendships can fade away, so he invested time and effort to maintain them through visits, phone calls, presents, invitations, and offers of help. He managed to stay in contact with some of his schoolmates for nearly six decades and with many others whom he had met over the years, naturally without ever using social media. Mom's colossal contribution to cherishing these family friendships lied in treating guests and friends in a kingly manner, with her endless tenderness, smile, and sublime feasts. I can hardly recall a visit where the guests weren't flabbergasted by what was served after many hours of magician tricks in the kitchen and by the style of its presentation.

There was a friend to be found in every situation. Our furniture was designed by one, the garden by another. There was a friend helping with legal issues, another one fixing the gas boiler, or giving advice on the skills children should develop for a successful future in times of uncertainty. In return, dad helped them to build or renovate their houses, or he was just a dedicated, dependable friend. Until today, people feel confident to share with him their most private issues. Sometimes individuals he doesn't know very well share with him details he doesn't want to know. Dad radiates trustworthiness, possesses skills to recognize the true causes of personal and relational problems, to foresee their effects and give most of the time the right advice. He has the ability to reflect deeply. He is one of the very few people whom I know to have many of the characteristics of those Abraham Maslow calls *self-actualizers*.

When the Covid-19 vaccination program was being rolled out in Slovakia and it was dad's turn to get the jab, his sister suggested that to avoid queueing he could get an appointment at a doctor who was her friend. Dad vaguely knew the doctor as well; she was the daughter of a former director of the local agricultural cooperative (a highly respected position during the communist era), a friend who prematurely passed away nearly thirty years earlier. Dad called the doc to get an appointment, and he was met with utmost kindness, care, and willingness. So much so that the received attentiveness felt utterly unusual. When dad showed up for the appointment and the unexpected attention continued, he asked the doc what the reason for the unprecedented treatment he was receiving was. She said it was because dad changed her life, and she would be forever grateful to him. Dad did not understand. The doc continued to refresh his memory. About fifteen years earlier they briefly chatted at the wedding of my cousin, dad's daughter-in-law. The doc was in her thirties, still single, and without a partner. With his usual directness and conviction about motherhood being the primary role of women, dad told her that she had very little time left, her biological clock was ticking, and if she ever wanted a family, she should prepare a plan and begin to work hard not on her career but on finding the right man. This conversation made such an impression on the doc that she did exactly as she was advised. She was now living in a happy marriage with wonderful children, and she was thankful for it to one person only—my dad. We can never know when our honesty may turn into someone else's most striking inspiration or when its fruits may come back to us in the most unanticipated ways.

It is not so much the perfect home, vacations, education, and support mom and dad provided that makes me proud of them but their virtues, which were highly appreciated by many. They were channeled to me not only by setting an example but also by the endless hours of debates and discussions during which we scrutinized innumerable components of the world, life, and ourselves, dissected personalities, relationships, problems, and solutions, learned appreciation for everything small, simple, and basic, shared guidance to see reality in the right light, develop passions and goals, educate and cultivate ourselves. People's expressions of respect for mom and dad, praise of who they are and what they stand for, or the occasional applause for the noticeable closeness, harmony, openness, and effectivity in our family are some of the elements reflecting those virtues and the environment that hatched my many inspirations and continues to inspire me on the slow path toward self-actualization.

2

MATURATION AND MATRICULATION

"The more sand has escaped from the hourglass of our life, the clearer we should see through it."

– Johann P. F. Richter (Jean Paul)

Adrian is twenty months older than I am. He has always been a remarkable source of stimulation. I looked up to him when we were children because I always felt he knew a lot more than I did. He radiated more sophistication. He was always prepared to give me a hand with homework or pass me his reports from two years earlier, which helped me to improve my own. It evoked both pride and a sense of challenge when I saw the smile on the faces of some of the teachers, as they realized I was the little brother of one smart kid they taught not long before. We attended the same schools from first class elementary, all the way to our doctoral degrees.

Adrian was talented, curious, and interested in a variety of things. He liked to draw, write poems, read book after book (faster than I could ever dream to, although that changed as I began to read more and he less), and he formed well-grounded opinions, which he was able to defend. Our occasional disagreements were compensated for by a friendship built on unshakable trust reinforced by a union against our parents in most of the intergenerational conflicts. But it doesn't take long in a person's life to begin to be shaped by various forces beyond those in one's family.

I looked up to the guys and girls in my fencing club who, despite being only a year or two older, were so much more experienced fencers that they regularly attended World Cups and World Championships all over the world. The club's head coach Oszkár Forgács was a kind and patient old man known by the entire town. Oszi *bácsi* (uncle Oszi), as he was known to everyone, was always in a good, youth-loving mood. We were his grandchildren in a way, and he felt the responsibility of his guardian role. He cared for our results in school, and he made sure we were always behaving with courtesy. Dozens of printed quotes of wisdom were on display in his office, and he lived by them. He treated all of us equally, as he taught us honesty, ambition, perseverance, and tussle. He wasn't giving orders but asked us instead to do things, then thanked us for completing what we were asked. He had been one of the best fencers in postwar Czechoslovakia, a national champion multiple times, who represented his country in the World Championship already in 1938. He established the fencing club in 1962 and remained its soul and coach with a foil in his hand every evening until he was eighty-one, long after I left the club in 1995 to concentrate on my studies.

The club in the little town near the Danube River became without doubt the best in the country, producing most of the national champions and young individuals successful on the European and global fencing stage. Some of Oszi's apprentices became renowned coaches. My fencing career lasted only about seven years. Training three hours every workday and traveling to tournaments across Central Europe most of the weekends was becoming a burden as the negligence of homework was not in mom's vocabulary. When a decade later I visited a fencing club in Denmark with the intention to restart training, I was stunned to learn that one of my former coaches enjoyed an international reputation. I was treated with respect purely because of the professionalism he and his athletes were generally known for.

I was often attracted to the feeling of knowing, and I was impressed by knowledgeable people who wanted to pass on to others what they knew. They made me strive for merit perhaps because I believed it might elicit similar admiration and praise. Knowledge is like a drug; it inspires learning. Among my relatives, it was two of my older cousins who seemed especially mature and wise to me when I was in elementary school. Marika, who was in high school, helped with ease to solve my math Olympiad problems. Her sister Csilla was in medical school and advised me on the biology competition.

I was captivated by the historical Latin phrases that my history teacher in fifth grade occasionally cited. I collected them and learned them inside out. *Hannibal ante portas*; *Quo usque tandem abutere, Catilina, patientia nostra?*; *Roma locuta est, causa finita est; Per aspera ad astra*. I asked Mr. Klačman, the historian with one glass eye who used to be my father's teacher some decades earlier, if he could get hold of the *Pater Noster* for me. A few days later, he handed over a piece of paper with the typewriter-written text, and it remains one of the very few texts that I learned by heart and can still remember thirty years later.

Most kids in my class feared the strict math teacher who taught us four years in a row, from fifth to eighth grade. He was funny, kind but authoritative and demanding respect and obedience. He often stressed us with surprise exams, which caught some of us unprepared. But we were proud to have him as our teacher. He was the school's principal, and our class of pupils specially selected for extra focus on math was the only one he taught. He used to give us voluntary math challenges and reward those who solved them. I hated it when I couldn't provide the solution the next day. He referred to the difficult problems as "college math", and it raised my curiosity about what college math might really look like.

I developed an admiration for him. When he asked for help to bring supplies to the class, I always volunteered because it meant a visit to the principal's office. We built a relatively friendly relationship over the years, facilitated, naturally, by my performance in class. I found it overwhelming when he asked me one day to sit down on the sofa in his office and chat for a while before class. What impressed me most about him, however, was something about his name, which stood on everybody's transcript of records at the end of every school year. In front of it was an abbreviation I had not yet seen before. Dr. Imrich Sokol. There is only one way to explain to a child what a doctoral title represents: it is a designation of someone bright, who studied in school diligently for many years.

I visited Dr. Sokol in his summer house for the first time nearly a quarter of a century after I finished elementary school. Now in his eighties, he demonstrated the same vitality and humor as I remembered from my childhood. He proudly showed me around in his vegetable garden and introduced me to the neighbor's cat that loved to stay around him more than at home. With a beer in our hands on a warm summer afternoon, I interviewed him about his professional life in the public service, most of which passed during the Cold War era. The oral history of the former director of the country's once second largest elementary school, spiced with political anecdotes and reflections on his private life, happened to be awe-inspiring. He remembered exactly who I was, and the summary of my adult life and career made him exclaim: "I knew you would eventually turn out to be someone."

I don't remember all the careers I ever dreamed of pursuing when I was a kid. My early interest in planes made me want to become an air navigator (not really a pilot), and at some point I dreamed of becoming a taxi chauffeur, when I just couldn't wait to be old enough to drive. I didn't want to become a firefighter like most children, I didn't want to be rich and famous either, and I played with the idea of becoming an astronaut when I was in college, when my fascination with space exploration and science was reaching new heights. After my mother expressed her secret wish that one of her sons becomes a doctor, I decided, without a particular attraction to medicine, that I would be the one. I took it seriously. In my early and mid-teens, I was reading about famous doctors and human anatomy, and I subscribed to the Czech periodical *Domácí Lékař* (Home Doctor).

Much earlier than that, however, I wanted to be an inventor. Just an inventor, without any affiliation to a specific field. Once when I was playing with my Rubik's cube (which I learned to solve only recently), I asked my mom why it was called so. She explained that it is named after its inventor, the Hungarian Ernő Rubik. I found inventors and inventions captivating until Adrian explained to me that becoming an inventor will hardly be possible without becoming something else first. It was disappointing news.

I was a curious kid. When my parents' friend showed me how she dyed wonderful ornaments on white t-shirts, I went home and experimented with the technique. When she showed me the brooches she made of leather, leaves, twigs, and flowers, I began producing them. I gave one to my favorite girls in class on Women's Day, and I sold the rest to the guys who wished to give a present to their mothers.

I was in fifth grade when we looked into a microscope in natural science class for the first time. I was blown away by what I saw. I asked the teacher if I could take the device home for a few days, and she did not hesitate to agree. A couple of weeks later, dad bought me the latest version of the same microscope. I spent the entire summer slicing off thin pieces of petals and leaves, placing the specimens on the slide, looking at the cells, trying to draw nature's vividly colorful artwork into my dedicated notebook, and browsing my parents' encyclopedias to find the Latin name for each examined plant. When dad wasn't convinced that I needed a new toothbrush after several months, perhaps a year of use as the TV ads recommended, I compared a new and an old tuft under the microscope and victoriously presented the scientific evidence for the bluntness of the used brush.

One day around this time, I stopped at the local bookstore on my way home from school. It may have been the first time that I entered a bookstore on my own. I wasn't particularly fond of reading long novels, poetry, or story books. But I liked books, the way they looked, the touch of them, their smell, their power to help you know stuff. I browsed the books published by the local publisher, which were standing next to one another. They dealt with the Silva Method of meditation and mind control, hypnosis, theory of dreams, and learning about people by reading their faces. I bought them all with the pocket money I was able to save up and began reading the Silva Method. I was determined to put the new knowledge to the test.

Valika was three years old when mom was getting increasingly frustrated with her need of a diaper overnight. Although there is nothing unusual about it by today's standard, most children in the culture of the times were trained to be in control much earlier because it was a prerequisite for being accepted in daycare. I recorded on my cassette player a few minutes of repeated instructions to either stay dry until the morning or wake up and go to the bathroom. Enlightened by Silva, I played the recording by Valika's bed every night ten minutes after she had fallen asleep. Wet nights turned into dry nights just a few days later, and they remained so even after I stopped playing the recording. The success was sweet. It reaffirmed that knowing stuff isn't all that bad.

Unfortunately, our school system was doing its best to make us know the wrong stuff. Equations, laws, theories, and hard facts came before practical knowledge and creativity. I was terrible at taking a chance, and so I felt ready for the next day in school only when I felt absolutely confident that no question, quiz, or surprise exam could surprise me. So, I read and recited and read and recited until nothing important was missing from my monologues. No wonder that school was hardly to my liking. One day my father gave me a book about learning to learn. The tricks of effective learning and self-motivation turned out to be an important asset with many more years in school ahead of me.

Although we lived next door to the town's only high school, my parents strongly recommended that I commute an hour to the country's capital, Bratislava, and attend a school with a much better record. I was suddenly the only Hungarian in class, and it meant new challenges. I spoke a different language at home, I watched TV channels broadcasting from the neighboring Hungary, I knew different jokes that were often impossible to translate. Yet, being different wasn't more embarrassing than being among the top students. I never experienced problems emerging from my ethnic minority status.

High school was changing my fields of interest. Astronomy, history of space flight, twentieth century advances in physics, especially in the theories of the atom and relativity, chemistry, geography, one more fascinating than the other. One year, my geography teacher decided to regularly play a relevant documentary in class. She asked for a volunteer who would track down such programs on the television and record them onto a video tape. Although we didn't have National Geographic or similar channels, paying a little attention to the two Slovak public channels could satisfy the demand. It is perhaps this responsibility I volunteered to take that had been the early source of what has slowly developed into a passion—the observation and understanding of lands, nations, peoples, and their cultures.

>«

A fresh source of inspiration appeared when my parents signed Adrian up for a foreign exchange program in the United States. Visiting the United States was a significant undertaking in our part of the world in the mid-1990s, just a few years after the end of the Cold War. Once my parents offered the opportunity to me too, my dream was to follow Adrian's example and take part in the program the following year. He returned one summer later both physically and spiritually more mature. An eighteen-year-old who was fluent in English, had seen the U.S. from east to west, understood the American life, felt comfortable at huge airports, and knew about hot rods. Every story he told from his American adventure pushed me further in my desire to transform in a similar way. At the end of the summer of 1996, it was my turn to begin exploring parts of the world remote from Central Europe. At the age of sixteen, I was *en route* to Clarksville, Tennessee, where I would spend the following ten months.

Ironically, only a few years after the fall of the Iron Curtain, I was now living in the heart of the Western Bloc, the part of the world that I was once taught in school to consider my enemy. Visiting America, a superpower now "on our side", whose image was at the time still overwhelmingly favorable back home, was an unforgettable experience and a dream coming true.

I was coming from a country in which a couple of years back communism demanded pupils to greet their teachers with a loud "Honor Work!" instead of "Good Morning" and which made us recite and believe in a lot of empty idealistic rhetoric. Now I appeared to be in a place where every school day began with everybody standing and vehemently pledging, with hand on heart, allegiance to the American flag. It took me a while to fully discern and understand the text that kids and teachers were parroting without thinking. I was obliged to stand, but I could not convince myself to pledge anything to anyone, certainly not to a flag. Coming from the Hungarian minority in Slovakia, and thus being bilingual and feeling binational, I never developed an unshakably strong attachment to my own nationality and nation, or rather nations, and I wasn't about to do so to America. On top of it, the Pledge of Allegiance didn't seem to me any different from the similar propagandistic inculcations we had to put up with during the 1980s.

Another irony of my stay was that I was living with a single host dad, Vincent Hernandez, a veteran from the Vietnam War, a warrior against communism, who later guarded the iron curtain from its Western side in Germany. He was unlike my parents. His past and his principles had distanced him from his family. He talked to his parents about once in ten years, he was divorced, and gradually lost contact with his daughter after she graduated from high school. He was a military man, who had been on active duty for twenty-two years, first in the Unites States Marine Corps, then in the United States Army. He then continued working for the military until his retirement. At the time of my stay, he was an occupational health and safety professional at Fort Campbell, Kentucky, the home of the 101st Airborne Division of the U.S. Army. We often toured Fort Campbell together. Vince had free access, I entered unchecked as his son.

When he came across the word *macho* in my schoolbook while helping me with my homework, he pointed at himself, indicating that it is what he used to be when he was young. Fearless, adventure- and adrenaline-loving, who fought in the jungle, stole trucks for the U.S. Marines from the U.S. Army, and jumped out of planes and helicopters so often that his knees were now paying the price. It felt like I was staying with a hero. Perhaps not yet *my* hero but certainly someone who could be classified as a hero, if his younger years were made into a Hollywood war movie.

On the first day after my arrival, Vince showed me photos of him in uniform, taken on the front. He told me about his onerous training in the Marine Corps and his family's "war tradition". His grandfather fought as a marine in World War I, his father in World War II, so it was his destiny to fight in Vietnam. He arrived in Vietnam shortly after turning eighteen. It was unimaginable to me, as I was approaching that age in a perfectly comfortable setting. In his late teens, he requested two six-month extensions to his deployment after his first year of service in the armed conflict. He voluntarily returned to Vietnam even after a three-month recovery in a Hawaiian hospital from a nearly lethal landmine injury, which would have normally secured his discharge. He did not do so from patriotism during a war he considered pointless but, ironically, for the feeling of security. Young soldiers did not see in war the risk of dying. On the contrary, it meant income, privileges, provision of basic needs, and some fun too. I was getting a retrospective taste of the American 1960s, which was very different from the sex, drugs, and rock 'n' roll depicted in popular culture.

There were firearms and plenty of ammunition in Vince's house. I found different guns in the basement and a pair of pistols in the bedroom. Holding a weapon other than a pellet gun or my fencing foil was bizarre but exciting at first for a boy coming from a place where no Second Amendment existed. One weekend we visited Vince's sister and her husband in the countryside of Missouri. The morning after the first night, Vince called me into his sister's and brother-in-law's bedroom. A large gun safe stood in the corner, its door was open. The king size bed was entirely covered with firearms, dozens of them, from tiny pistols, revolvers, to shotguns, and semiautomatic rifles. I was asked to choose one or two that I would like to try to fire and learn from "dad", a former sniper trainer, to properly use. I was speechless and somewhat frightened.

I did not know what to make of this strange new environment, which was supposed to be my home for the following ten months. It wasn't until much later that I began to understand and appreciate the life and personality of my host, who was unlike anyone I ever knew. But Vince possessed features that reminded me of my father and mother. He was candid, thrifty but generous, and he loved to travel, read, and learn. He had principles and an incredibly strong will. He was able to look back at his memories of war, pain, and suffering with positivity and remain cheerful and witty. When he almost lost his life to a diabetic attack couple of years after my stay, he proved a miraculous recovery against all odds. He began to run long distances, half marathons and more nearly every day, and he defied the doctors' conclusion that he would live on daily insulin shots for the rest of his life. He never needed any. He demonstrated what some of his physicians believed may be theoretically plausible but basically unimaginable in reality.

Vince took good care of me. He cooked every day (but demanded that I prepare my lunchbox), he took me to the opera a few weeks after my arrival, helped with my homework, made me feel secure, and set the right set of rules, balanced between my freedom and his strong sense of paternal responsibility for someone else's child. Not that any agreement was strictly necessary with the obedience that I was equipped with from back home. Vince wished in fact that I would hang out more with girls and my schoolmates. But I didn't feel for it. My English was disgraceful, I was reticent, homesick, sad, and lonely in the beginning of my American adventure.

The thought of having another eight or nine months ahead of me was terrifying. I couldn't imagine how I could handle such an eternity in the New World. I saw some refuge in my faith. I restarted the long-abandoned evening prayers and they seemed to help. Every few days I wrote long letters to my parents, relatives, or friends back home. Since email had not yet replaced snail mail at the time, I couldn't wait to get home from school and check the mailbox to see if there was an envelope with familiar handwriting and a Slovakian stamp waiting for me.

The principal of Clarksville High School decided that I should be in senior class, although I had completed only two years of high school back home. She had experienced European kids being ready for senior year at a younger age, and she thought graduation would be fun for me to experience. I failed five of the six subjects after the first six weeks, despite spending long hours into the nights browsing my English-Slovak/Slovak-English dictionary, in order to complete my homework. Vince had to be called in for a meeting. There wasn't much he could do. I wasn't lazy or stupid, I just couldn't understand what was said in class. The fact that I excelled in math served as the evidence.

I imagined I was considered a "pitiable immigrant from the other side of the world". The kids in school seemed to be sorry for me. In the beginning, they were asking whether I know what a microwave was, whether we had flush toilets back home, whether I had seen a car before coming to the U.S., whether Slovakia was a city in a country called Europe, and when will I return to my home in Russia. They had no idea that I grew up in a larger house than most of them, that I had traveled outside my country more than most of them had travelled outside their state, that we had two Western cars in the family (one of them being the same Ford they knew all too well), that I likely had an equally comfortable and secure childhood, or that someone in their class came from a culturally and socially much more developed place than they could ever imagine, where kids and their parents never had to worry about the cost of healthcare and their college education. And I was just from an average middle-class family. They had no idea that I had never seen the kind of poverty in communist Czechoslovakia I was seeing in their neighborhoods and across their powerful and wealthy country (although some of it did arrive in Central Europe eventually with capitalism).

Making friends started off slowly, but eventually I did meet a couple of nice guys and girls who occasionally drove me to the Cumberland River or to the local Catholic church. I spent a lot of time with our neighbor, Chris. She came to the U.S. from Germany when she was a young girl, and Vince and I used to call her *Oma* (grandma in German). She knew my culture and always tried to please me with her European style cooking or took me out for a drive at the weekends. My other "grandma", Edie, was of Polish descent. She had a troubled past, living with a husband with a Slovak name, a tough military man nursed by Vince until his death after he lost his legs. Edie lived a few blocks away, now with an old man named Bob, who was rarely seen without a well-chewed cigar in his mouth. They both drove a crimson Cadillac and lived in a house of cataclysmic disorder, where every bit of floor and furniture was constantly covered with stuff, nothing having its permanent place, making it impossible to sit down or place a mug on a table without moving magazines, statues, souvenirs, candle holders, crystal, or dishes on top of another pile of such items first. I loved the fact that Bob used to meet Elvis Presley during his military service in Germany. He told a couple of anecdotes about their brief encounters, and I felt cool about knowing someone who had met the rock 'n' roll legend.

I often helped Chris, Edie, and Bob with garden work, which earned me the pocket money that came handy when Vince decided to take me to visit his sister in California during Christmas, show me San Francisco, and make me walk on fire on New Year's Eve. Vince requested that I earn the price of my flight ticket to California. I thought it was fair, since he found the small jobs for me to do so, just like my real dad used to do back home. The trip to the West Coast was exciting; my first visit to a Chinatown, the boat tour around Alcatraz, and the ride on the manually operated cable car felt like Hollywood classics. And I survived the walk on fire, performed literally and of course barefoot. First I did not think it sounded like fun, but it was in the end. I only burned my foot a tiny bit when I lost focus on my third walk over the four-meter stretch of glowing ash.

When another exchange student, Altin from Albania, started having problems with his host family, Vince offered the program coordinator to take him in. We were supposed to become brothers, but the sharing of household only lasted a few weeks. Altin was weird. He had changed host families several times and developed problems in each of them. He soon began to give me threatening looks and kept whispering me that he would kill me.

Every morning after Vince left for work, Altin and I waited for the time when we should walk out in front of the house, where the yellow school bus would soon arrive. We were usually sitting in the living room, listening to the radio. To my ears, Altin had a terrible taste in music. I disliked his channel of noise, so after a week or two, when one morning I came to the living room earlier, I gathered the courage and changed the station to my favorite oldies channel. My move was not met with acceptance. As soon as Altin entered the living room and was confronted with *Oldies 96.3*, he went back to his room and came out with one hand in his pocket, apparently holding something or pretending to do so. He told me that if I didn't change the channel back, I would die right away. I wasn't a fighter type, so I tuned in to 102.5, and in the evening I called my exchange program coordinator. Altin was moved out the next day. We were told soon after the incident that he had escaped from his next host family, and no one knew his whereabouts.

I was not happy the first months in America. I was counting the days remaining until I could return home. I began to put in perspective everything that was happening to me. I was learning to better appreciate my home, my family, my past, my life just as it was. But as spring approached and my American experience entered its second half, I began to enjoy it more. Once I became fluent in English, my classmates could not comprehend how I could "all of a sudden become so smart," how on Earth I could know everything we were supposed to know in school. My grades were at the top of the class, without spending much time on school affairs at home. Some of my teachers shed tears when waving goodbye on my last day at Clarksville High.

I enjoyed especially U.S. history and U.S. government. I even became a little patriotic, although I still saw the Pledge of Allegiance as unnecessary. One day our history teacher, Mr. Wherry, invited a guest speaker to demonstrate the uniform and life of a Civil War soldier. Three or four classes were gathered in the auditorium. At one point, the guest announced that if he were our history teacher, he would offer five extra points for anyone who could at that moment tell the dates of the Battle of Gettysburg. I had watched the epic war film about the battle a few weeks earlier, so I knew the answer perfectly well, but I didn't want to look too smart in the crowd. I was convinced that someone among the hundred American kids would know the date of the most decisive battle of their most important war. But when all of them remained silent for everlasting minutes, I raised my hand and provided the answer. Mr. Wherry's jaw dropped. "He's a foreign exchange student from Europe," he yelled in embarrassment.

Experiencing America in the 1990s, at the age of sixteen-seventeen, was probably a monumental factor in the development of my personality, which I might still appreciate only to a limited degree. It was a dream before getting on the Delta flight bound for New York JFK in Prague. A dream shared and an experience envied by many back home but a hardship in reality. I was desperate the first days after my arrival in my new home; I could not imagine how I could possibly endure through the ten months that were ahead of me. Despite everyone's good intentions and the effort made by Vince and my two new "grandmas", a good part of the stay remained a struggle. Yet, it may well be that it is the combination of the dream and the struggle that brings true value to an adventure. Or maybe we often like to emphasize the good in every experience and let the bad memories somewhat fade. But I greatly value today what that year provided me with. I cherish the memories of both the joyful and the strenuous moments. They taught me resilience and forbearance; they reinforced in me what I used to hear so often from my parents, that learning and diligent work is the only way to evolve and achieve things.

The echoes of my early American experience continued to teach and stimulate long after. The well-intentioned but somewhat pretended parent-child relationship between Vince and me has transformed with time into friendship. Friendship in which I call him dad, he calls me son. We have been meeting regularly over the following two decades, both in the U.S., Europe, South America, and the Middle East. As we grew older, Vince began to share more of his personal memories. He recounted joyful as well as distressing stories from Vietnam and from his later service all over the world and his efforts to learn to live a more emotional life in stronger personal relationships. I listened in wonderment. The first-hand accounts of war and its impact moved me and began to develop my pacifism. Although there were elements of active service that Vince described as fun, just like most soldiers would, he did not believe in war, and he considered it fundamentally wrong. The older I was the more absorbing his experiences and observations became. I was happy for the times and place I was born in.

After his retirement, Vince took up active service in the Red Cross' disaster relief efforts. He traveled across the country to help alleviate suffering after natural disasters. He continued to read and reflect on a broad range of topics, travel the globe, explore histories, observe cultural, social, and political environments, look for connections, try to understand the world, and question long established views (like the American exceptionalism that most Americans believe in). We continue to learn from each other through galvanizing discussions about America and the world, and about some of Vince's passions, including history, gardening, healthy lifestyle, and volunteering.

»«

It is not only regarding achievements in school and career that one should try to look up to others and emulate their behavior. In a person's life, there are immaterial moments that have the potential to touch the heart and generate happiness, appreciation, and admiration. These are instances when others express their affection, trust, respect, generosity, humility in front of us and toward us. We can seek such moments of magic for our spiritual growth, learn to recognize them, cherish them, and let them inspire us. We also need to learn to enjoy the emotional fruits of giving such moments to others.

You have likely met a person who was always so cheerful that you wondered if her optimism was real. One who smiles all the time regardless of the circumstances and can transmit her ease and joy without effort. I find such blessed individuals stimulating. The power of a smile is immeasurable, especially in the many everyday instances when we face people we had never met before, or in situations that demand an apology or showing consideration. The more challenging it is to give a smile, the more rewarding it becomes. Because no matter how difficult the situation is, a smile is most often rewarded with a smile. And the more we apply it, the better we become at it. When I get an undeserved smile, I'm reminded of my silent desire to share more smiles. Life becomes so much more enchanting with them.

During one of our many childhood family vacations at Lake Balaton in Hungary, I was on a boat trip with my parents. One of the sailors in a white uniform was wearing a beautiful gilded-looking anchor on a chain around his neck. It had a tricolored pattern woven around its shank. I told my dad that I loved it, and I would like one if we could find out where it can be purchased. Towards the end of the boat trip, my dad approached the sailor and asked him where we could obtain the fancy item. The young man took the anchor off the chain and handed it over to me. I never forgot the astounding incident, and although such moments do occur every now and then in a child's life, I often dream of encountering opportunities that would allow me to please children in a similar casual manner.

My maternal grandfather Vili was one of the most loving and peaceful men I knew. He was always calm and sensible. He had authority in his family, yet he never raised his voice. Some of my early childhood memories are associated with *papa* (grandpa). He was diagnosed with Parkinson's disease at the age of fifty-nine, and I do not have recollections of him living without the tremors, flexed torso, and difficulty with walking and later talking. He took a nap on the divan every day after lunch. When I was spending time with him, he often asked me to lie down next to him and play "Who falls asleep first". He counted to three and the one who began to pretend snoring first (sometimes loudest) was the winner. It was difficult to judge who grunted and rattled sooner or louder, but he was eventually the winner because he soon fell asleep. I rarely did.

I loved to race against him from one end of the yard to the other. He did not refuse the contest even when he could barely walk. He tried to be helpful in the garden despite the physical constraints. He supported himself with a walking stick in one hand and worked with a rake or a hoe in the other. Or he sat in his garden chair and helped shell peas and beans. Grandpa never missed his cheerfulness, never missed a Sunday mass. After he was no longer able to walk the five-hundred-meter distance to the church, he followed a mass on the radio.

Grandma was his tireless full-time "nurse" over his last fifteen years with the illness, and she rarely expressed a sign of complaint. She fed him, gave him his medicine, woke up three times a night to turn him to his other side or help him get up and go out to the bathroom. (My mother would eventually end up in a similar role when this once energetic woman struggled with severe dementia well into her nineties.) It was on his deathbed that the doctors realized he was born with one kidney, which was now utterly demanding retirement after having had to deal with truckloads of medicine over the years. I was told I was his favorite grandchild. And he was my favorite grandparent, the one I occasionally found myself talking to in my thoughts.

I have been blessed over the years with friends who continuously trusted me, even with their most personal concerns. I especially enjoyed such friendships with girls, free of any mutual romantic or intimate attraction. Friendships and spiritual connections *between* genders are different from those *within*. I felt the responsibility of my role as their emotional garbage bin when they shared with me their confrontations with parents, boyfriends, or obsessively jealous spouses, their financial constraints, or childhood traumas. I was there to jump in the car in the middle of the night and rush to provide a shoulder for the tears of loneliness when one's father forgot her birthday, or to take another out to theater when the pressures of school and private troubles felt unbearable. These friendships were reciprocal. They were there for me whenever I needed to cope with issues of the heart. Regardless of whether the joy of soothing can be considered philosophically selfish rather than generous, the mutual confidence meant the world to me. Being there for someone is wonderful, and so is the feeling that we do not have to confront troubles on our own.

Zuzana Palečková, my high school classmate, was the only friend who regularly wrote me letters during my year of absence spent in Tennessee. She was mature, compassionate, and we understood each other from the first day we met in school. She studied culturology after graduation, became manager of Bratislava City Gallery and later of a major bank's foundation, supporting education, cultural programs, awards, and organizing invited talks by Nobel laureates and Pulitzer Prize winners. She invited me to art auctions, presented me with valuable artwork and art books, and passionately described her powerful experience of regularly visiting the pediatric oncology department at a hospital as a volunteer friend to those most unfortunate children. She later initiated our mutual long-distance adoption of two Kenyan children, which continues to this day. With time, we became soulmates who considered each other a precious gift and remained deeply connected despite distance or extended periods of limited communication. No information is too private between us, as we know we would always try to understand but never judge one another.

Zuzana is the only career and success-oriented woman (although she allows nothing to come before family) whom I have heard speaking especially critical of feminist women and their excessive ego. It began with her frustration with the teachers at the university she attended. She considered me fortunate for studying at a technical university with an overwhelming majority of male mentors. It was also her way to show admiration for my choice of career, which was at the time considered difficult and somewhat unattractive. I was the only one from our class of thirty-five who opted for a technical education. Two thirds of the class went on to study economics or management.

Zuzana wasn't raised to regularly attend church service, but she demonstrates a strong (but rational and pragmatic) faith and a deep sense of spirituality. She doesn't hesitate to draw strength and wisdom from any culture, art, religion, philosophy, or science. Her approach to work, life, and people is characterized with analytical mastery, intelligence, generous heart, and morality. It is especially the last one she often struggles with in jobs with pervasive unfairness, corruption, and authoritarian leadership, which she refuses to be bent by. She communicates through words caressing the soul. Her exemplary courteousness, respect, appreciation, and love for others remain a profound source of inspiration.

A few male friends are like brothers to me. These friendships developed during the final years of my university studies. Shared history, expat status, similar attitude towards life, and comparable values served as the foundation. We talk over our everyday lives, our families and work, troubles and pleasures, and the world in general. There are no secrets, no hard feelings when our opinions differ, only trust and compromise.

Jan Babiak and I began our poorly paid doctoral studies in Slovakia on the same day, we shared an office during those three years, we travelled together to conferences and shared hotel rooms, and we defended our works on the same day. Then we travelled a lot more together. No longer to conferences, yet we still shared hotel rooms. We always do. Regardless of what we can afford, we want to minimize costs, maximize experience and authenticity, and have ample time to discuss our impressions, observations, local history, politics, personal stories we encounter, their reasons and implications. Every trip is a project, a well-prepared expedition, a journey of intense learning.

Everywhere we go we visit a church, say a prayer, and if possible, we attend Sunday mass. If we understand the language, we discuss the sermon. If we don't find a Catholic church, we enjoy any other. They all have the capacity to bring about tranquility. The Orthodox in Sofia, Armenian in Isfahan, Catholic in Hanoi, Georgian in Tbilisi, or many in one—the Church of the Holy Sepulcher in Jerusalem.

What connects us is our past, our similar childhoods in Czechoslovakia, the appreciation of the opportunities we enjoy but our parents never had, the willingness to work tirelessly for the goals we set, the sacrifices we make, the thankfulness for every little thing life provides, and the respect for virtues and faith. Some of Jan's inspirations resemble my own ones. He has been influenced by the endeavors of his grandparents, who managed to demonstrate achievements despite their refusal of communist party membership. He draws strength especially from a complete and spiritually rich family, from his mother, who studied theology in her spare time, and from his love for the colorfulness of the world and its nature and cultures, which helps to destroy prejudice and protect against disrespect, judgmental behavior, and negative views about others. Jan greatly appreciates the positive effects various Christian communities had on his life, especially the youth in the local parish and the older members of the Focolare Movement and the Salesian Society, from whom he learned much throughout his boyhood.

Growing up in a small town, my opportunities to be

part of such communities were limited. I was blessed instead with the presence of Father István Morovics. He became the parish priest in my grandparents' village, Bacsfa, when I was thirteen. He was sixty-five. Questionable stories surfaced about him in the little traditional community, which felt robbed of its very formal and conservative young priest after he was replaced with the older, more outspoken Father István. He was loved by some, hated by others.

Father István wasn't an ordinary village priest. He was an academician, author, founder of an elementary school. His sermons were incredibly stimulating and never political. They were pervaded with wisdom, associations, and emotions. If they had been public lectures, they would have qualified as some of the best I have heard. Dad, who rarely had time to attend Sunday mass, used to ask the rest of the family to summarize Father István's sermons while we were gathered around the table for Sunday lunch. He believed they deserved to be not only discussed but recorded and published. These orations touched on a myriad of spiritual and real-life topics. Once I asked Father István how long he usually worked on his Sunday sermons. "All the time," he answered.

I often had the impression that for most of the congregation, his sermons were too intellectual, too complicated to comprehend; their complexity obscured the message that he intended to convey. When I challenged him with my observation, he answered, "I'm not worried. One cannot step into a bathtub full of water and come out dry".

In my late teens, I was often in conflict with my father. Adrian and I rebelled most often against his high demands on our time. Dad disliked it when we slept in on weekends or when we did anything he did not consider useful (especially watching television). He demanded over the weekends our help with his ongoing projects, which there was never a shortage of. We found some of them unnecessary. We objected to his decision to totally renovate our barely twenty-year-old house, which to us seemed to be in perfect condition. It meant very little free time over the summer and interference with the summer exam period. Our different opinions on a variety of subjects, from family roles to values and priorities in life, caused further friction.

One such day, when I could not find refuge anywhere and by anyone's side in the house, I walked the six kilometers to Father István's church, rang the bell of the parish office and asked him to have a chat. We dissected the issues that bothered me, and I learned that there was a place where my soul could always find peace. From that time on, I regularly visited Father István. We talked about history, news, girlfriends, unrequited love, parents, God, marriage, politics, Buddhism, Islam, abortion, euthanasia, dogma, poverty, anything that came to our minds. We told each other incredible personal stories as well as jokes. He could talk about everything. He possessed a massive knowledge of history, philosophy, theology, sciences, and cultures. He understood the workings of nature and the secrets of humanity, he was well-travelled and spoke several languages. He had written two dissertations. The first one in Hungarian in 1954 (on artificial insemination), the second in Latin in 1966 (on the Eucharistic transubstantiation according to Thomas Aquinas and Duns Scotus). He had been studying spirituality at the Pontifical Gregorian University in Rome, but in fact he studied all the time.

He was proud of being assigned to Bacsfa, the little village of my ancestors with few hundred inhabitants, many of them nuns in the local convent. It has been a site of pilgrimage since 1715. That year, according to the records, tears of blood were repeatedly seen shed by Virgin Mary on the painting standing above the altar. The tears were collected on a chalice cloth, the painting was locked in a room, and the room's windows and doors were sealed. Soon after, the picture was seen on the altar, while the seals of the chamber where it had been kept were unbroken. The miracle was investigated by experts from Vienna and several committees under the Archbishop of Esztergom in Hungary. Pope Clement XII authorized the pilgrimage to the site in 1737.

The event is celebrated every year with an outdoor mass attended by thousands of visitors and numerous clerics. One year, Father István asked me to deliver the welcome message in honor of the invited bishop. I lacked the skills to write an adequate spiritual welcome note. He dictated fluently, without preparation, an impressive text that I learned and recited. I felt extremely shy and unconfident. It was the first time I spoke into a microphone in front of a crowd. To make it worse, Father István asked me to do it jointly with a girl from Bacsfa, a fellow student at the university, to whom I was much attracted to, and he knew it.

It was difficult to surprise him with a piece of information he wouldn't know or wouldn't be able to relate to. When I told him I was about to continue my studies in Denmark in indoor air sciences, a field not yet broadly recognized in Slovakia, he was able to reflect upon it, offer a substantiated opinion, and of course recognize God's workings behind the journey I was embarking on. He also expressed a warning before my departure; he said I had to be strong because I was going to an ice cave. He wasn't referring to the unpleasant

Scandinavian weather. Over the following years, as I was slowly penetrating the deeper layers of the Danish society, I often came to remember his spiritual metaphor.

Father István could offer a view on every issue I ever raised with him, especially on the ones related to human relations. Many people question the skills of those living in celibacy to understand the challenges of marriage, parenting, or sexuality. But Father István knew it all much better than most others. He constantly studied, and he empathized with so many people from all walks of life throughout the decades. Members of his flock came to him with mountains of problems, many more serious than I could ever imagine. From the shame of extramarital pregnancy to the inability to conceive and the fear of conceiving due to medical reasons. Some had dilemmas over abortion, others over a handicapped fetus. Several of these stories ended with what many would consider a miracle. Father István prayed, gave his blessings, hope, spiritual and emotional support, and those feared or unwanted children became, against the odds or expectations, their parents' most precious gifts, most uncompromised sources of happiness. He considered them his children.

He expressed harsh criticism of unethical political decisions and of individuals who led immoral lives. On the other hand, he appreciated disapproval of his actions, although not many in the parish dared to openly convey it. Dad was one of the few who did not hesitate to extend his objection when he thought the father took wrong decisions regarding construction works around the church and the convent and regarding the related financial matters. Dad was frustrated when he noticed poor quality or inefficiency, so he offered his assistance. He also questioned the father about his limited ability to attract more young people to the church. Father István rarely tried to defend his position. He thanked dad for his openness and criticism because, as he said, it made him think and learn.

He valued knowledge and education highly, but he especially praised those who lived an honest, God-fearing life, one of family and human values. He could speak beautifully of simple and poorly schooled people, whom few found anything to praise about. He used his own benchmark when speaking about others. There was space for everyone among those he looked up to. Everybody belonged among God's children.

Planting the seeds of his moral and spiritual convictions was his primary goal, and in my case he seemed to reach fertile soil. I liked the way he was able to appreciate the most unnoticeable beauty in others. I began to emulate some of the ways in which he talked about people. One day, after an emotional, friendly chat I had with our family's intimate Dutch friend, Tonny, about the troubles of life and my conflicts with dad, I expressed to mom and dad my gratitude for the kind of person I thought Tonny was. I must have used Father István's approach of overwhelming approval because my parents noticed something was unusual. Dad reminded me that I had never spoken so pleasingly about my own mother, who deserved it at least as much as Tonny did but rather many times more. She could listen like Tonny did, and she did so much more for me, in fact every day of my life. I hurt her feelings that night. I should have realized who deserved true praise in the first place. That night I learned that I had to be myself, I had to be fair, and I had to try not just to praise others behind their backs but to do so while looking in their eyes. Just like Father István did. He could embarrass anyone with endless compliments. It is the most difficult to exercise it with those who deserve it the most. Perhaps it is therefore that I still struggle with mastering such a salient virtue.

The father's faith was impressively steadfast and incredibly forceful, perhaps even considering his priesthood. Whatever was the theme of our discourse, Jesus and God soon appeared in his otherwise pragmatic sentences. His rhetoric wasn't an attempt to convert or strengthen one's faith. He simply saw God's grace in everything. His conviction was unshakeable, and the strength his faith provided him was immense. It had the power to inspire, even evoke envy in the observer regardless of the existence or absence, depth or shallowness of his own faith. When I was talking to him, I often had the feeling that faith might truly be able to move mountains. It wasn't just a cliché; it was a genuine feeling that an inner power enabling us to achieve anything exists. I find it much more difficult to experience such moments of conviction without having someone like Father István radiating it upon me. He believed God was holding his hand throughout his entire life, especially in the hardest of moments. There were many of them.

He began his studies in a seminary during World War II. When his father was sent to the Eastern Front, István became the breadwinner of the family of six. They hid others in their home, while themselves were hiding from rains of bullets, air raids, and massacres perpetrated by German and later Russian soldiers. István himself was held at gunpoint by a Russian soldier. It was the neighbor who yelled at the soldier in that dreadful moment, begging him not to fire at the young pastor wearing a soutane. On the 14th of August during the war, the eve of the Assumption of Virgin Mary, István's mother told her children that whatever they would ask from the Virgin that day, it would come true. They had not heard from their father for months. They wished he were there again among them. At half past four that afternoon, a ragged pauper opened the gate and entered. It was István's father, barely recognizable, weighing forty-five kilograms, wearing tatty clothes, yet holding a couple of sweet drops that he might have been collecting over weeks for his children.

Years later, Father István met the successor of Saint Maximilian Kolbe in Niepokalanów, Poland. He received a bronze medallion in the very same room from which Kolbe, the later venerated Conventual Franciscan friar, was taken by the Nazis. The medallion carried the engraved date of Kolbe's death. He volunteered to die in place of a stranger with a family, when ten men were chosen to be starved to death in an underground bunker in Auschwitz. The date was the same when István's father returned from the front. István wanted to know the time when Saint Kolbe had passed away. The head of the monastery said it was half past four in the afternoon, and the sky was shining blood-red. For the rest of his life, Father István symbolically considered Saint Kolbe the savior of his father.

I recalled the story the day when my son Jonatan was born. My wife Gina felt the first light contractions at four o'clock in the morning. She woke up, sat by the window of our second-floor apartment and was looking down at the intersection of two streets bathing in the sanguine light of sunrise. Suddenly a bang woke up the rest of the street. A car nudged a motorcycle, the rider fell, slid into a parking post, and remained still. All of it unfolded in front of Gina's eyes. Ambulance and police arrived within minutes. The driver of the car, a young English-speaking foreigner, was first in a state of shock, then babbled repeatedly that he was blinded by the rising sun and could not see the motorcycle coming.

It was summer, the windows were open, we could not avoid hearing every detail of what was happening. Soon after, the contractions intensified, and we drove to the hospital. Jonatan was born in the afternoon. Then I checked the local news in my attempt to find out about the motorcyclist's condition. The young man, father of two small children, succumbed in the hospital.

When we arrived home with Jonatan a few days later, dozens of bouquets were lying around the ill-fated parking post. We laid one of those Gina had received after giving birth. I couldn't stop thinking about the meaning of it all. Was it merely a coincidence that did not deserve attention? Or was there a message concealed in the events of that day, a deeper conundrum to be pondered about? How vulnerable a newborn is, and in a sense we remain so for the rest of our lives. Within a few hours, we witnessed the end of one life and the beginning of another. Could they be related in the same spiritual way as István's father's survival was with the martyrdom of Saint Maximilian?

After the war, István's family became stateless, as some Hungarians in Czechoslovakia were stripped of their citizenship and their properties. A couple of years after he witnessed the deportation of Jews, he now witnessed in similar horror the deportation of fellow Hungarians from his hometown, first to forced labor in the Czech lands, then later to Hungary. Nevertheless, he remained determined to become a priest, and his perception of Christ's and His Church's protection has never faded.

He completed his studies and was ordained during the times that were the hardest for priests. His ordination was postponed due to military service and forced labor. Thousands were taken to labor camps. He was one of the very few penalized young priests-to-be who returned home. Thanks to teachers and colleagues, of whom he spoke always warmly, his dream of becoming a priest became reality in 1951.

Many of his friends and colleagues were imprisoned or disappeared forever over the following years. The communist secret police were constantly in his footsteps looking for a pretext to do what the brutal regime did to thousands of other priests over the decades. But, as he said, God always placed the right words on his lips and made him take the right actions to safely elude the dark men's intentions.

After freedom resurfaced, Father István gradually lost his sight. Masses became more and more difficult to celebrate during the last two decades of his life, but they remained equally rich in experience. He praised God for taking his sight and letting him suffer "just a fraction of what Lord Jesus suffered".

He was grateful for having personally met several "saints". They were mainly priests and bishops imprisoned, tortured, or killed by the communists and since then beatified or canonized. Among them was Blessed Pavel Gojdič, bishop of the Greek Catholic Eparchy of Prešov. Father István met him at a theological course in 1946. Gojdič was imprisoned after the communist regime illegalized the Greek Catholic Church. He was interned over some time in Bacsfa, when the monastery was turned into an internment camp for priests, decades before Father István became the parish priest there.

I met Alexandra, Zuzana's close friend and fellow student, during my years at the university in Bratislava. My conversations with this kind, artistic, and spiritual girl taught me important lessons. Once when we were exploring my struggle with painful, unrequited love, Saša, as she was called by everybody, told me: "Everything is exactly as it should be, we just need to comprehend it." This statement has been resonating with me ever since. Saša came from a troubled family of devout Greek Catholics. Her responsibilities for her neglectful and alcoholic parents and a brother suffering with disabilities outweighed any support she could ever get from her family. She searched for the meaning in everything, including hardship. She believed everything happens for a reason and we can't influence everything in life. Life is easier when we try to see certain things positively, identify the purpose in them, and accept them as they are because they might hold value for us. She was spiritually so much more mature than I was. But she wasn't more fortunate with developing romantic relationships. We jokingly agreed to get married when we reach forty, if we both remained single until then. We didn't.

Although Saša found comfort in her deep faith, that faith had its frailty at times. I remember I was somewhat surprised when I heard her talk about her seemingly steadfast faith being challenged and shaken. Especially because Zuzana had once told me with excitement about the beatification of Saša's relative by Pope John Paul II. I thought such family faith must be rock solid. When I heard the story, it struck me that it might not be a coincidence after all that Saša's last name Gojdič was identical with that of Father István's hero. My friend in the big city was referring to the same person who meant so much to my friend the priest in the village. One of his favorite saints, who once spent time in Bacsfa, turned out to be family with my friend.

Father István was especially proud of his encounters with two individuals who later became saints. He celebrated masses on various occasions with Pope John Paul II, both in Slovakia and above the tomb of Saint Peter in Rome on the fiftieth anniversary of the pope's ordination. They talked with each other several times. Father István brought back from one of his trips to Rome small images of John Paul II and miniatures of his bent cross, both blessed by the pope himself. I was a teenager when he gave me one of each. It filled me with delight, and I cherish the items ever since.

The most important encounter in Father István's life was that with Mother Teresa. They had met several times, in Bratislava and Rome, but the most powerful was the meeting during a study trip in Berlin in 1986. Mother Teresa wrote in his breviary the following message in English: "Be humble like Mary, that you be holy like Jesus. God bless you, m. Teresa". It remained Father István's most precious relic.

He was requested to retire in 2008 and he left the parish. He lived with his sister in Bratislava and occasionally celebrated masses in a nearby chapel. In 2011 he published his memoirs. It was a fascinating reading, and it inspired me to take Father István for a tour, visit the places he mentioned in his brief autobiography, refresh memories, and relive stories. He was enthused about the idea. It was one of the most heart-warming days of my life. We visited parishes and their churches in countryside villages and towns in southern Slovakia, one by one the places where he had served over the six decades since his ordination.

Although we came unannounced, he rang the bell of

the clergy house everywhere we stopped, and we were welcomed with the highest respect and gladness. He personally knew the priests currently serving at each place, and they knew him well even though years have passed since they had last met. It felt as if time had stopped since he moved away from these places decades ago. He gave me a guided tour of each church, explained its history, told ages-old stories about the local residents, showed some of the frescoes he painted when he was young. Then we said a prayer and moved on to the next parish.

We did not need a map or a GPS. Despite his loss of vision, he was perfectly in control of the direction. He knew every turn, every curve on the road, every house and bus stop, as if he had driven there the day before. But he was nearly blind for the last fifteen years, and he had not been to some of the places for thirty-forty years. In the village of Csúz, which he had visited last time in 1967, he guided me with utmost precision to an old, worn-down house and asked me to stop the car. He said it was the house of his former cantor, and we were going to visit him. He rang the bell and hollered the cantor's name. I expected an embarrassment. What if the cantor and his wife were long dead? What if the house has been sold? How can he pay an unannounced visit with such a confidence to a house he has not visited for nearly forty-five years?

The cantor's wife opened the door. She stood there in disbelief, not knowing what to say or do before she started calling the father's name, yelling to her husband to hurry over and meet the precious guest, and finally opening the gate for us while still uttering words of bewilderment. She immediately recognized the father. They met last time about fifteen years earlier, when the cantor and his wife travelled to attend one of Father István's anniversary ceremonies. They spoke of their memories of the sixties as if they had just ended yesterday. They talked about local families, about the successful years when communist newspapers reported the village's extraordinary watermelon yields, and about how the young father used to bicycle through the village, making the girls turn their heads to stare at him.

The cantor, now walking with difficulty, happened to still be the cantor. He drove us in his ramshackle Lada up to the chapel and opened its door. The father described the church's renovation that he carried out half a century ago, he gave a complete explanation of all its paintings and frescos, and then the cantor asked him to bless the church and all of us who were gathered there. It was a memorable day for everyone.

When we were coming out of the church at the next stop in Galanta, a town of sixteen thousand, where Father István had been serving between 1967 and 1970, a local resident recognized him with insecurity. After the two chatted over fifteen minutes, the old man expressed his wish to confess. The father was always prepared to offer the words of absolution. He could turn the often-feared confession into an absolute pleasure. He asked me for a moment of patience, walked with the man to the nearest bench, sat down, and administered the Sacrament of Reconciliation.

Gina and I visited him a year later, when Jonatan was two months old. We met in a pastoral center, where he was in the caring hands of sisters and other fathers. He couldn't get out of bed, and he talked with difficulty. He was preparing for the biggest journey of all. He was willing to baptize Jonatan, but there was nobody available to first administer upon him the required absolution. He asked therefore for Jonatan to be placed on the bed next to him. He ran his fingertips through his face to "see" him. He complimented the softness of his skin, prayed over him, and blessed him. Father István passed away two months later. His wish was to be buried in Bacsfa. His resting place is a few steps from that of my grandparents Vili and Erzsi.

3

MEETING BIG SHOTS

"Example is not the main thing. It is the only thing. … Only as a man has simplicity can his example influence others."

–Albert Schweitzer

My encounters with highly inspirational people and environments began to intensify during the last years of my studies at university. I chose to study building services at the Faculty of Civil Engineering of the Slovak University of Technology. Dušan Petráš, a professor at the Department of Building Services, was one of the most internationally recognized members of the faculty. He was the dean at the time, and we felt privileged to have a class with him. He was different from other teachers. He spoke several foreign languages, travelled extensively, and often lectured abroad. In the then relatively authoritative school system, he gave the impression of an academician with vast knowledge and authority but at the same time respect, kindness, humility, and goodwill towards the students. He regularly asked us in class to express our worries or comments related to the faculty and our studies. We felt a certain level of equality and empowerment.

Adrian studied building statics at the faculty. When he was offered to spend one semester in Bochum, Germany, and later a year at the Polish Academy of Sciences in

Warsaw, I was convinced that I want to undertake part of my studies abroad as well. The bilateral agreements between universities, the funding opportunities, grants, and programs that facilitated such study trips were substantially more limited around the turn of the millennium than they are today. Slovakia was not a member of the European Union, and studying in most countries entailed a tedious visa application process.

It was therefore like winning the jackpot when Dušan announced one day during lecture the opportunity for two students to spend a year (the final semester of our studies and one additional semester) at the Technical University of Denmark (DTU) outside of Copenhagen and write a master's thesis there. All costs were to be covered by the Danish university. Dušan spoke highly of the place where his own career began in the early 1980s. I was immediately determined to pursue the opportunity. After a brief telephone interview purposed to verify the adequacy of my English language skills, I was accepted. One month later I landed in Copenhagen, together with my classmate Oto, a guy with a very similar upbringing and values, who would be my soulmate for the following eleven months. I was embarking on an experience that would give my life a totally new turn in every respect.

Dušan prophesized that the two semesters spent at the International Centre for Indoor Environment and Energy would be an adventure of a lifetime. It was the institution where he was a doctoral guest student twenty years earlier and to which he was thankful for his own successful career. The Center was the famous research institute led by the renowned Professor Ole Povl Fanger, the father of thermal comfort theory and one of the big names in the field of indoor air quality. We had seen the name in our textbooks back home. Now we faced the man for whom we had such a respect that we didn't dare to start a conversation, and we waited instead for him to approach us first.

Ole was a legend in the field. He lectured around the world, and he was a prominent member of numerous organizations, committees, advisory boards. He was frequently receiving honorary doctorates and honorary professorships around the globe. During the following few years, he became the Danish scientist with most honorary degrees. His office walls quickly filled up with awards, prizes, and diplomas to the extent that there was no space for more. He had celebrity status in academic and scientific circles. Little did we know at the time about how consciously he worked for it, sometimes going to such extremes as to request an award in return for an invited talk or other high-profile favor.

Ole was a self-loving person who adored success, fame, and glory. He enjoyed it with style. Everywhere he travelled, he visited the best restaurants, ordered the best wines, and demanded that they be served at the correct temperature, which he always checked with his personal wine thermometer. He never hesitated to send back wine when its temperature wasn't by the textbook. He returned from his trips with gifts for his personal secretaries, whom he refused to share with the rest of the institute despite pressure from the university administration. He had an iron will and demanded his wishes to be satisfied with perfection. Although the research group benefitted from his charisma, some of his attributes were atypical for a Dane and silently criticized by many.

His humble attitude to students was, however, truly inspirational. He treated us very politely and with a sense of equality. The fact that a person of his caliber could make us feel so comfortable was startling for me in the beginning. He ensured that every student working on a master's thesis at his Center was part of the team. Students were listed together with the staff on the board in the entrance and on the Center's website, and they were invited to all social events, such as welcome parties, receptions, Christmas dinners, and summer picnics. The first lecture of the Center's flagship course, fittingly called Indoor Climate, was given every year by Ole himself. At the end of it he took a picture of the class and memorized the names of all course participants. We were made to feel special. Ole's research group had a reputation even within the university itself.

On the first day after our arrival, Oto and I were introduced to our new colleagues and the other students. Ole then asked us to sit down in his office, and he described some of the ongoing scientific projects among which we could choose one to work on over the next months. They covered ventilation and air distribution, air cleaning, chemicals in the indoor environment, thermal comfort, human exposure and perception, effects on health and productivity. Studies were performed in different environments, from offices and residencies to schools and operating rooms, in the laboratory with numerous full-size climate chambers as well as in the field. Later I would spend time reading on the Center's website about the various research areas that the group covered, and I found most of them absorbing. I would eventually have the privilege to work in most of these areas and environments over the following decades. But for a rookie sitting on Ole's sofa, it felt almost disappointing that we had to select one project that would then be the focus of our thesis, without knowing much about any of them.

We chose a project (investigating the causes and

effects of air pollution caused by used ventilation filters) without knowing clearly what it would entail. We met our supervisors, Geo Clausen and Jørn Toftum. Few months later, our co-supervisor Charlie Weschler arrived from Rutgers University in the United States for one of his numerous extended visits. While Ole was a leader, a legend, one the Center has benefited from long after his premature death just three years after my arrival, it was Geo and Charlie whose mentorship and later friendship would turn out to have an immense effect on me.

Ole's legacy reached much beyond Denmark. Relatively few Danes worked and studied at this cosmopolitan institution that he had created. Students came mainly from Central and Eastern Europe and Asia. The scientific staff was assembled from among the best in the world. Scientists from around the world were popping up for shorter visits or longer sabbaticals. Guest lectures by recognized experts were frequent, and the lectures in the Indoor Climate course were given every week by a different lecturer, mostly distinguished foreign academicians. Within a few months I met people from dozens of countries and universities, including top ranking schools like Harvard, UC Berkeley or those in Hong Kong, Tokyo, Singapore, and elsewhere.

The professor most popular among the students was Jan Sundell from Sweden. Jan was divorced, had adult children, and the world was his home. Both at DTU and on his frequent travels to foreign universities and conferences, he bonded with students, he inspired them, gave them dreams, laughed and partied with them, he lived with them. Jan was one of them, and they loved him in return. Several times a day, he walked into the student office to jokingly tease them or initiate an interesting conversation about the countries of the world, universities, smart students, publishing science, or anything that fascinated him. Then he took a few pictures. A camera was always hanging on his belt, and he documented with it everything. Not more than a few minutes could pass without a shot. In my first year at the Center, he invited all students at the institute to his riverside cabin in central Sweden to hike, fish, cook on fire, chop wood, drink plenty, sweat in the sauna, and jump in the freezing cold river. It was a professorial gesture I had never experienced before. Not even after.

Jan loved science. He was one of the early pioneers of modern indoor air science, and he was a fierce advocate for more health-oriented research in the indoor climate and ventilation community. He was respected around the globe for his contribution to the field. He knew the world, and the world knew him. Ole recruited him when the Center was established and consulted him about the world experts he should attract to shape his new research center into the top-notch institution it soon became. Jan knew well all the field's top scientists. It was him who had largely attracted the numerous big shots to Denmark, including those who would shape my career and to some extent my way of thinking over the years to come.

Jan was an engineer by his first education. After he realized how much health-related knowledge he lacked while writing national guidelines for the built environment and ventilation, he completed a medical degree in his forties. He became extremely passionate about elucidating the impact of indoor air on children's health. He started up large studies involving tens of thousands of children in several countries on three continents. He inspired additional such studies in his absence, including the one Geo started soon after Jan's departure from the Center. It was the one which would become my bread and butter for the first years after the completion of my doctoral degree.

Jan was well-read (once he estimated that he read on average about five hundred pages a week), well-travelled, and very open-minded and liberal. We caught him once listening to Polish rock music, which he did when he was supervising students from Poland. Geographic and cultural differences never meant a barrier. He followed the funding opportunities that enabled him to continue his passionate search for answers to the question why children suffer from allergic diseases and what role ventilation plays in it. He came to Denmark from Sweden, then continued to the United States. In his later years he eventually decided to settle down in China. He loved China and knew the country better than most Chinese. He was proud to live there, and he was convinced that it was the place to work with the smartest and most diligent students one can dream of.

It was his modesty and undemanding nature that impressed me the most. He gave an impression of an unpretentious workaday man. When he was cleaning his office before moving to his next destination, he pulled down a pile of papers, envelopes, and plaques covered in thick dust from the top of the closet. "These are the awards and recognitions I received over the years," he said. Unlike Ole, he never cared to display them. Interestingly, both attitudes can be equally powerful in inspiring not only dedication but also simplicity. One does it by overdoing the display of success, the other by ignoring it.

Jan was diagnosed with cancer in early 2018, and his remaining time was estimated to be less than a year. He returned to Sweden for medical treatment. By fall, we knew he wasn't doing well. He was going through extensive treatment sessions, which we heard were torturous for him. Then one day, we (his former colleagues at DTU, including myself) received an email from him announcing that he would pay us a visit within a few days. We didn't know what to expect. He was coming between two treatment sessions. He asked us for help to find a place where he could stay, but every affordable hotel and hostel around Copenhagen was fully booked. Eventually, I offered him to stay in our house, and he gladly accepted. Some of my colleagues thought it was a daring offer from me, but it came to me naturally. An old friend and colleague of Jan, Hal Levin from California, who happened to be spending time with family in Milan, flew up to Denmark to see him, very likely for the last time.

When he arrived, Jan was in better shape than we had expected. He looked older and had lost his eyebrows (he used to keep his grey hair unnoticeably short already for years, so his baldness didn't surprise anyone), but he was energetic, and his mood was as we remembered it. He came with a specific goal. He was working on a book about the history of indoor air science. He needed to find his master's thesis on home ventilation from 1969. He believed it was the first study reporting actual measurements of ventilation rates and airflows in dwellings. He had looked for it everywhere, in Sweden, in China, at home, and in his offices. His library, which remained at DTU when he left a decade earlier, and his moving boxes full of reports, books, and articles still stored in the Center's basement were the last places he had to look. The thesis was in one of the boxes.

I felt honored to have the opportunity to host one of my earlier role models, who was now a friend. Our rich conversations on our way to work and back, and in the evenings with a drink after dinner, touched on everything from his childhood, parents, failed marriage, and children, to traveling, the future of indoor air science, and his disease. I shared with him an early version of this book and its predecessor, *Reflections on the World of Human Inspirations*. He agreed with most of what he had read, and he admitted that he had always thought we were soulmates. He made one last plea to me for a more health-based approach to indoor air research (as opposed to energy, comfort, and productivity as primary drivers), which he spent a lifetime advocating for. He believed I should take over that torch. Suddenly I remembered that in the early years after we had first met he also believed that among the many students he had met I was the most promising to become a future indoor air scientist, which I now was.

Jan spent nearly a week going through the decades-old papers, meeting notes, and reports in his archive. He was still refining his knowledge of history. His passion never faded. (He wrote an editorial shortly before he passed away, likely from his hospital bed.) When I drove him to the train station on the final day of his visit, we said goodbye with a sense of optimism about the treatment he was getting and about another chance to meet in the future. But deep inside of me I felt the burden of my consciousness of the fact that I was saying goodbye to a dying friend for the very last time. Jan passed away in May of the following year. His book was never completed.

David Wyon was another big name attracted by Ole to work at the Center. He was a professor of applied psychology. While studying at Cambridge, his physics professor Antony Hewish, who later received the Nobel Prize for the discovery of pulsars, told him not to even consider doing anything else but science. That is what David has been doing ever since. He set the stage for studies investigating the link between indoor environment and occupant performance already in the mid-1960s, forty years before I entered that still relatively young theater. David had a remarkable career behind him. He had been developing statistical methods and conducting research for corporations such as Kellogg's, Johnson Controls, and Volvo as well as for research and academic institutions around the world. His brother's story was equally inspirational. He developed unique engineering capabilities and solutions in the field of heavy lifting and moving, and established a company that could solve giant moving challenges that few others dared to tackle.

David embraced new opportunities with enthusiasm. He assigned little priority to attaining personal wealth. He and his family moved twenty-four times over the years, and he was proud of the fact that his children had greatly benefited from this lifestyle. They were ahead of their peers in school, spoke multiple languages and later reached leading positions within their fields. David remained active in research, teaching, publishing, and consulting even after he officially retired and moved to the place he considered best for life, the French Riviera. All this was unthinkable for someone like me. I had just made my first temporary move for which I was considered a rare bird back home, where people mostly settled down where they were born. The haunting tradition of taking a firm decision about the future and avoiding floating through the world of uncertainty clashed with my desire to explore and experience the unknown and unpredictable.

My new colleagues travelled all the time. Doctoral

defense in Asia, lecture in Europe, meeting in the United States, all within a week or two. Such schedules were unexceptional, but it was new, very new to me, a kid from the former Eastern Bloc, where the academicians I knew were primarily teachers and practitioners who perhaps never left the country with a work-related purpose and who did not speak foreign languages, except perhaps some remnants of much forgotten Russian.

I began to understand why Dušan was an exception back home. He had been walking in my shoes twenty years earlier. His father was a chief engineer in a factory in Slovakia, who was keen on providing his son with a good education. He spoke several languages himself and recognized already during communism that speaking Russian would not be sufficient in the future. During the period of normalization in Czechoslovakia, Dušan secured an invitation from Ole and managed to obtain permission to spend six months at DTU. He arrived a German speaker, left an English speaker. Ole arranged for him a tour across Scandinavia, visiting various companies and universities. During the following many years, he often pulled the strings to help Dušan's career and his international reputation. Those six months remained to be some of the most influential in Dušan's life.

Over the years I realized how many lives around the world Ole had influenced, how many people learned a great deal from him and remain thankful to him. As I meet reputable individuals from around the globe who have been enthused students or guests at the Center decades ago, I encounter proud accounts of Ole's care and mentorship. For example, Shin-ichi Tanabe, the leading Japanese professor on the built environment at Waseda University in Tokyo, recalled his amazement upon arrival for an extended stay in Denmark as a young researcher in the 1980s. Ole personally picked him up at the airport and drove him to his accommodation, where a flower on the table and champagne in the fridge awaited him after the long journey.

Mustafa Muhaxheri from the University of Prishtina in Kosovo appreciated Ole's sense of responsibility for his family's happiness and well-being during his sabbatical in Denmark. When feelings were blue and economy tight, Ole purchased flight tickets for the family to visit their home country. He later did everything in his power to help Mustafa and his family settle temporarily in Denmark when they had to flee due to the Kosovo War.

I was becoming part of this family of grateful mentees, the last generation of students who would remain thankful to him for the chance to study and work at his Center and for shaping their careers. Students who came from the world and took their experiences back into the world, expanding the pool of those who carried on Ole's international legacy. And his legacy was the Center's legacy.

»«

The place swelled with knowledge, curiosity, diversity, teamwork. It was international, multicultural, global. I found the scholarship and excellence, but also humility and simplicity that radiated from the more senior colleagues, sensational. They did not act superior. Students, academic staff, and administrative staff treated each other with equal respect and elegant, casual politeness. To my initial amazement, they called each other by first names and addressed nobody with academic titles. Naturally, I had to learn to do the same. Young and old, we were mostly expats, we were equal, we were becoming friends. We worked, learned, and celebrated together, and we enjoyed each other's company. It was the right place to soothe the thirst for learning. Learning about anything—science, cultures, languages, social relations, diversity, about each other but most importantly about ourselves.

It took a while to get used to the atmosphere. We regarded the PhD students, who often co-supervised master's students, as authority and the professors as practically legendary. The whole environment was one big pot of inspiration. The country, the campus, the facilities, the staff, and, perhaps most importantly, fellow students, our officemates, their cultures, personalities, their slightly different projects, their ideas how to spend time together (like when a few of us decided to spend months to write, design, rehearse, and perform a burlesqued puppet show for everyone at the Center). Our office with a dozen international master's students was boiling with enthusiasm. (Master students were assigned their own office space, and working on the thesis was a full-time engagement.) While most Danish students followed the official work hours between 9:00 and 16:30, international students didn't mind working around the clock. There were evening discussions, night-time lab work, and plenty of fun too. We had no families, no real homes to go back to every evening. We lived at the Center. The stimulating effect of the environment on us foreigners was likely enhanced by the places we were coming from.

Most of the students were from Poland, the Czech Republic, Slovakia, and Bulgaria. These countries had still been in the claws of the Soviet Union less than fifteen years earlier, and they had been going through a political and economic hurricane since then. None of them was yet a member of the European Union. Studying in the

West meant going through a wearying visa and immigration process. Although all of us remembered having a happy childhood, we had clear memories of communism with its modest lifestyle, shortages of certain goods, and the endless hours of waiting at the border when crossing to a neighboring COMECON country. We had briefly travelled in the West during the decade following the fall of communism, some of us had lived there for some time during our teenage years. These experiences further reinforced the shared political and social skepticism toward our home countries. Once we found ourselves in a world-renowned research environment at an acclaimed university, everything could motivate and excite our freshly independent college minds. Perhaps it was no coincidence that several of us went on to become academicians, some right there in Denmark.

It might not have been a coincidence that amid all these impressions and novelties I fell in love with a fellow student and good friend at the Center. It was the second time that I developed feelings of romantic love during my university studies, the second time as an adult. Second time painful, unrequited. And it was the second time that after about a year of constant, dreadful attempt to interpret every word and every move as a possible sign of mutuality, a year of pathetically devoting most of my efforts to finding ways to impress, convince, and win her over in my silent desperation, I realized that, taken everything together, the best thing that had happened to me was that my love remained unreturned and therefore eventually began fading. Maybe it was emotional fatigue, maybe disillusionment, but my eyes certainly began to see things clearer. Not so much the subjects of my admiration but especially my circumstances and myself in them. The story of the shy girl from Bacsfa with whom I attended every lecture in the first year at the university, and the story of the energetic, confident, and athletic Pole with whom I spent at DTU most of the work time and free time the final year before graduation, were diametrically different, yet, with a few years of emotional freedom and piece between them, *my* stories of the two seemed similar. What remained in the end was friendships, and so I escaped again the unanswerable dilemma I often pondered: when it comes to that decision, is it the genuine friendship or the romantic relationship, which so often endangers friendship, that is worthier of commitment?

During my first months as a student at the Center, most of the scientific staff and doctoral students were preparing for the Healthy Buildings 2003 world congress in Singapore. When the organizers were obliged to postpone the conference by six months due to the SARS outbreak, I began to play with the idea of participating. I asked around to learn what it takes to join such an event. Then I drafted an article and received Geo's and Charlie's support, with the amelioration of my first, rather substandard attempt. The Center agreed to cover the conference registration fee, and my father helped find among his friends and business partners sponsors willing to financially support my trip. He provided the largest contribution to my unusual project, and Vince bravely sent me from the other side of the Atlantic two hundred dollars in an envelope.

It was an incredible experience to deliver my first presentation in front of a substantial crowd of experts, to meet scientists from all over the world, and to see my colleagues from the Center among the most prominent delegates, organizers, and keynote speakers. I discovered that my affiliation with DTU triggered a certain degree of recognition. It meant credibility, confidence in the quality and importance of the work, and a full lecture hall during my fifteen-minute presentation.

I was determined to enter a PhD program after the defense of my master's thesis. It made little sense to do so without proper guidance and facilities at my *alma mater* in Slovakia. I wished to stay in Denmark, but a funded PhD position was unavailable. Dušan turned out again to be the key to a solution. After Oto and I returned with the master's thesis in our hands, he arranged at the faculty that the course credits we had obtained in Denmark would be accepted as equivalent to the credits we missed back home while we were at DTU during the final semester of our studies. Official credit transfer from another university was not yet established at our faculty, but Dušan, sitting in the dean's seat, made sure that the new skills we came back with would be recognized and that our graduation, already postponed by an extra semester spent in Denmark, would not be further delayed. In January 2004, we defended our thesis for the second time. (The defense in Denmark couldn't be recognized, despite the high grade we received and the fact that David Wyon thought the extent of our thesis was comparable to a doctoral dissertation.) Then he offered me a doctoral position under his supervision in Bratislava and free hands. I was allowed to have Geo as my co-supervisor in Denmark, have my ongoing project at DTU as the topic of my PhD, and spend as much time there as I wanted, as long as I completed the minimum course and teaching requirements at the Slovak University of Technology. I could start in the fall, and Ole was willing to employ me as a research assistant at DTU until then, further extending the head start I was already having for my PhD.

I was in a privileged situation. The media repeatedly criticized (and continues to do so) the state of education in Slovakia. Every time I came back from Denmark to visit my parents, there was a pile of newspaper articles waiting on the desk in my room. Dad, who probably thought I might end up becoming an academician in Slovakia, used to save for me the ones that dealt with the problems of the education system. None of the articles offered a reason for optimism. After about ten years, I stopped receiving the articles. Perhaps dad realized that their chances to impact my career, in whatever direction, had faded away, or simply because the articles continued to parrot the same, year after year, without impact on the reality. I was safe from all this. The experience I had with my supervisor was almost entirely the exact opposite of the one my sister would have with her master's degree advisor ten years later.

Valika studied environmental management at Comenius University. During her final year, she, along with a few other girls, selected a supervisor whom she found, given his publication record, to be among the most skilled in the department. It happened to be a mistake. He not only didn't supervise her, but, by his inability to communicate and by his self-centered attitude prioritizing his own interests, he nearly caused Valika to fail to complete her studies after she had excelled in all subjects during five years and had passed her final state exams with top marks.

This gentleman (or not) kept postponing the laboratory work for months, cancelled meetings minutes before the agreed time (and sometimes after), or he just did not show up without prior notice. He often didn't answer mails or phone calls. The final laboratory data to be analyzed were delivered to his students just days before the deadline for thesis submission. Several girls were treated similarly, one encountering health consequences from the months-long stress over the near-failure of her final thesis.

The censors delivered their evaluation of the thesis prior to the defense. They were harshly critical of the quality of the data and its scientific value. The supervisor disagreed with the censors and ensured the girls that the data were of good quality and that he had plans to publish them. However, when the time came to defend his students, he did not appear at their defense. Was he perhaps afraid of a prick of conscience if faced with his own responsibility for his students' performance? The incident resulted in a certificate that read: "Master's thesis defended at second chance; final grade D", along with substantial financial losses caused by the two months longer study period and postponement of job seeking.

As a scientist, I also found it disturbing that the data that this department's "top scientific employee" (as claimed in a letter by his superior) planned to publish in an international journal was considered nonsense by his peers. It reflected the state of teamwork and the general atmosphere within the department. Since I understood the hierarchical structure in the academic environment in Slovakia and the routine reference to academic titles in salutations, I took the liberty, as an associate professor at a much higher-ranking university, to write a complaint letter to the head of the department and express my concern about the treatment these bright and enthusiastic young ladies had received over several months prior to their defense.

The response I received was humiliating. I was scolded for "letting myself be provoked by my sister to write a shameful letter full of lies". I was told to talk to her and hear the truth. And that was what I did. It turned out that her supervisor, upon seeing the letter, admitted the truthfulness of what was written in it and accepted responsibility for it. Unfortunately, he only dared to apologize to my sister, but he wouldn't concede to his superior. It wasn't the bravest behavior by a "key employee" and deputy head of the department, who should take responsibility for handling such situations instead of fearing for his relatively untouchable position. All I could do was to reply to the derogatory letter suggesting that this time the department head ask her deputy for a true account. I never received another response.

I was certainly happy about the direction in which my life and professional development were heading when I was at the same stage in my studies. But not everybody thought international experience was prestigious in any way, or that academic degrees were worth much. One day, as I was waiting for a bus to commute to the university, a car stopped at the bus stop. Its door opened and Pista, my former classmate from elementary school, asked me if he could give me a lift to Bratislava. I jumped in and we talked about our lives since elementary school, which we had finished about a decade earlier. As children, we lived close to each other, and we helped each other to catch up with assignments when one of us was ill or missed school for another reason. During the ride, I told him I was still in school, just like his two older brothers, who were also studying engineering. Pista laughed with a friendly mockery in his voice. "What will you do with that degree? It means nothing in today's world. You're wasting your time like my brothers. Look at me. I earn more money than you ever will as an engineer," he said. Unfortunately, too many at the time would have felt that he wasn't far from the truth.

I smiled and I was silently glad for "wasting my time" in the school bench a little longer. Pista finished masonry school, but, as he told me then dressed in a suit and a tie, he was working as a representative of a certain company, selling their products. I never saw him again. A few years later he was working as a security guard, became a hitman and was jailed for killing the ex-mayor of a town in southern Slovakia. The media talked first about life in prison for financially motivated manslaughter, but he got away with twenty-five years and a four thousand Euro fine payable to the mayor's widow for damages during the shooting. If he just had been inspired a little more by his brothers.

»«

The salary of a PhD student in Slovakia was a miserable income. (On the other hand, the low income was perhaps the price of generous availability of PhD positions at the faculty and their relatively liberal distribution across the departments.) Travel grants were limited, and they rarely matched the costs of living in Denmark. The Center, upon Geo's suggestion, provided a financial supplement during my stays at DTU. It was an insignificant amount in Danish terms, but to me it meant a fortune. I had everything I needed and much more. It would have been incomprehensible (and illegal) for Danish candidates to join a three-year PhD program for such income, but I could not dream of better conditions. I was fortunate and grateful. I was ready to begin working twice as much as most Danish doctoral students, for less than third of the income they earned.

Dušan wasn't always easy to work with. He was very busy with leading a large faculty, and he had plenty of industry-related projects, which made his colleagues and doctoral students often hard-pressed. But he was the only one in the department whose doctoral students nearly always successfully finalized their studies. He created the necessary conditions for them. He secured opportunities for international experience and satisfactory (and legal) extra income from external industrial projects. In return, he demanded high performance and compliance.

My case was different though. So was Jan Babiak's. Dušan wanted our studies to run in parallel, and he arranged that Jan's PhD was also a joint effort with DTU. We were working long hours every day without much supervision and without any extracurricular tasks that Dušan often burdened his students with. We did not desire supplementary income generating activities, and he respected it. He knew we were dedicated to delivering a work of internationally recognized quality and that we were in good hands with our Danish advisors. He appreciated the fact that as one of the few ones, I was about to credit indexed scientific journal publications to the faculty. We were assigned an isolated office one floor above the rest of the department, and nobody was supposed to disturb us with irrelevant duties routinely dumped on doctoral candidates. He defended us when some colleagues loudly envied our frequent travels abroad, referring to our English language skills and scientific output.

Dušan inspired us by his moral and social determination. He was visibly comfortable with the fact that I was of Hungarian nationality, which represented a minority that many Slovaks considered remnant of unfavorable times in the country's history. I met very few Slovaks in my life who indicated dislike towards my minority status. But in the case of Dušan it wasn't simply neutrality. He knew that Hungarian students at his faculty were often among the highly performing ones. He recognized that the history of Slovakia cannot be understood and fairly interpreted without the history of Hungary. He was well-travelled to understand that the beauty and values of the world are vulnerable to emphasizing nationalistic differences. He had several Hungarian friends, and, to my surprise, he was no stranger to Hungarian music of the 1960s and 1970s. He listened to it, and, rather unusually among Slovaks today, he attended concerts of his favorite Hungarian performers, such as the rock band Omega and the pop, folk, and beat singer Zsuzsa Koncz.

He was a pedagogue. He understood that education isn't only about performance, academic success, and revenue generation, it is also about standards of humanity. He tried to extend moral guidance to his students and younger colleagues. During cozy, informal conversations, he sometimes recommended certain healthy traditions and moral rules that he thought would be to our benefit in the long run. He wasn't a religious person, but he believed in the message of the Ten Commandments being the universal guide to basic human decency. He believed in the power of ethics, honesty, politeness but also marriage and family. Our student-supervisor relation metamorphosed with time into friendship. Dušan helped where he could. Not only in business-related issues, but he was ready to support us in our private challenges as well. He tactfully enquired about our love life and partners. He wanted us to be happy. When Jan went to a conference organized by Dušan in the Tatra Mountains in the north of Slovakia, Dušan offered him to stay for a few days longer and enjoy a skiing holiday with his girlfriend. I was also given the opportunity to join, with the hotel expenses being covered by the conference agreement, even though I was not participating in the event.

He was devoted to the development of the department, the faculty, and later the entire university as its vice-rector. Perhaps unusually for the environment and the times, he did not work for personal gains, he did not accumulate wealth nor ran a private company along with his official duties. He drove a rather old, unexceptional car, he used an ancient phone, he scrimped and saved where he could and moved from an apartment to a new house in his mid-fifties, when his savings finally allowed it. When the non-digital 35 mm camera was long the thing of the past in everybody's mind, he refused to give up his twenty-year-old little compact apparatus, for which he had difficulty buying films.

After he retired from university and faculty leadership, he became department chair. He declined the large chair's office and remained in his small one packed with documents to the extent that the door could not fully open and no more than three people could stand in the reasonably-sized room at one time. He turned the chair's office with its couch and elegant furniture into a common room for his colleagues to socialize.

A few years after Jan and I finished our PhD, Dušan was asked to consider the position of minister of education. When he briefly discussed it with me, I was struck to hear that he was considering the offer under one major condition. He would under no circumstances turn his back on his doctoral students and the department. He wanted to make sure his existing students would continue receiving his attention and that he would formally remain in his professorial position in order not to jeopardize his department's accreditation.

He found new challenges attractive even though they sometimes brought along personal difficulties with rivals and opponents. This one was inviting not because of the opportunity to abuse the corrupt political system, as many in such positions did. He recognized the flaws that had long been lingering in the education system, and he was determined to address them. When the elections did not produce the result desired by the government, the offer was called off. Given his moral convictions, it was probably best for him not to get sucked in by the political machinery, which rarely left one with dignity unharmed.

Dušan gloried in tales of his travels around the world and friendships with upper class individuals. He wasn't flawless. But his contacts with CEOs and influential people came mainly with his hard-earned leadership positions at the university and in the country's professional society for environmental engineering, and with the many related professional activities. They brought him not only participation at receptions and reliable tennis partners but especially job opportunities for his students and sponsorship for his many different projects at the university. He didn't just think of himself, his responsibilities, and his career. He valued attitude, skills, passion, and he helped them flourish. He utilized his successes for the benefit of many. And he extended a certain degree of moral example in an age of deteriorating values, which helped young people develop principles and preserve them unscarred.

»«

During the periods of my doctoral studies that I spent in Denmark, Geo was the one who cared about the development of my career most. He guided me in my project, supported my ideas and signed without reading (much like Dušan) every document I ever needed him to sign when I wanted to travel to a conference, apply for a grant, or be in Denmark rather than in Slovakia. When he invited a distinguished guest visiting the Center to his home for dinner, he invited me too. I felt privileged to join the company of my supervisor, his family, and renowned scientists within our field. It taught me to extend such invitations to both more senior and younger colleagues later, when I got in position to do the same.

My doctoral project allowed (and required) me to continue to intensively work with Charlie Weschler. He was our chemist since Ole invited him to be a visiting professor at the Center in 2001. He was now spending with us several months every year (and he would continue to do that for more than twenty years). He was increasingly influential in shaping my career, but he was also a role model whose personality I wanted to emulate.

I first realized what a gem Charlie was at my first conference in Singapore. I was an unknown novice, and I knew only my colleagues. It seemed as if all the nearly thousand participants knew Charlie and as if he knew everybody. I was repeatedly reassured over the years that my colleagues did not exaggerate when they claimed that we work with the greatest indoor air chemist of our time. Charlie was held in high regard wherever I mentioned his name during my work-related travels. Everybody wished to have him on board. And he was on board all over. He was a guest professor at several universities and an advisor to various institutions, projects, and a great many students around the world.

Charlie wasn't a lifetime professor who had taught thousands of students, course after course, year after year. He worked at Bell Laboratories and its successor institutions since his studies in the mid-1970s, then retired and became adjunct professor at Rutgers University in New Jersey when he was fifty-three, shortly before I met him. Yet, he touched the lives of many students and academicians in the U.S., Europe, and Asia over the years. I came across several individuals who claimed he was their most influential mentor or the reason they entered our scientific field. He became one of its most productive and most cited authors, and he was probably busier since his retirement than ever before. Everybody loved him, everybody wanted to work with him. But few had that privilege.

The collaboration with DTU allowed me to attend more conferences and become increasingly passionate about science, traveling, meeting new people, and experiencing a diversity of cultures. These interests were particularly intensified by meeting one guest of the institute who embodied all these elements. Professor Kirk Smith of the University of California at Berkeley was on a one-year sabbatical at the Center during my doctoral studies. He spent a lifetime studying women's and children's exposure to air pollution from household fuels and the related health effects in developing countries. He worked tirelessly to improve the environmental conditions and save lives through science, awareness, and policy. He ran investigations in countries like Guatemala, Mexico, India, Nepal, Laos, Mongolia, China and inspired countless others to pursue such work all over the world. He collaborated with the World Bank and the World Health Organization and contributed to the assessment reports of the Intergovernmental Panel on Climate Change, which was awarded the 2007 Nobel Peace Prize. (I would later meet several officially recognized contributors to the Nobel Prize awarded to the IPCC.) His research and advocacy were especially recognized in India, where his advice to the government led to schemes promoting the use of clean fuels and clean cookstoves to avoid the toxic effects of burning firewood and other biomass. What an honor it was to attend his lectures, work with him, observe his appreciation of cultures, hear his reflections on global challenges, and be invited by him for dinner in the nearby Vietnamese restaurant.

Living in two very different countries and traveling between them back and forth made me realize what an effect my surroundings were having on me. I increasingly appreciated and respected my host country, where I saw that citizens proudly and selflessly contributed to the common good and where the wealthiest had a long tradition of philanthropy, presenting their nation with everything from charitable trusts to museums or an opera house. My criticism grew towards my home country, where prosperity was measured in individual riches, and the wealthiest knew no limits nor decency on their journey to greedy success. The option to return to the town I grew up in did not seem any longer the most natural or wisest thing to do. I was now a different person. There was a shift in my perceived personality, an adjustment to the new environment. My attitude, my world views, and my opinions began to take shape in a new light. The world was becoming my home, I was becoming its citizen. Nurture complemented nature. And it did so rapidly. In fact, I was a different person in Denmark and in Slovakia. Every return to Slovakia for longer than a short family visit became difficult. The way I thought and the way I talked was switching back and forth. I observed that it quickly adjusted to the local environment after each move, which frightened me even more. I was struggling with the adaptations of my persona to the two worlds. With the personality shifts between two countries and cultures, one known for critique and discomposure, the another for positivity, content, and easygoingness. And I preferred my own self in Denmark rather than its equivalent in Slovakia.

I spent the little money I was able to save up to undertake a research stay at the University of Texas at Austin. It only lasted a little over a month, but it provided me with an array of uplifting encounters. I met professors active well into their late eighties, a Mexican doctoral student who, from solidarity, activism, to save money and send to his poor family, or for another reason, lived in a tent and walked everywhere within twenty kilometers, and an extremely generous Iranian housemate, a professor with poor English, who willingly answered all my questions about Iran and his life there that he tried to replace with a new one in America for the benefit of his family. I toured wonderful museums, where I got a rare chance to see and contemplate the world's first photograph and one of the original Gutenberg Bibles.

My host at the university, Professor Richard Corsi (later dean at Portland State University and University of California, Davis), impressed me with his unparalleled love for students and teaching and the energy he was able to extract from them. He considered students the giants on whose shoulders he always stood. In the beginning of every semester, he wrote a new song incorporating the names of every student and played it on his guitar in front of the class. Rich later spent three months of his sabbatical at DTU, where I could try to return his generous hospitality that I enjoyed in Austin. When his department opened a tenure track position in his group, he wished that I would apply for it. It was a tempting offer, but I remained happily loyal to DTU. Over the years, we remained in contact through occasional emails, and we met at a few conferences. His closing plenary talk at Indoor Air 2024 in Honolulu was one of the most inspirational talks I've heard. Rich always radiates utmost love, care, compassion, and interest in me and my life, but he does that towards everyone and all life on Earth. "He wouldn't hurt a fly" is meant literally in his case. Combined with his elegant humor, endless humility, and great wisdom, he is as pleasant a company as one can be. When I recently described to him the complicated but positive developments in my private life, my efforts to build a perfect relationship with my children, and the two books I've been working on in the past few years, he became an instant fan and added, "We often speak about legacies surrounding our careers, but these pale in comparison to the legacies we create in our relationships with those we love and care for in our lives".

My landlady Donna Johnson was a devout Democrat in a strongly Republican state (although in its mostly Democratic capital). She was in her eighties and worked as a volunteer at the Lyndon B. Johnson Presidential Library several days a week. We were compatible from the first moment because of our shared interests. I listened to her attentively as she talked about her family's history, American history but mostly about politics. Donna had a passion for American politics for a very long time, and her views were enlightening. She had been prepared to hear John F. Kennedy's speech in Austin from a front row seat on the eve of the day he was shot. She spoke about that day with emotions. Now she loved Senator Obama, and she was certain he would become president one day. She did not dare to predict that it would happen just two years later. When I met her again in 2011, well into the Obama presidency, she said she was convinced it was the best thing that had happened to the United States in recent years. Then she pulled out with pride his autographed portrait picture.

Donna told me about her friend Gene Hodge, who served as tail gunner on a B-24 Liberator in World War

II. During a bombing mission over Vienna, his plane was shot down, and the crew bailed out over Slovakia. When Gene heard about me staying in Donna's house, he wanted to talk to me on the phone and send me a dedicated copy of his book *A Taste of Glory*. Gene described how the incredibly friendly and caring Slovaks had saved his life, treated him like their son, and helped him evade capture when Slovakia was under a pro-Nazi puppet regime, risking their lives day after day over months to hide him along with other downed American fliers.

When he could no longer bear the responsibility for the danger he caused to his benefactors, he decided to break out to the Russian front. He was captured by the Gestapo and a perilous month began, lasting until his liberation by the Americans in Austria. During this time, he entirely relied on his deep faith in God to help him make it through. Gene returned to Communist Czechoslovakia for the first time three and a half decades later in the effort to reunite with his Slovak heroes. Since then, more reunions with fellow fliers and benefactors followed, and close friendships developed. It was an emotional story, a walk through history, witness to its fascinating impact on destiny, all made ever more authentic by talking directly to the tale's protagonist.

>«<

A year after visiting Austin, I handed in my doctoral dissertation in Slovakia. Following the defense, my father thanked Geo, to my embarrassment, for his fatherly care while I was in Denmark. I began to look for a job. I was driving to Prague for an interview at Ingersoll Rand, where a former doctoral student of the Center was working at the R&D division. Halfway between Brno and Prague, the highway was suddenly closed due to a major accident. I did not make it on time for the meeting. I was disappointed at first, but a phone call I got a few days later from Denmark made me think that sometimes these things happen for a reason. Geo offered me a two-year contract as a post-doc at the Center. I was hesitant in the beginning. I wished for something that would last longer. After years of uncertainty about the future as a student, I wanted to settle down, I wanted a little more security. I did not know in 2007, shortly before the start of the Great Recession, the most severe global financial crisis since the Great Depression in the 1920s, that the corporate world out there didn't necessarily offer lasting security either.

Geo patiently asked me to think about it, and he added a simple piece of advice that sounds like a cliché now (especially after having read works about the human mind and decision making) but had its effect back then (and might have it next time again). He said I should listen to my heart because it knows best. I also recalled his earlier reflection that some of his more daring friends, who often changed work and moved between countries, might have had more interesting lives than those who needed a constant sense of security like himself. There was nothing really I wished more than to extend my time at the Center, which was one of the most absorbing periods in my life. It refined me and increasingly defined me. I told Geo on the phone that if I should listen to my heart, there would be nothing to think about. I wouldn't hesitate for a second to accept the offer. That was what I did, and I never regretted it.

The opportunity to continue learning and growing in a stimulating environment among wonderful people came with uncertainty. My first contract at DTU was limited to two years; a permanent position was never in sight. I did not know what would come next. I was a foreigner in a country the language of which I did not speak. I was uneasy to return to my homeland, where I did not see opportunities to utilize what I had learned. Question marks appeared over when and where to settle down, what would it mean to be a foreigner for many years to come, and whether I'm ready to perhaps settle down with someone of a different nationality, since I was now having less and less contact with fellow Slovaks and Hungarians.

Most friends and relatives back home could hardly understand how someone could live with such uncertainties. They did not walk in my shoes, they did not see me with the eyes of someone who had travelled the world, knew similar lives, or had opportunities outside the borders of his native country. They lived in their own world, a comfortable one, and even if not, in any case a convenient one, where they knew exactly what to expect. Few could comprehend why I gave up the elegant, modern house that my father had slowly completed for me while I was undertaking my doctoral studies without the suspicion that those studies might keep me distant for a while, or even forever. But I didn't hesitate to exchange the luxury property for rented rooms, tiny apartments, and the opportunity to continue to mature in a whole other dimension.

Mom and dad never tried to hold me back in my endeavors with such earthly arguments as a house waiting for me to move in. They never doubted the worth of time and money spent on education. Or did they? When it began to be clear to my mother that she might not have me near her for some years, she questioned briefly whether providing "too much" education, studies abroad, and knowledge that cannot easily be exploited back home was worth the effort. She thought that perhaps the conventional path followed by most of my schoolmates and friends would have secured my presence and protected me from unnecessary challenges and uncertainties. Although there was some truth in her contemplation, mom eventually realized its selfish nature and was proud of my decision to accept the job in Denmark.

I was hired to work on a project that was Jan Sundell's legacy. We were looking for associations between the built environment (mainly ventilation and chemical exposures) and asthma and allergies among children. We collected an extensive questionnaire on the environment and respiratory health from more than eleven thousand children under six years of age on the island of Funen in Denmark, and we selected five hundred whose homes and daycares we wanted to inspect and perform measurements in. I was asked to recruit and lead a group of about twenty students (some older than me) who would complete the job in small groups staying for a few days at a time, or as their schedules allowed, at our rented base in Odense, the hometown of the prolific writer H. C. Andersen. We were operating with up to four groups of two, each assigned a rented car, leaving the base for a new assignment on an hourly basis. Another team in the house was typing in the collected data, and one person was continuously on the phone, standing in front of a wall covered with large sheets of calendar with hourly slots, recruiting the families that agreed to be visited. We worked seven days a week over a period of three months. To anyone observing the house, our activities must have resembled something like a secret CIA operation.

After two years of postdoctoral fellowship, my contract was extended. Then it was extended again. I was promoted to researcher and finally to associate professor. My office seventeen years later is still next to Geo's. He made a great effort throughout the years to ensure that I'd stay, especially as part of the staff's salary had to be covered by external funds. He secured projects, carefully managed them to make the resources last longer than expected and gave up having doctoral students so that he could finance me instead. He prioritized high quality science over any other academic performance indicator. I began as his instrument, and I tremendously appreciated it. What better way exists to learn science, gain experience, and embark on the path to academic reputation, which I admired in the professional role models I had met in recent years? I continuously progressed, and I loved flying in my small, private, invisible intellectual balloon, which I knew would be punctured (and patched) every time I talked to a more accomplished colleague.

It was always clear to Geo what was best for me. I knew I could freely steer my own development, but my confidence in his judgment didn't allow me to question his recommendations and guidance. He was also attentive to my contentment. Right after my full-time employment began, he and his wife Maria tried to match-make me with a girl because they didn't want to see me fall into a state of loneliness. Later, Geo was accommodating with respect to the well-being of my newly established family. Although Danes rarely interfere in their colleagues' private lives, we were able to discuss topics that belonged in the domain of friendship rather than colleagueship.

Charlie continued to spend two to three months every year at DTU. Geo was the golden ring in the chain. He acquired the funding for the projects that supported both Charlie and me and kept us busy. I tasted the wonders of multidisciplinary science. We worked with indoor air quality, ventilation, air cleaning, occupant comfort, exposure to particulate and chemical pollutants, indoor chemistry, epidemiology, and public health. The study on children's health, in which we measured various chemical pollutants in homes and daycares, moved me in the direction of chemical exposures. We spent a decade studying human exposure to phthalates (chemical compounds for example in plasticizers) and other semivolatile organic compounds (abundant chemicals indoors with potential health consequences, which are happy to be present both sorbed on surfaces and flying around in the air). When I obtained funding for a three-month-long guest professorship, I invited Professor Glenn Morrison, a rising star in indoor air chemistry at Missouri University of Science and Technology and a friend of Charlie's, to join the party. After Charlie, together with Bill Nazaroff of UC Berkeley, ran his models suggesting that some airborne semivolatiles for which the skin was believed to act as a perfect barrier can in fact penetrate the skin directly from air without contact with the source, he came with the ingenious idea to experimentally test the hypothesis. The three of us teamed up with two great minds, Tunga Salthammer, yet another excellent chemist at the Fraunhofer Institute in Germany, and Holger Koch, one of the world's leading biomonitoring experts. (Biomonitoring measures chemicals and their metabolites in biological substances, especially urine and blood.) We performed several fascinating and unique experiments proving on our own nearly naked bodies sitting in a climate chamber with our head fitted in an oxygen treatment hood supplied with clean air that some phthalates and nicotine can penetrate the skin directly from air. The next step was to look at the role clothing plays in dermal exposure. This was Glenn's expertise.

The months when Charlie was at the Center were the most enjoyable and productive. I learned all the time. It was like being on steroids. To work twelve to fifteen hours a day to complete as much work as possible within the time frame of Charlie's visit was the most natural thing to do. I hated the sudden realization that I must sleep when I looked at the clock at 2 a.m., and I couldn't wait for the morning to continue what we set out to complete.

We authored numerous scientific papers together. Charlie returned my early manuscripts with so many changes that I felt not only embarrassed but sorry for him too. It could have been easier to write the text from scratch than to rewrite after me. I carefully examined all his edits and asked for explanation when something was unclear. A few years later, he began to compliment my writing. A couple more years, and I began to receive some sections of my manuscripts back with only minor edits. It was a mini triumph but especially a lesson that science doesn't allow shortcuts, it doesn't accept bribes. It can take a decade to see a little progress in the illumination of a scientific conundrum but also in one's own academic competences. It helped me appreciate the extraordinary effort renowned experts must have made before reaching recognition, often at an advanced age. No youngster, however assertive or confident about his abilities, can compete with the experience and knowledge of those who have spent a lifetime learning, searching for answers, and putting their hypotheses to the test.

With time, Charlie became not only an amazing mentor but a great friend as well. Knowing him and working with him now for almost two decades has been a blessing. He is not only an inexhaustible source of professional inspiration but also a magnificent source of inspiration in general. He can talk about anything with an enviable overview. Whether it is about art, nature, cultures of the world, sports, politics, his love for beer, films from around the world that inspired him over a lifetime, or science in general, including fields that have little to do with his own professional interests, he always provides a well-grounded opinion, which comes along with an immense willingness to listen, learn, and compromise.

The reason for his likeability is his unparalleled kindness, humility, generosity, considerateness, compassion, and gratitude. He compliments the ordinary, emphasizes the self-evident, appreciates the quotidian. Charlie's behavior reveals his delicacy but not his prominence. His respect and politeness towards everyone know no boundaries. He devotes equally courteous attention to the cleaning lady in the corridor and to his colleagues or friends. He keeps an eye on everybody in a conversation and makes sure no one feels left out. He never forgets to credit those who deserve it, even for the most minor contribution to his efforts. But he sometimes entitles himself with a "stupid" or a "just a chemist" for the smallest mistake.

Soon after I received my doctoral degree, Charlie asked me before a conference whether I would be willing to look at his slides and give feedback on his lecture. I was honored by his confidence but doubtful that I could find anything to recommend this champion presenter. I was puzzled. Could the apprentice improve anything in the work of his master? (I did offer a couple of minor comments, which likely originated from my lack of full understanding of the topic. Of course, Charlie saw it as a demonstration of my cleverness that helped him rectify his errors. I did not see it that way.)

It was also humbling to hear Charlie talk about the completeness of his extended family, the cheerful annual family reunions, which have brought together generations for decades, and his equally remarkable siblings. Frank, a doctor, regularly volunteered to help the poor in Haiti, and Ted has been inspired by Warren Buffet to the extent that he decided after his retirement as a successful hedge fund manager to try his luck and meet his role model. He was the top bidder in two consecutive years to win a private lunch with Buffet. He became Buffet's right hand, his top investment manager, at a time in the business magnate's life when one would think his machinery was well-oiled and his closest team had long been established on firm grounds without need for change. It was captivating to hear of the wealthy brother who remains humble and generous, a financial steward of education for the extended family's later generations, who understands his responsibility towards the society that enabled him to achieve what he has achieved.

Charlie believes that coming from a Catholic family and attending Catholic schools had an immensely positive effect on him and his family regardless of the gradual loss of his religious belief throughout his life. He and his wife Lulu, who is equally humble, appreciative, and passionate for knowledge, form one of those few adorable couples that continue to inspire me to be a better person.

Geo and Charlie have been masters of encouragement and motivation. They paved my way to a career I had never even dared to dream of in my earlier years. But more than that, they demonstrate an indescribable work culture that I will try to emulate and pass on to the next generations. My father captured it well one day about ten years after I began working with my two mentors. He said he was astonished at the fact that all those years I had not once mentioned a trace of criticism of my closest colleagues and my boss, nor a hint of disagreement. It was utterly unusual, nearly impossible in the world he knew. This, together with Geo's attentiveness and Charlie's repeated visits, was among the main reasons why I declined job offers from other universities. The combination of the professional opportunities and the personal relations I had with my colleagues could not be easily outclassed.

»×«

My full-time employment brought collaboration with more people through international projects and, for the first time, solid pay, which allowed me to visit foreign places and meet people from all walks of life. My inspirations were rapidly growing. I was impressed especially by individuals who achieved something despite unfavorable conditions or who, like Charlie, were giants in what they were doing but acted as if they were insignificant. One of those in the second group was Jack Spengler, probably the biggest name in the field of environmental health and the built environment.

Jack's appearance was always casual, his behavior unpretentious. It would have been difficult for the unacquainted meeting him on the street to tell whether he was one of the most recognized scientists from the most prestigious university or a local janitor. He was able to talk virtually to anyone at a level that put his dialoguer in the driver's seat. Young or old, newcomer or veteran, scientific staff or technician, nobody felt belittled when talking to him; every remark received his full attention and an uplifting response. But it was hard not to feel humbled when he was asked to share his expertise. Boy, there was wisdom.

Jack, together with Jan Sundell, Ole Fanger, and a few

others, was one of the early pioneers of the field. He was involved in some of the landmark studies that shaped our understanding of the importance of indoor air quality for health. His encyclopedic knowledge of past and ongoing studies around the world was impressive. He could provide a powerful idea or advice on any project. During his career, he shifted the focus of his research several times. He was a true expert in environmental pollution, personal exposure, indoor air quality, epidemiology, and environmental sustainability. He advised the World Health Organization, the U.S. Environmental Protection Agency, the Federal Aviation Administration, and when his excellence was needed, he wasn't far from some of the top people in the U.S. government. He never considered slowing down. As the recent COVID-19 pandemic unfolded, Jack, approaching eighty, embarked on the busiest period of his life.

Jack's legacy reached every corner of the world. Numerous leading professors, university leaders, entrepreneurs, and other influential persons around the world had in common a PhD degree obtained under his supervision. He was a true role model for so many people out there and for so many students constantly around him, whom he was always determined to help the best he could. And most of the time he could and would. In 1988, he co-founded a successful consulting company bringing together dozens of hygienists, hazardous materials managers, engineers, microbiologists, risk assessment specialists, and other professionals to solve complex environmental and engineering problems. Many of the employees were his former doctoral students. The company was employee-owned, and when he finally decided in his mid-seventies that it was time to quit, understanding well that he was certainly not in need of financial gains, he passed his shares to his employees against modest or no compensation. Jack's famous generosity reached me too, and his invitation to visit Harvard and work with his team I will cherish for the rest of my life.

When our son Jonatan was born, I was, thanks to the generosity of the Danish government towards its public employees, entitled to a three-month paternity leave with full pay. It was the perfect opportunity to accept Jack's invitation and immerse myself in the kingdom of intellectual inspiration. When most funding agencies refused to support my trip, I was determined to minimize costs and finance myself the missing part on top of a small travel grant and Jack's contribution covering the cost of accommodation. I packed up the family and left to explore Boston, absorb what Harvard had to offer, and analyze some fabulous datasets on onboard environmental conditions and passenger and crew responses collected on eighty-three transcontinental and transoceanic flights all over the globe. And so, Jonatan visited both Harvard and MIT before he turned one year. Perhaps it will inspire him one day to return and find out on his own what a stimulating place it is.

I knew Jack for about ten years before this happened. He was first on the advisory board of the Center and visited us every few years to evaluate our activities. I presented my work in front of him for the first time just a few months into my first visit to the Center as a master's student. He was later one of the advisors for a large Danish project I was working on, and over the five years it was running, we met at the annual meetings, which were usually two-day retreats with ample time to socialize. Geo often expressed to me during these meetings his admiration for this giant and legend. My office was now, for a short period, next to his.

The two months I spent at Harvard were the most intense and intriguing I have experienced in terms of inspiration. I felt the same keenness, although at a more mature level, as when I first arrived at the renowned International Centre for Indoor Environment and Energy at DTU as a visiting master's student a decade earlier. The Centre felt back then like a nest occupied by heroes, from hand-picked students to brilliant professors. A place where students were treated with collegial respect, where each research topic was so fascinating that I couldn't decide which one I should first devote time to. A place visited by guest scholars and advisors from even more prestigious places (both Jack and Bill Nazaroff from UC Berkeley being among them). It was the place where my appetite for an academic career, which doesn't let curiosity sleep, had been awakened. But the place where others perhaps still arrived with the expectations and dreams that I brought with me on the first day slowly turned for me into something a little more than a common workplace. Inspiration can be like a drug. At some point we begin to need more because we love what it does with us. Harvard evoked the same feelings of excitement as the Center did eleven years before. It was the excitement of the environment with more intense manifestation of intellect and talent, where thought-provoking events and inspiring people swarmed like honeybees. An environment that for so many of its own fellows is just the venue of everyday routine.

Harvard was flooded with brainpower, mastery, and wisdom. The number of open seminars, workshops, debates, and lectures offered on campus was overwhelming. Many Harvard employees don't appreciate in their everyday busyness all the fantastic opportunities that surround them. But I was there to try it all. I could have spent my entire time going to fascinating events and soaking in tubs of information. A casual chat at a reception with the dean of the Harvard School of Public Health and former minister of health of Mexico (Julio Frenk), lectures on volcanoes and human migrations, placebo studies, or leadership in public health, signing of a new book about science versus God (Amir Aczel: *Why Science Does Not Disprove God*) or about the final days of the Soviet Union (Serhii Plokhy: *The Last Empire*), a public conversation with a former U.S. ambassador to NATO and Greece (and currently China) and Under Secretary of State and national security advisor under several presidents (Nicholas Burns), a former presidential candidate (John McCain), and President Obama's spiritual advisor and head of the White House Office of Faith Based and Neighborhood Partnerships (Joshua DuBois) were just the main events I could fit into my schedule. But the Harvard event calendar was inexhaustible; there was something to everybody's taste, all the time, all open, all free. And the Massachusetts Institute of Technology with a similarly rich repertoire was within spitting distance. Some of the best and brightest in any field of interest could be found in town. Not only their sheer knowledge but their personal stories too could make passion burst into flames.

A conversation with the director of the National Institute of Allergy and Infectious Diseases, Anthony Fauci, was one such thrilling experience. He has been one of the first and most influential pioneers of understanding and tackling HIV/AIDS in the 1980s and 1990s and one of the most cited scientists in the world. But he didn't talk about immunology. Instead, he spoke about personal experiences and reflections on leadership in challenging times. He had advised five U.S. presidents (seven since then; all since Ronald Reagan) and developed programs saving millions of lives. When HIV/AIDS first surfaced and was followed by hysteria and wide demonstrations demanding answers and help, and when the disease was so stigmatized that no public official wanted to have anything to do with it, he was one of the first to invite the demonstrators in his office and listen to what they had to say. He recognized the need for research and did all he could to secure funding for it. He was instrumental in developing treatments, policies, and relief programs that now enable a long and active life for people with HIV around the world (including the President's Emergency Plan for AIDS Relief, PEPFAR, the largest global health program focused on a single disease in history until the COVID-19 crisis).

It was also stimulating to hear his reflections on the diplomatic skills needed when his policies and recommendations that could have saved lives were not seen by the president politically well-timed or when he opposed the president's views on tackling a given public health challenge. Since the time I met him, Fauci's leadership skills have been put to the test by the Ebola outbreak and especially by the COVID-19 outbreak, which put him as a lead member of the White House Coronavirus Task Force in the world news on a daily basis. He later served as President Biden's Chief Medical Advisor.

A few days after my arrival in Boston, I was invited to a doctoral defense of one of Jack's students. The presentation and its presenter made me somewhat belittle my own efforts during my doctoral training a few years earlier, no matter how hard I thought I had been working. Catlin Powers travelled to the Himalayan plateau in Western China as an undergraduate to study climate change and outdoor air pollution. After she was repeatedly challenged by the local families asking her why she was looking for "smoke in the crystal-clear sky" when there was plenty of smoke from their stoves indoors, she decided to postpone her studies at Wellesley College and stay in the remote village to help solve the problem. Catlin grew up living in almost a dozen countries around the world, so she knew well what it takes to adapt. She embarked on a journey that turned her into a scientist, inventor, and public health entrepreneur, all while working on her degree.

She became passionate about helping the nomads. She began to develop a solar stove, which came into being after fifty-four prototypes. When Harvard heard about her progress, she was encouraged to pursue a doctoral degree on her project. She was offered an individual program to rapidly finalize her college degree at Wellesley. Her work wasn't funded by the university or her supervisor's projects. She secured grants and research prizes. She learned some Chinese and Tibetan, and she frequently returned to the villages to test and develop her invention and to live with the nomads to understand their needs and culture, which she found crucial to her success. When the word came that she had contracted a parasite infection that could cost her life, her Harvard advisors, including Jack, took responsibility to locate her (no easy task under the given conditions) and evacuate her to a Hong Kong hospital.

Catlin co-founded the tech company One Earth Designs, which developed renewable energy innovations and made her products available around the world. She continued to travel and face the unique cultural, economic, and political challenges in each new country where she decided to distribute her invention. She was determined to achieve her goal of improved health for poor rural populations at significantly reduced fuel use. I learned with time that she and her company had not only received prestigious prizes and recognitions before she finalized her studies, but she also served on various boards, advisory committees, and panels of leading social change organizations, including the Clinton Global Initiative, and on juries of various entrepreneurship and environment awards and prizes. She was one of a kind among the doctoral students even in Harvard terms.

Although I shared an office with Catlin, her busy schedule allowed me to meet her only one more time before my stay was over. She invited me for a Hong Kong style hot pot lunch. Two years later, I was asked to suggest a young plenary speaker for the Indoor Air 2016 world congress in Ghent, Belgium. I could not think of a better candidate. Catlin accepted the organizers' invitation, and it was now my turn to treat her to dinner after her talk. And she treated me with an unforgettable conversation in which the world became more transparent, its big problems little, struggling people happier, life more harmonious, and my spiritual energy more abundant. This person of inexhaustible kindness, compassion, perpetual smile, and devotion to improving lives remains probably the most inspired and most inspirational young person I have met.

The gratefulness for the opportunity to observe and the pride in having tasted the boiling stew of fascinating intellectual ingredients present at Harvard continues to fill me with enthusiasm for my job and much beyond. I'm grateful to all those mentioned in this chapter whose contributions, small or large, have helped my professional (and closely related personal) development. But I'm also thankful to many others who have made an impression on me but haven't been mentioned here. As I got to work with more professionals in the field and befriend some of them (and perhaps as I became myself a minor source of inspiration for a few), there seemed to be space for more professional "celebrities"—hard-working experts whose achievements were recognized by others. No matter how good one is, he is never alone in his success. And the more I worked with people across disciplines, outside my own niche, the more I realized that plenty of minor stars can be found everywhere. They may be considered stars within a different homogenous group of few, who are no-names outside their circumscribed comfort zones.

Most often, those of our personal connections we consider big names are big names only within a given field and among a few with whom they share expertise. It became clear with time that most of the professional people who have inspired me inspired relatively few others. They didn't mean much to my friends and neighbors and were considered only my colleagues even by my family. To students they were only teachers, to many of their academic peers they were fellow scholars of equal rank, whose publications were read mostly by few others within the field (at most a couple of hundred or thousand who were equally unknown outside of it). I even saw less stardom in the people I once admired as I got better at my job and more accustomed to working with them. Fame in science is a byproduct of diligent (most often ordinary) work and its impact, or at least others' perception of its relative importance, which in academia is rarely appreciated beyond a specific community. Professional fame is often confined to a narrow group of people who work on similar problems and equally believe in their work's significance. They establish their own societies, organize their conferences, publish in their journals, read each other's articles, and hand out awards among themselves.

The people I used to consider stars weren't perhaps unique in the vast world of all academia and scholarship. Perhaps their inspirational power, while possibly unchanged for new people who meet them, may change with time among old friends. But our heroes, who have once shaped us, are to us never trivial. We continue to treasure them, and they will remain *our* heroes. Everybody can be somebody else's hero. And our heroes can come from anywhere. Even from the most unexpected of places.

4

VOYAGE TO ANOTHER VIEW

"One of the signs of passing youth is the birth of a sense of fellowship with other human beings as we take our place among them."

– Virginia Woolf
(Hours in a Library)

What a joy it is to be among brighter people than us. It is the only way not to fall into complacency, recognize our limitations, and continuously learn and evolve. We need from time to time to join circles in which we feel somewhat little and unimportant. Not ones that discourage us or make us feel worthless but circles that motivate us to try to grow up to their level. The cascade of inspiration often occurs naturally in our professional life. But what about the other domains essential for our completeness?

Growing up in a modest, simple countryside environment, although not too remote from opportunities, can make a person under certain circumstances more motivated, more deeply inspired by sources taken for granted by those living a flashy city life. On the other hand, one can then sooner reach the perception that he is intellectually outgrowing those around him. Whether this is just an illusion or truth generated by the rudimentary nature of the reference point, standing out in some aspects of life should not be counterbalanced with total ignorance in others. Even if we reach heights in education and career, we need to realize how unenlightened we may be in other fields and especially in life's true wisdom, which is the root of contentment.

We need not only to be among brighter people but also people who are wiser regardless of their occupation, successes, or failures. We need to walk through life with open eyes and open minds, observe the diversity of human destinies, contemplate them, and adopt their lessons. There is wisdom in everyone. We can build our own wisdom from many small elements that we encounter along the way. But first we need to encounter them.

In my late teens or early twenties, I realized how much I enjoyed talking to older people from all walks of life. I loved their stories, memories, reflections on the past, present, and future. With time, I began to enjoy listening to both older and younger individuals. Cross-generational observations were captivating. They were especially thrilling when experienced across nations, cultures, religions, political systems, and histories; they reflected a broad variety of destinies and wisdoms drawn from them. The most exciting way to obtain a myriad of such viewpoints and "truths" is traveling!

My zeal for travel, both mental but especially physical travel, may have been awakened by my father's stories of his early adventures. His ride on a Jawa Pionier scooter to the Romanian coast when he was sixteen and hadn't yet had a driver's license, his adventures as a bachelor in Crimea, where he sat in the chairs of Churchill, Roosevelt, and Stalin at the venue of the Yalta Conference of 1945, or his two trips with my mother from communist Czechoslovakia to Western Europe, which became possible only after arduous visa processes preconditioned by leaving their children at home as "hostages" of the state, a guarantee of return from behind the Iron Curtain, were stories I listened to with awe.

My parents' three-week honeymoon in 1977, much delayed by the months-long visa application process, took them to Venice, Verona, Florence, and Rome. When my mother became sick one day due to her pregnancy with Adrian, they decided to get away from the tent floor and the car seat for one night and treat themselves to a hotel room. It cost them most of their never-seen-before valuta, of which a strictly insufficient amount was allocated by the regime to every approved traveler. Credit cards were unheard of, and Eastern and Western countries didn't trade each other's currencies.

Their Škoda 100 (which later broke down in Austria on the way home and thus further stressed the budget) was therefore stuffed with three weeks' worth of food supplies from home, dishes, cookers, cutlery, sleeping bags, and a couple of valuables that they hoped to trade for cash when needed. And, of course, a small amount of Czechoslovak korunas, which they were obliged to report at the border when leaving the country and again when returning. When upon return they were unable to present the exact amount indicated in the documents, the officers made them unload the car and unpack every piece of luggage. After a few hours, my mother expressed her irritation with a sigh and a reference to the unappealing ending of the honeymoon. The evidently surprised border guard showed his humane face for a second and said, "Why didn't you say so in the beginning? Pack your stuff and go. Congratulations and goodbye".

The second trip took their white Lada 2105 and a cramped caravan, filled with canned food and products from the latest hog killing, to Paris and the Swiss Alps in 1988 while my brother and I enjoyed our summer vacation at our grandparents. Obtaining visas to Germany, France, and Switzerland took almost two years and several fruitless three-hundred-kilometer trips to the nation's capital, Prague, where the embassies were located. The few hundred Deutschmarks and French and Swiss francs from the government and a few pieces of tradable Bohemian porcelain sufficed for the essentials, like the warm water in the camping shower, which ran ridiculously short every time a precious foreign coin was inserted in the automat that seemed like technology from the future. When the Lada, struggling in first gear, could no longer continue the fight to reach the top of a mountain pass (taking the tunnel was unaffordable) and the engine gave in hundred meters before relief, all they could do was leave it in the middle of the road despite the jam of angry muscle cars behind them and wait for a miracle after the VAZ carburetor took its rest. After weeks of longing for an ice cream, my father finally treated my mother to the magical delicacy towards the end of the trip. And himself with the only beer he could afford during the vacation.

My parents could never forget the obstacles cast under their feet before and during these trips that shaped their understanding of the world at that time. But they never wanted to forget. We spent lots of cozy family evenings over the following years viewing the hundreds of diapositives from these trips while listening to my parents' recollections and letting them stimulate our own desire to get to know the world. They continue to cherish these adventures, which, if they had waited a few years, would have been achievable without obstacles but would surely have tasted very different. We visited some of the places as a family a quarter of a century later. The opera in the first century Roman amphitheater Arena di Verona was a very special treat for me, and I can only guess how seeing Carmen until the end under the clear summer sky must have felt for mom and dad, whose first (and financially much more burdening) attempt to see the very same opera all those years ago was cut short by pouring rain and lightning striking at the feet of the frightened dancers on the stage.

In 1989 and 1990 my father was working in Makó near the Hungarian-Rumanian border, supervising the construction of a milk powder plant, the glory of which would not last long. Soon after its completion in the fresh age of capitalism, it was acquired by the Italians and dismantled, as if from dust it came to dust it returned after a very short lifespan. Dad came home to visit us every other weekend, and my mom had to handle the two boys and the household with my sister in her belly. Dad took us back with him several times to visit the center of the Hungarian onion farming and home of one of the largest international onion festivals. The regional cookery offered some fabulous delicacies like the goulash made of deer, boar, or other animal, and the equally paprika-based *halászlé*, fisherman's soup, mostly prepared by dad's friends in a traditional cauldron over open fire. Visiting the local market with its muddy floor and disorganized arrangement turned out to cost dad much more money than expected. The country freshly liberated from communism (or just we in our ignorance) saw people using new creative ways to make money. It was our first time to observe the fraudulent shell game performed by confidence tricksters, and we were learning the cost of naivety the hard way.

One day we crossed to Arad, a nearby city in

Romania. My memories of the town are blurred, but I recall the extremely bad roads, very poor conditions, and the warning of dad's friends in Makó to be very cautious, not to stop for anyone on the road, perhaps not even the police, which may be fake, lock the car even when sitting in it, and always watch our belongings. A few months had passed since the bloody Romanian revolution of 1989, the collapse of the communist regime, and the hasty show trial and execution of Nicolae Ceaușescu. Signs of law and order were sparse, poverty widespread. I got myself a traditional pan flute, the *nai*.

A couple of years after the Velvet Revolution, my parents decided to break the routine of family vacations within Czechoslovakia and Hungary, which used to be virtually the only destinations that made sense to consider during communist times. Even though the latter had been a friendly communist nation, the border crossing usually required hours of queueing and nerves of steel. The mountains of Slovakia and the beaches in Hungary with their fragrance from corn on the cob distributed by vendors passing between lying beachgoers and stands selling pancakes, *lángos* (deep-fried flatbread), or swim rings and water guns still evoke the sweet memories of the hiking and skiing trips in the former and the summer tours in the latter. Instead of the Tatra Mountains and Lake Balaton, we visited the Istrian peninsula of the newly formed Croatia in the summer of 1993.

Visiting the former Yugoslavian state was a rather unique experience. Although Yugoslavia was communist ruled, it had a status of a semi-developed, semi-Western, independent country before the fall of the Iron Curtain, and my luckier classmates bragged about having visited its majestic coast before I could even dream about it. It was the country where many of the episodes of our childhood favorite, Winnetou, were filmed and where my siblings and I saw the sea for the first time. Glimpsing it for the first time was a moment I was intensely looking forward to, with my excitement continuously growing as the road got us closer and closer to the coast. It felt like a highlight of my life, understandable only to those coming from a landlocked country.

We visited the island of Hvar the year after. The war on the coast had just recently come to an end. The inland road via the beautiful Plitvička Jezera National Park near the Bosnian border was still closed and considered dangerous. A part of the road we took, perhaps by mistake, was winding through deserted villages, passing bombed houses and road signs perforated with dozens of bullet holes. Destroyed bridges were replaced by pontoon bridges, and the traffic was policed by soldiers. A strange feeling was slowly overpowering us, although we did not feel danger. Many foreign cars followed the same route in the height of the tourist season.

Everything was new to me. The mountains melting into memorable beaches, the lemon and olive groves, the sweet figs plucked from the trees along the roads, the *ćevapčići* and *pljeskavica* (grilled dishes of minced meat) feasts as well as the refugees. Hvar wasn't damaged by the war, but some hotels housed those who had escaped the fighting and did not dare to return or had no home to return to. The summerhouses were in use by their owners year-round for the same reasons.

We befriended an older couple living in their summerhouse. János was a Hungarian from northern Serbia, and his wife Anna was German. They never imagined they, at an advanced age, would have to flee one day. They went down to Hvar during the war and didn't dare to leave. Being considered Serbs, they feared that their *kuća* (house), if left vacant, would be looted or destroyed by local Croats, and the risk of confiscation was also real. There were indeed many formerly countrymen now suddenly living in neighboring foreign countries who waited a decade or more after the war to get their properties back.

Sándor was a refugee from the north of the war-torn country. He was staying in the nearby hotel, and he also spoke Hungarian. We met him several times during the vacation. He showed us his favorite place to swim, a pristine assemblage of rocks in a remote part of the peninsula known probably only to him, where he often walked out when he desired solitude. We listened with awe to his accounts of what had happened over the past years and how he miraculously escaped after someone had pulled him out of a mass grave. It never occurred to us that these circumstances and encounters might in any way negatively affect the magic of our vacation. Quite the opposite, we returned the following year and rented the lovely apartment that János and Anna had completed next to their summerhouse. It was only in 2021 that I went back to Hvar again, with my parents, wife, and children, and we revisited with nostalgia the mostly unchanged places so vividly present in my Croatian memories from childhood.

During the following years, as my parents' income improved, we began to regularly visit Western European countries. Ski Amadé near Salzburg was our new skiing destination, and during the summers we visited Venice, the Dolomites, Côte d'Azur, and the Benelux states, where Peter and Tonny were always ready to host us or provide us their house while they were in Slovakia. Adrian and I eventually spent a year in the United States. The real breakthrough in my passion for traveling, and with that for understanding the world, came with moving to Denmark for the first time. It was the second time I moved from home for nearly a year, although this time it turned out to become a longer-lasting commitment. In contrast to the experience that I had in the U.S. six years earlier, this stay, characterized by personal independence, more mature age, and a very different purpose, was a joy from the beginning. I experienced for the first time an international campus, a melting pot.

Colleagues, guest scientists, students, and classmates came from all corners of the world. I signed up for Danish language lessons even though I intended to leave Denmark at the end of the eleven-month program. (It took eventually way too many years before I could use Danish at a solid conversational level partly because of the international academic environment in which I remained to work to this day.) I also learned to converse in basic Polish. Ania and Basia, my two new Polish friends, fellow students, and office mates, refused to speak English to me. For about a month, I was having no idea what they were saying to me, but Polish, Slovak, and Czech gradually became three shades of the same tongue in our group. Others could not comprehend how we from the three countries can babble in our own distinct languages and still lead a perfectly complete conversation with each other.

I was making new friends, encountering a variety of languages and cultures, people with vastly different lives, views, and attitudes, and I began to follow the international news, in the times when the American wars in Afghanistan and Iraq dominated them. These floods of inspiration awakened my passion for geography in its broadest sense, and it has not come to rest since. I gradually became fascinated with different countries, their nature, traditions, history, politics, and the impact of these on the way people live in them. I asked my new friends lots of questions. From the structure of a sentence in their native language or spelling of their names using their alphabets or characters to their national holidays, meals, and topography of their lands. The conversations often inspired me to explore the map, look up photos on the internet, read articles about the places I found most exciting and ultimately dream of visiting them.

And I found every place exciting. The list of countries I desired to visit became longer than what time and money could possibly allow. I was a student with a small scholarship in an expensive country, and I chose to continue under these circumstances for another three years as a doctoral student. But I was longing to see the wonders of the planet, learn them, live them, and understand them, gain appreciation for life and its countless miracles, big and small, through experiencing the endless diversity with all its beauty and troubles.

I was ready to set concrete travel goals. I used every opportunity and a big portion of my modest savings to see the world. I was optimistic that with time my work would help me get to new, more distant places as well. I aspired, following the examples of my supervisors and senior colleagues, to see the world through what I knew and what I could share with others—through working on the international scene. I knew there was a long way to build the knowledge and recognition enabling global travel, but the first opportunities for work-related travel soon appeared.

Participation at conferences paid for by the university or travel grants was a good way to see cities and to fund the expensive airfares to regions where staying a few extra days was then inexpensive. My first trip to Asia was to the conference in Singapore. It was a tropical escapade in the middle of the miserable Danish December. It was special, it was different. Different were the people with their skin colors, ethnicities, and religions, the tropical smells, the flavorful tastes, the scorching sun, the moist air, the monsoon rain, the left-hand traffic, the four official languages, the order and cleanliness, the unprecedented development, the multitude of electronic stores. It further awakened my appetite to explore near and far.

Two years later, I attended a conference in Beijing. I arrived in China after a few-hour stopover at Sheremetyevo airport in Moscow for which I obtained a visa at the Russian embassy in Bratislava to be able to visit Saint Basil's Cathedral, Red Square with Lenin's mausoleum (the venue of flashy Soviet military parades the images of which were still vivid in my memory), the fearful Kremlin from afar, and the new Cathedral of Christ the Savior. In China, I had invited Yuexia, who had been my officemate few years earlier in Denmark, to show me a few places after the conference. I figured that partly covering my friend's expenses (she lacked the means at the time) would be cheaper and allow for a more authentic travel than the alternative option of hiring a travel agency. Given the immense language divide and the limited time I had, traveling on my own wasn't a viable possibility. Yuexia was thrilled to travel with me to Xi'an, visit its Terracotta Army, and bike on the top of its majestic historical city walls, and especially to guide me through Guilin and bamboo raft around Yangshuo, where we explored the caves, rice fields, and the windings of the Li River between the magnificent karst mountains. Some of the places were popular among tourists, but it was unnoticeable to me, as the tourists were mostly

Chinese, and I was tasting the magic of traveling with a local friend. We biked through remote villages, passed farmers wading barefooted in the deep mud of their rice paddies as they arduously tried to maintain control over their ox-driven plows, we slept in motels of local families with their kids in open-crotch pants running around, ate in the most authentic places that only locals knew. The fact that it was also Yuexia's first time in this part of China, made the adventure ever more enjoyable.

At the time of my visit in 2005, China was already on its path to economic boom and tremendous development. But it offered plenty of what I had (and had not) expected: not only the magnificence of the Great Wall and the Forbidden City, the awe-inspiring culture, glorious temples, sublime parks but also underdevelopment, poverty, disorder, and the national sport of spitting in public, outdoors as well as indoors (with its own historical and cultural reasons). There were two subway lines with a few dozen stations operating in the mighty, overpopulated Beijing. When I returned just a couple of years later, I found a complicated network of nearly two dozen lines with over four hundred stations, each so long that the ends were invisible when looking from the middle of the platform. When I took a train from Beijing to Xi'an the first time, I was advised to choose a connection with the shortest possible train number to avoid the discomfort of dirty, overcrowded cars. I ordered tickets for the two-digit number connection, and the travel agent didn't want to believe that it really was my choice. I didn't find it particularly expensive, but I understood the agent's reaction when I arrived at the platform. A lady in uniform welcomed me at the car door with a bow and a smile and guided me to my elegantly decorated shared four-bed berth, which featured a flat screen TV at each bed, a silver vase with fresh flower on the table, and "room service". The more than fifteen-hour ride felt like a luxury. The second time I visited China, the new bullet train network crisscrossing the entire country allowed me to reach Shenzhen near Hong Kong in the south from Beijing in the north in eight hours. It was experiencing rapid development, technology, and determination at their best.

>«

Conferences, project meetings, seminars, research stays, and invitations allowed me to visit numerous places over the years after these early business trips. I usually went prepared to every new place, even if just for a very short visit. At the minimum, I familiarized myself with the map and read the Wikipedia page of the country and the city of my destination, with a few detouring clicks on links to major historical events, tourist attractions, or phrases in the local language. Besides the time spent in meeting rooms and restaurants, I could often squeeze in a brief cultural event or a few hours, maybe a day, of exploring. No matter how busy I was, an early morning hike in humid Hong Kong or in the Rhodope Mountains in Bulgaria, trying to spot a whale at Point Lookout on North Stradbroke Island outside Brisbane in Australia, a boat trip to the Suomenlinna sea fortress in Helsinki, city swimming in the Rhine in (or rather floating with the current through) picturesque Basel in Switzerland, tasting delicious pastry in Lithuania, learning about the traditional way of life in Dubai Museum so remote from the bizarre and kitsch reality of the city today, not to mention the observation of just about every element of the Japanese society wherever one looks there still provided plenty of opportunity to learn and reflect. Reflect especially on my own belonging.

Every introduction (other than a roundtable where I was obviously coming from an academic institution in Denmark or Slovakia or both) carried the sense of burden of my unclear nationality. "Where are you from?," sounds the most frequent first sentence in a foreign country, which I must have heard a million times. "I'm from Slovakia," I answer most frequently. "But I live in Denmark," I add often. "And I'm actually Hungarian," I say less so often, and it initiates a conversation about the region or about the blurry difference between citizenship and nationality, which in English most often refers to the country where you were born and officially belong, or the one that issued your passport, but not to your language and the culture you most identify yourself with. "From Slovakia? So, you're Slovak." "No, I'm a Hungarian. My mother tongue is Hungarian." "So, you're from Hungary." "Not exactly, I'm from Slovakia." "How?" "It's history. There's a Hungarian minority in southern Slovakia… No, we didn't move. The borders did." I didn't always feel for this debate. I felt European. I often thought of the dilemma I would be facing if a conflict broke out between Hungary and Slovakia. Whose side would I fight on, and who would be my enemy? What would be the role in that fight of my fellow Hungarians living in a country foreign to me and what of all the Slovaks living in the country I call home? My vague concern wasn't different from that of the proud and well-integrated Swabians living in Banat or other Germans who lived in Hungary and Transylvania during the past turbulent centuries so elegantly portrayed by Claudio Magris in *Danube*, or the endless ethnic minorities, immigrants, and colonists who remember their roots but are happy where they are, away from their homeland.

I soon found professional tourism, with its meeting

rooms, elegant hotels, and sporadic sightseeing, unauthentic and its destinations sometimes unattractive to satisfy my passion. I was drugged, I needed more. I didn't like to be a tourist as much as I wanted to be a traveler. Even the camping trip with friends from DTU, which took us around entire Iceland (claiming that our studies in Denmark provide us the one and only opportunity to visit the place), a visit to Tenerife, the home of another new acquaintance from DTU, or the road trip in Portugal and Andalusia after a conference in Lisbon began to feel like joining the masses of foreign visitors in seeing the very same places and going home with identical photos and memories. Not that the roaring waterfalls, glaciers, and geysers of Iceland, historical towns like Cordoba, or the lunar landscape of Mount Teide and the breathtaking coastline of La Gomera, and all the moments of planning, learning, problem solving, and endless joy shared with my travelling companions weren't inspirational. They form a very important part of my memories, and they take a prominent place in my heart. I was just longing to try something different.

A pilgrimage to the Holy Land had been on my to do list for a while. Because I invited my parents to join (as an expression of gratitude for completing the house I never got to live in), and because I was largely ignorant about the true situation in that part of the world, we opted to take an organized trip with a travel agency. It turned out to be a trip that would not only take me back to the Holy Land but would profoundly change my life.

It was humbling to visit Nazareth, the Sea of Galilee, Jericho, Masada, the Jordan River, Bethlehem, and most of all the unparalleled Jerusalem. Going in the footsteps of Christ awakened many impressions and thoughts. But observing the blend of religions, cultures, and histories, the political and social challenges, the vast differences and yet similarities between two peoples that made this little piece of land dominate the news since I could remember, was equally fascinating. Or rather it would have been. After seeing the mesmerizing places mostly from the window of a bus crowded with Slovak pilgrims praying ten Hail Marys between the stops and guided by Slovak priests and tour guides, I had to admit (again) that this traveling style was far from appealing. I wanted to know more about the truth as seen by the local people.

The opportunity emerged most unexpectedly. I found the receptionist in the Santa Maria hotel in Bethlehem attractive. My dad insisted on taking a picture of us. I had no idea how to ask a girl in a predominantly Muslim region, although dressed in Western style, for a photograph. But when I did so and she happily agreed, nothing seemed more natural. Later I saw others taking pictures with her as well. We chatted briefly, and I asked her for her email address to share the photo. I sent it to her after I got home from the trip. It was she who wrote to me again a month later, asking me how I was. This led, to my surprise, to a persistent email communication over the next few months, which taught me things invisible to any tourist who goes to Israel and Palestine for a perfectly pre-planned trip with a group. It faced me with my utter ignorance, it opened my mind, my senses, my desire to explore; it made me try to understand the incomprehensible. And it eventually gave me a friend, a partner, a better half, a constant source of inspiration.

Gina wrote to me about the relative openness and modernity of her society and of her family. I was learning what I probably should have already known: it wasn't a taboo for a Palestinian girl to communicate with a Western guy and complimenting her would not get me in trouble. But I also heard about the importance of a girl's purity and reputation contrasted with the relative freedom of men. I learned about the many Christian Arabs living in harmony with Muslims. I realized that being Arab is not synonymous with being Muslim (and certainly not with being dangerous as the news and the political rhetoric often want us to believe), and both Christians and Muslims can be either conservative or liberal, or even both at the same time. I could sense the intertwined roots of cultural features, the blend of Eastern traditions and modern Western influences, fingerprints of various religions and convictions, which made the differences between Christians and Muslims sometimes clear-cut, sometimes very blurred.

I was also told about the daunting effect of Palestine's isolation from the world on people's values and attitudes towards each other within society. I began to understand what decades of occupation and closure behind a segregation wall, which could be crossed only occasionally with a special permit valid until ten o'clock in the evening on a given day, can do with a nation's mentality, dignity, and sense of self-worth. But it seemed to me that some people living in this undeserved "prison" can learn to be content despite the bitterness of the ghetto-like circumstances imposed upon them. And this was just the beginning.

When Gina saw my interest in her country, she asked me to look at the website of a history professor at Bethlehem University, which contained articles about Bethlehem, Palestine, Arab culture, and the history of the Middle East. Only later it was revealed to me that the professor was her father, Adnan Musallam. When Gina learned that I worked with environmental issues, she shared with me the website of The Applied Research

Institute – Jerusalem, an organization dedicated, among others, to the research of the impact of the occupation on the country's environment, natural resources, and agriculture. It was an institution based in Bethlehem, and Adnan was a member of its advisory board.

Gina turned out to be one of those Christian Arabs, an Arab Christian, a Catholic just like me. She had travelled in Europe and the United States, she had a college degree, and she turned out to be an American citizen. I was asking myself: Could this Palestinian receptionist, who was anything but what an ignorant European biased by misguiding news would expect, surprise me more? Half a year after my first trip to the Holy Land (just after I submitted my doctoral dissertation and was determined to travel in Africa, but the travel agency cancelled the trip), I decided to visit it again and experience it the authentic way. Gina and her family invited me to stay in their home. They routinely hosted foreign visitors coming with different purposes—friends, distant relatives, descendants of Palestinians who emigrated generations ago, volunteers and activists from Europe and the Americas. It was my first encounter with an immeasurably generous hospitality that I had not experienced before.

On my way to Tel Aviv, I made a three-day stopover in Istanbul. I wanted to feel the atmosphere of the city on two continents, the capital of the Byzantine Empire, Constantinople, and of the once vast Ottoman Empire, which occupied Hungary for more than 150 years and stretched from North Africa and the Persian Gulf all the way to my home in southern Slovakia. Little legacy of those years, besides rare signs in architecture and the baths in Budapest, remains visible in Central Europe. And so, where else can one concurrently taste the East and the West with such intensity if not in one of the most significant cities in history, which has been an imperial capital for sixteen centuries and a bastion of both Christianity and later Islam, a city with a majestic past witnessed by the nearly fifteen-hundred years old construction, the marvelous Hagia Sophia?

The young Israeli student sitting next to me on the flight to Tel Aviv eagerly described his skiing trip to Canada that he was returning from right in the middle of the scorching summer. What a luxury, I thought, which I had never had the chance to try, although I was living in the most developed part of the world. The customs officer at the airport found it suspicious that I was returning for the second time in half a year, so a little routine questioning followed. To avoid unnecessary complications that visiting friends in the occupied territories would have certainly caused, I pretended to be a tourist going to Jerusalem without having any personal contacts in the country, and my illustrated city guide was supposed to confirm it.

I took a shared taxi van, *sherut*, from the airport to the checkpoint that I was supposed to cross to arrive in Bethlehem. The driver refused to take me all the way to the checkpoint, and he dropped me about five-hundred meters before it, near the Tantur Ecumenical Institute. I walked down to the checkpoint. It was early morning, and the place was crowded with Palestinians trying to cross and get a ride to Jerusalem on their way to work. They usually queued from four o'clock to make it through the humiliating checkpoint on time. The sight of the tall concrete segregation wall, frequent watchtowers, endless barbed wires, and Israeli soldiers in bulletproof vests pushing around the Palestinian men and women with their semi-automatic rifles and occasionally forcing them to partially strip before passing the metal detectors, was bizarre and frightening. I looked like a tourist, so I was simply waved through.

Spending a week with Gina and her family was extremely inspirational. I was given a tour of the Church of the Nativity, the old town, and Bethlehem University. The day when Gina obtained an exit permit from the Israeli authorities, we visited Jerusalem. This time I was able to walk the entire Via Dolorosa without the time restrictions of group travel. I visited all four quarters of the old town, the Jewish, Muslim, Christian, and Armenian. I could spend as much time as I wished in the Garden of Gethsemane on the Mount of Olives and in the Church of the Holy Sepulcher, which encompasses the Golgotha and the tomb of Christ. I did visit again the Wailing Wall, but it would require several future attempts before I could finally access the admirable Temple Mount with the Dome of the Rock and the Al-Aqsa Mosque a couple of years later.

More importantly, however, everything was so different than what I remembered from six months earlier. I saw everyday life, its comfort, and its struggle. I met Gina's and her family's relatives, friends, and colleagues, people from all walks of life. We barbecued in the evenings, partied on the weekend. I was one of them. The Palestinians treated me like their brother and their son. As if the less they had and the more they struggled, the more generous, friendly, hospitable they were regardless of their religion.

I was also absorbing a different kind of experience at the same time. I now saw with my own eyes the true face of the decades of occupation. I visited the refugee camps, where generations of families continue to be born and to die and where the elderly still hold the keys to the beautiful villas on the other side of the separation barrier, which once belonged to them. They could hardly accept that those keys would probably never have the chance again to unlock the gates that had long forgotten them and now serve their new undeserving masters.

In the Palestinian city of Hebron, I walked the streets with the few houses occupied by Jewish settlers. The fragile peace on those streets, where no Palestinians were allowed and their businesses were long forced to close, was protected by roadblocks, checkpoints, and soldiers, some of whom said to have come from the U.S. The presence of soldiers may have been a sign of peace for the settlers, but, as the local Palestinians described to me, it meant harsh restrictions, violence, and harassment for them.

I heard people complaining about settlements being built on confiscated land, olive trees being uprooted, and houses of innocent people being bulldozed (among them, at a later time, the house and restaurant of Gina's brother-in-law's family) by the neighboring country that claimed something that did not belong to it based on questionable arguments and outdated yet effective laws, violating human rights, international laws and conventions, and United Nations resolutions. I was touring a land that was largely erased from the map, a land that was perforated by oppression and had few patches remaining for its own citizens to move in and live in without restrictions. I was observing how the victim was labeled as aggressor, the aggressor convinced the world that it was the innocent victim, and nobody dared to see the truth because the cataclysm that took place decades earlier perfectly justified it all and made the world fear to object. A new world view was slowly taking shape in my mind.

Gina and her family described to me their memories

of the Second Intifada during which they were often hiding in the basement while their newly built house was under a shower of bullets and their neighbor was torn into dust by an Israeli airstrike. The house standing at the bottom of a valley was frequently in the middle of a crossfire. Gina showed me, in her otherwise neat and renovated room, the holes hiding in the back side of the wardrobe caused by bullets that penetrated the window. They were the reminders that the subsequent renovation works left unpatched. Adnan proudly described Gina's effort during these horrifying days to study by candlelight for her *tawjihi*, the final high school examination. I was impressed.

These images were fundamentally different from the one I got from the young gentleman I met on the plane, who was on his way home from his summer skiing adventure and who was now just on the other side, the modern, safe, and rapidly developing side, of the art-covered eight meters high concrete wall patrolled by armed soldiers. They were different from anything I had ever seen or heard. Mind-blowing was to hear when people said their lives are good in the West Bank, I should just go and see how they live in Gaza. My childhood suddenly seemed so idyllic. I was learning to reflect upon my own life from a new perspective, upon fortune and destiny, upon the fairness of the world and the principles of collective responsibility (and collective punishment). But the answers seemed more remote with every question that popped into my head. And feelings were slowly awakening towards this lovely receptionist, who was now a good friend.

Every time I returned to Bethlehem, new impressions and adventures awaited. Arriving at Tel Aviv airport was stressful. The persistent questioning by the intimidating officers trained to drive visitors to inconsistency in their answers deterred me from reciting the same fabricated purpose of my trip. I was going to cross to the occupied territories, and this usually triggered a long, meaningless interrogation. Who do I know there, where do I know the person from, how did we meet, where do I come from, where do I work, can I prove it, how can I work in Denmark if I have a Slovak passport, and why did I fly from Vienna if I am not an Austrian citizen? I had to patiently explain again and again to the different officers asking the same questions what they certainly knew very well, namely that Europe is a free place where we can move between the countries for work and that direct flights to Tel Aviv are not operated from every airport in every country. I usually mentioned Adnan as my contact in Palestine; he was a fellow academician who also taught at universities in Israel and had a clear record.

Leaving the country was equally annoying. On my first solo visit, my return flight was scheduled to leave early in the morning. I had ordered a *sherut* to pick me up on the Israeli side of the checkpoint in the middle of the night, so I could be at the airport the recommended three hours before departure. I was told the checkpoint was open all night. Adnan drove me there. When he was approaching the crossing with its fearful, cylindrical watchtower, he slowed down and turned the car's interior lights on to avoid misunderstanding by the soldiers, who could consider the car in the middle of the night a threat. The crossing point for pedestrians was closed. I ran to the main gate for vehicles. I tried to awaken someone's attention but to no avail. I realized I could do nothing but wait. The chance of making it in time for my flight was becoming slim. After about an hour, when a few cars and a bus lined up, the soldiers opened the huge, clumsy iron gate. I was the only pedestrian queueing between the vehicles. One of the soldiers was standing behind a short concrete protection barrier in the middle of the road, holding a semi-automatic-looking rifle. He carefully examined with his flashlight the passengers in the cars in front of me, looked at their documents and waived them through. Then it was my turn. He checked my passport and I walked on.

I did not know whether the *sherut* was still waiting for me. I knew that if it was, it would be standing hundred meters down the road behind a roundabout and a curve. I began to run, following the cars on the road. Suddenly I heard a loud yell from the loudspeakers: "STOP!" My heart was pounding, I felt as if a gun was being pointed at me. The invisible soldier ordered me to enter the nearby building and go to the hall where Gina and I crossed a few days earlier as pedestrians after a perfectly humiliating security check. There was no one. I came out again, only to be rushed back by the frightening loudspeaker to wait. Everlasting minutes later, a sleepy, unwilling soldier started up the metal detectors and let me through. To my surprise, the *sherut* was still waiting for me. I was asked to pay for each passenger who booked a ride but did not wait to be picked up at the agreed address and time because of the tardiness I caused. It was a fair request, a price worth paying for still being able, with a little luck, to take my flight home. I could not blame the two such individuals, who must have been cursing at the unreliability of the service but hopefully could arrange alternative transportation to reach the airport on time.

When I finally reached the airport, I tried to check in after another unpleasant questioning. Every content of my baggage was first thoroughly checked for traces of explosives. One item seemed suspicious to the security officer. I was asked to place my small Jerusalem guidebook in a large, empty cardboard box and personally place it into a special elevator in the check-in hall. I did not know at what special place on the plane the book was traveling and for what reason, but it was waiting for me on the baggage carousel after arrival.

Another time at check-in, I was escorted away and asked to strip down to my underwear without receiving any explanation other than the usual "This is a routine security check". Later, when I travelled with Gina, we were obliged to travel via Amman in Jordan. Palestinians are not allowed under any circumstances to use Ben Gurion airport in Israel (except with a special permit, which is granted rarely and mostly in connection with, of course, close business ties to Israel). Instead, they must go through an even more arduous and humiliating half- to full-day effort to make the seventy-kilometer trip between Amman and Jericho via the Allenby/King Hussein border crossing, which is the only exit and entry point for most West Bank Palestinians traveling abroad.

Because Israel controls the border crossing between two Arab nations, Jordan and the West Bank, foreigners here are entitled to the same disrespectful, often hostile treatment as the locals, unless they travel with an organized tour. As if they had to be made to understand that setting foot in Palestine means entering enemy territory, which, on the other hand, Israel claims to possess. I was made to wait hours before I got back my passport. My totally legal request to receive the entry stamp on a separate piece of paper and not in my passport, a service routinely offered at other points of entry because an Israeli stamp can hinder admission to several other countries, was denied, and my new passport was maliciously stamped. My luggage was taken from me and tossed unto a pile with dozens of bags of traveling Palestinians, and I felt like cattle, just like the locals, when soldiers guarded the crowd at gunpoint, far not as elegantly as a shepherd guards his beloved sheep. The meanest were the young girls who clearly enjoyed the authority bestowed upon them by the uniform they wore. Misanthropic were particularly the Russian female officers, who didn't speak any other language than Russian, and, as it was commonly believed, they rarely knew much about Judaism, if they were Jewish at all.

It became clear that all Palestinians without exception, and all their friends and supporters regardless of their country of origin, are considered enemies, perhaps even potential terrorists. General defamation has been a national policy for decades. Interestingly, Gina's American passport never meant much in Israel. The only privilege it occasionally brought was when Gina tried to cross to Israel without a permit, pretending to be an American tourist. It worked a few times, but it was always nerve-racking. Especially the one time when we were driving on the highway between Jericho and Jerusalem, and we arrived at a routine checkpoint. The rental car had Israeli number plates. I waived two foreign passports and expected to be through as was usually the case. But the officer wanted to see our tourist visas or entry stamps.

I began to browse my passport first. I knew the right stamp was there somewhere among the many overlapping ones in a nearly full passport. I was hoping that the officer would become impatient and let us go before I found it. But he waited tenaciously, and he demanded to see the stamp in Gina's foreign passport as well. I browsed it page by page, reached its end and its first page again, pretending that I can't find what is certainly there. When he saw the long queue the cars behind us had formed, he eventually gave up and let us continue our journey. We were once again relieved. It never occurred to us that we could have tried to argue that we had lost the stamp note or forgotten it in the hotel. Tourists in Israel can ask for the entry stamp to be given on a separate piece of paper, due to restrictions on visiting certain countries with a passport that contains an Israeli stamp. Lying, however, wouldn't necessarily have been a more comfortable or secure approach.

My incredible travel adventures were somewhat absurd. It was illuminating to witness the bitter resentment but also the traces of sympathy between the two sides. My new Palestinian acquaintances were empathetic about the horrors of the holocaust, while some Israelis, both Jews and Arabs, expressed solidarity with the Palestinians and opposition to their country's discriminatory policies. Friendships occasionally developed between the two sides. When we were renting a car in Jerusalem, the rental company required that we provide an Israeli address. An address in the West Bank was a no go; rental cars were not allowed to be driven to the occupied territories. Gina called a Jewish Israeli friend of her mother who allowed us to use her address and offered help with anything we might need while in Israel. Yet another situation was showing me how inappropriate generalizations can be.

My visits to Palestine and Israel didn't only teach about a place and its peoples, they inspired compassion towards an oppressed nation and helped to understand its indignation and resistance. I realized how little I knew not only about the Middle East but about every corner of the world, including perhaps my own backyard, regardless of how much I followed the news or read various sources. I felt the power of experience. I began to question what I thought was the truth. I wanted to know more, I wanted to constantly ask questions.

>«

Gina's father was a fabulous source of answers. Adnan was born in British Palestine before the State of Israel was declared. His first memories date back to 1948. As a four-year-old, he was standing in the window of their house, witnessing a massacre taking place outside. The first images he can remember are those of heads rolling down the hill in front of him on the street. It was the *Nakba*, the "Catastrophe", during which hundreds of Palestinian villages were destroyed and hundreds of thousands of Palestinians had to flee or were expelled from their homes without the right to ever return. It was a dark year for Palestine's future, just as it was a dark year for my own country, as it entered a lengthy period under a repressive communist regime. From then on, Bethlehem was part of Jordan until the Six-Day War of 1967 during which Israel seized the West Bank and other territories.

Adnan was raised by a stepmother after his mother passed away when he was just a child. His father served as member of the Jordanian parliament and later as the mayor of Bethlehem. Adnan was different from most young people around him. He cared little about politics or rebellion; he was striving for education. Trying to escape the legacy of his traumatic childhood, he travelled to the United States with the Rotary Club when he was eighteen. He was a promising young man, and he was given the opportunity to finish his high school studies in Wabash, Indiana. He continued to study political science, history, and Near East studies at Indiana University, served in the U.S. Navy, got married, became a father, and eventually received his doctoral degree in contemporary history and literature of the Arab world and Islamic thought (despite his Catholic faith) from the University of Michigan.

His divorce following an unhappy marriage, establishing a new family with another Bethlehemite, Gina's mother Salwa, getting their first daughter Hiyam, and the opportunities that emerged at the newly established Vatican-sponsored Bethlehem University for students of all faiths inspired him to return to Palestine, where he soon became chair of the Department of Humanities and dean of the Faculty of Arts. Although he was able to travel around the world, attend conferences, give invited lectures on minority issues, effects of occupation, diaspora, and other hot issues of the world, it was a decision he would come to deeply regret over the following decades, as the political situation deteriorated.

Adnan has lived in the United States more than twenty years. He is a proud American and an equally proud Palestinian, a professor of Middle Eastern history and culture, whose research focused over the last several decades on the life of Sayyid Qutb. Qutb was an impressive but controversial intellectual, writer, educator, and Islamic theorist, critical of the American materialism, consumerism, and sexual pleasures. His execution by the Egyptian government in 1966 paved the way to today's Islamic ideology and has inspired radical Islamism. Adnan authored the thought-provoking book *From Secularism to Jihad: Sayyid Qutb and the Foundations of Radical Islamism* about Qutb's life and its impact on the world as we see it today.

He also gathered a collection on Bethlehem's and the Holy Land's contemporary history with special emphasis on intellectual and press developments under British,

Jordanian, and Israeli administrations since World War I. At the time I first met him, he was working on a Palestinian oral history collection covering the last hundred years, on the history of Palestinian emigration and various historical aspects of the Israeli occupation and its impacts. He was the best person to ask about how Palestine and much of the region got where it currently was.

We talked for hours every time we met. We were often sitting on the large, sunny terrace of their elegant, modernly furnished house built of the stylish Jerusalem limestone, with the beautiful view of the valley, the steep hills of Beit Jala, and, in the distance, the highway bridge connecting two hilltops, inaccessible for cars with a Palestinian number plate. I was asking, Adnan was patiently answering. He elucidated the centuries-long Ottoman rule, the empire's partitioning in 1918 into the French Mandate for Syria and the Lebanon and the British Mandate for Palestine, the newly formed kingdoms on the Arabian Peninsula, the Turkish independence efforts of the early 1920s, and especially the Balfour Declaration, which accelerated the Zionist movement that existed since the First Zionist Congress in Basel twenty years earlier. Adnan especially enjoyed talking about the modern history, with which his life was so closely intertwined—the terrifying events that took place during his childhood and early adulthood, the more recent *intifadas* (the second as recent as early 2000s), and many rarely told details in between. He was always calm, demonstrating peacefulness and appreciation for what life provided. He was fair. As a lecturer in both Palestine and Israel, he was comfortable with acknowledging the mistakes both sides made over the course of the past century. He was, and still is, a true pacifist. "I can't tell what blood flows in my veins," he often says. He refers to the numerous peoples, ethnic groups, and cultures that are part of his homeland's history and eventually his own personal history, which has shaped who he is.

Salwa, a strong-willed, assertive woman with as much authority in the family as her husband (contrary to common beliefs about gender roles in the Middle East), used to run her grocery store in the past but then devoted nearly two decades of her life to nothing but raising their four girls. Born in Columbia and raised by descendants of earlier Palestinian immigrants (her mother only spoke Spanish and so did she until later childhood), Salwa was determined at an early age to return to her roots in the Holy Land. Life there seemed to be better at the time than in Columbia, and so she worked like a Trojan to bring back her parents and siblings as well. She rarely received for it the appreciation she deserved. Taking a decision so fundamental as to where to spend the rest of one's life can be extremely hard, but taking it when all options seem unfavorable is incomprehensible for most modern Europeans, including the many who struggle at most with the thought of leaving a nearly perfect place for an even better one.

Salwa's knowledge of the Holy Land's ancient history complemented my discussions with Adnan about modern history. It was her specialty as a tour guide, a career she began to pursue in four languages with a captivating passion around the time we first met. She used to be not only the eldest but the best in class while studying diligently at Bethlehem Bible College, where Adnan was one of her lecturers. Adnan and Salwa helped me realize that history is not a mere collection of facts, events, and years of their occurrence. It is a complicated science, a collection of many personal histories, results of political games, invisible wars of influence and interests in which human lives often lose respect and dignity. These lessons opened my eyes to how little we were taught in school about other regions of the world than the Western, developed Old Continent with is global domination, which has greatly harmed many people in many parts of the world, some equally rich, if not richer, in culture and history. How little we were told about reality. I began seeing the colorfulness of the world with its beauties and frights.

My seemingly perfect life turned into a cliché once I was faced with the destinies of those who struggled for existence. How can we in the Western world complain about the tiniest material inconveniences, like a slow internet connection, the unaffordability of something we don't even need, or the government's adjustment to the already rather low weekly work hours, when our brothers and sisters not far away are denied their basic human rights and needs? And if they under these circumstances brought about by a broken political system, immense economic challenges, corruption, war, and oppression can establish with honest work and decency a life with plenty of love and family harmony, contentment, and material privileges, including foreign travels and a lovely home like any other in Europe, then they deserve our utmost respect and gratitude for being tremendously inspirational.

At the same time though, I noticed the similarities in human destinies and values across vastly different worlds. Adnan's life has been so different from mine and that of my parents and yet so similar. The brutalities of 1948 and the occupation beginning in the late 1960s, the social and economic pressure on everyday lives, the lack of freedom and the early American experience, the passion for an academic career, the expatriate life and the ambivalence that comes with it were all too familiar to both Adnan and, even if partly indirectly, me. I was discovering how little the differences and immense the similarities can be between human beings and between societies, between their needs and yearnings, if we just look closely enough—something we are often told but rarely raised to comprehend and apply in the way we treat others. We let our differences in economy, culture, and religion, which are the consequence of myriad factors at play throughout the ages of the past and which are now largely hiding behind flags and some imaginary lines called border, outweigh the common traits that make us all humans, including our longing for love, respect, freedom, and understanding. In the name of these differences, we allow our smart but arrogant species not only to build and progress but especially, and for much longer in our history, to maltreat and destroy. I was increasingly appreciating the heavy burden that unfair and divisive nationalistic feelings can bring about. I don't recall any situation where the place I come from or the language I speak had an influence on the way I treated others, but if it was about to happen, I was now ready to stand up against it.

My parents, perhaps partly because of their own prejudices, were initially a little insecure about the way my relationship with Gina was developing. But soon I gained their absolute support and understanding, as they matured to accept the openness of the world, shortening of distances, and shrinking of differences. Gina and I received the sacrament of matrimony in the Church of the Nativity in Bethlehem a year later, during the fifth visit to one another (each lasting one to two weeks). Hundreds if not thousands of tourists surrounded us when we walked out onto Manger Square. I could not imagine a more sublime place for the ceremony. Our union began with five weeks of separation and a brief period of uncertainty about when and where we would be able to legally reside together. It unleashed an avalanche of administrative procedures in Palestine, Israel, Slovakia, Denmark, and the United States, appointments at embassies, ministries, immigration offices, police stations, and notaries, all spiced with subjective interpretations of the laws and with glitches in the various systems.

It was like one big journey that offered a glimpse of several hidden worlds. It was enlightening, exciting, and unpleasant. But the real journey was just beginning. Our marriage, just like any other, came with its own set of challenges. How big a role in them could be attributed to the international and multicultural character of our family and how much to personal differences not unique to it in any way could be the topic of another book, unlikely a fair one. Gina always seemed, even to her own family, to fit in with Western society better than with the one she came from, in which she often struggled with being herself. (She was always more cheerful, less strained when we crossed to Israel and left the conservative, closed Bethlehem, where people knew each other and nothing could remain private.) But giving up everything, job, friends, and family and moving to a cold, unknown place for a new life of uncertainty is a huge undertaking that few appreciate. Its effects are hardly predictable. I always considered our ethnic amalgam a blessing, never an obstacle. But I did wonder for a long time, despite Gina's almost unwarranted and certainly incredibly smooth and swift integration into the European and particularly Scandinavian society, how different our hurdles would be without the cultural element of our relationship, and even more, how much of the personal differences, not incomparable with other couples, could have their roots in what we had inherited from our own societies, cultures, personal little histories. Whatever is the true answer to this conundrum, both our union and its ethnic and cultural elements provided, as they always do, inspirations more powerful than any other. Inspirations that constantly alter one's certitudes and doubts, convictions and fears, decisions and actions. It is the biggest of all journeys.

5

CITIZEN OF THE WORLD

"Travel is fatal to prejudice, bigotry and narrow-mindedness, and many of our people need it sorely on these accounts. Broad, wholesome, charitable views of men and things cannot be acquired by vegetating in one little corner of the earth all one's lifetime."

–Mark Twain
(The Innocents Abroad, or The New Pilgrims' Progress)

My visits to the Middle East made me see traveling in a new light; they gave my globetrotting a new dimension. I was witnessing volatility, uncertainty, unreliability, all of which was teaching me resilience, adaptation, skills to get along in an environment of dysfunction. It also showed me the charms of a seemingly imperfect travel destination, its kindness and hospitality, its diversity and authenticity. Its power to teach. I was observing a miscellany of views and opinions, which reflected the complexity of the historical, political, and cultural contexts.

About a year before the Arab Spring, Gina and I visited Jordan and Egypt after one of our family visits in Bethlehem. Gina arrived in Bethlehem first, and since I was traveling later anyway, I decided to make a three-day detour from Amman to Syria before meeting the family in Palestine for Christmas. After the war broke out in Syria the following year, I often pondered about what may have happened to the two brothers who shared with me the taxi from Amman to Damascus and helped me communicate with the border officers, the students at Damascus university whom I saw while strolling through the campus just across the street from the rather modest National Museum, the vendors in the Al Hamidiyah Souq west of the grand Umayyad Mosque and Saladin's mausoleum, the gentleman who handed me a towel and a very sweet tea in an Arabic tea cup made of thin glass after an unexpected, rough but refreshing scrub in the beautiful, historical Hammam Al Malik Al Zahir, or the old women who offered me their sweets and drinks in the shared van during the ride to Maaloula, one of the three little towns at the foot of the Anti-Lebanon Mountains, where Aramaic is still spoken by a few individuals.

The windowless room I was given when I arrived in the charming palace-like Al Rabie hostel with its inner courtyard, featuring trees stretching up to the ceiling and an old stone fountain, was about four square meters. It was taller than it was wide and long. I only paid a couple of dollars for a night, and my initial surprise about the room, which must have once served as a storage room, disappeared after I got a few hours of daytime sleep following the night flight and the very early taxi ride from Jordan.

The cab on the way back to Amman three days later stopped a few times on the way, each time meeting up with another car, exchanging passengers, or asking me to get out of one car and jump into another, always without explanation. I was worried a bit at first, but then one of my fellow passengers that morning, Abdulrahman, assured me I was in good hands. "Just ask for me when you get there, everybody knows me. You don't even need my last name," he said when I told him I would be in Petra, where he worked, with my wife after Christmas. I never saw him again. When I inquired about him at the entrance to the archeological city, once capital of the Nabataeans, I was told there were too many Abdulrahmans working in Petra. This felt, after some time, like a classic way to obtain information (misinformation, to be more precise) in the Middle East, and it often repeated itself when asking locals for directions, advice, or just an innocent question. I never felt it was intentional. It was just the way things worked.

My good friend and frequent travel companion Jan and his girlfriend Kate joined us in our explorations of Jordan and Egypt. Visiting the well-preserved crusader castle at Al Karak, the breathtaking Wadi Rum with its rock formations in many shades of redness and its legendary stories of Lawrence of Arabia, the majestic pyramids in Giza, and the amazing Sahara dunes in Wadi El Rayan certainly offered scenes for some great photographic shots. But I enjoyed even more taking pictures of the guys sleeping on the cargo bed of a shabby pick-up truck racing on the highway, the bread distributors balancing on their heads (sometimes while biking) a wooden board with hundreds of loafs of bread, and the children driving a donkey-drawn carriage loaded with unfastened gas cylinders.

Our bizarre memories include a terrible deadly accident that slowed us on our way to Amman from the West Bank. Once we got passed the scene with the wreckage and the police cars, we saw the fire truck rushing to the site rolling down the cliff in a sharp corner just before its destination. The Jordanian roads turn slippery as ice when they become wet from a light rain.

After we had finally picked up our worn-out Mitsubishi Carisma from the rental company, we finally felt what freedom in the Middle East really meant. No more taxis, no more price negotiations to get to places. The Jordanians were kind and fair. We got frequently pulled over by policemen dangerously waving a barely visible red light in the middle of the road far from any major town in the darkness of the night. I ignored him the first time, thinking it was a kid playing a dangerous game by the side of the road. When Jan said it was a police officer, I stopped and backed up to him. As soon as he saw we were foreigners, he smiled, apologized, wished us a good night, and let us go. We were not once reprimanded for one of our headlights being dysfunctional.

The beauty, the historical richness, the kindness, helpfulness, and hospitality of the people of the Levant, and even the annoying but mostly lovely chaos, the constant honking, confusion, and mild complaint of the people we met, continued to fuel my curiosity in parts of the world that had not yet been spoiled by westernization, globalization, and mass tourism. After a little research, I came to a conclusion that Kyrgyzstan may be one of those few remaining unspoiled yet safe and approachable places. When I shared my thought with Jan, he noted to my surprise that Samat, his former colleague at the company in Germany where he worked, was a Kyrgyz, and he was repeatedly inviting Jan to visit his country. Samat made the hard choice to return from Germany to find a girl and start a family in his homeland, after he drove all the way between the two worlds. He now worked for the United Nations addressing the 2010 Uzbek refugee crisis, which had engulfed the Kyrgyz city of Osh following ethnically motivated violence. We agreed to travel the following summer.

We met very few other travelers during the ten days we spent in Kyrgyzstan. I could count them on my ten fingers. They were equally adventurous and respectful towards everything and everyone local. The experience was astounding. Not only because of events like the whitewater rafting in the Chong-Kemin valley, the stay with the nomads around Lake Song-Kul at 3000 meters above sea level, sleeping on *töshök* (cotton-stuffed mattress with embroidered cover) in their yurts, tasting the feast they served on the short-legged tables while sitting on the carpet sipping tea and vodka, riding their horses, trying to play goat polo, or tasting *kumis*, the fermented mare's milk, but also because we got to witness the destiny of another formerly communist country, which used to be under Soviet rule. We noticed features that reminded us of the Czechoslovakia of our childhood. The structure of Bishkek, the statue of Lenin still proudly standing on the main square, the identical concrete apartment buildings, the playgrounds and park benches, the lack of aesthetics. But while our country turned into a flashy, modern society with a restored history, renovated old towns, growing economy, and limitless travel and job opportunities, time seemed to have stopped in Kyrgyzstan with the declaration of independence in 1991. Everything looked almost the same as back then but accentuated with decades of deterioration and neglect, an abundance of disarray. We could hardly see anything that was built or renovated during the twenty years since independence. In Karakol ZOO, we felt genuinely sorry for the animals; the baby bear gave us a sad look from the cage made of rusty reinforcing steel and an unfinished brick wall, and the Przewalski horses had hardly any grass to graze below their feet.

The police weren't as forgiving as in Jordan; fines were to be paid for no other reason than being stopped, and this seemed to happen at regular, almost predictable intervals. People could not locate Slovakia on the map, but most of them knew where Czechoslovakia was. A man in his late fifties rejoiced upon hearing where we came from. He grabbed his guitar and sang a Slovak song on the sandy beach of Issyk-Kul, one of the largest and deepest mountain lakes on Earth surrounded by the peaks of the Northern Tian Shan mountains. It turned out that he had spent a few years in Czechoslovakia. He said to us with pride that the years he was living in the *developed West* of the then global East, which Czechoslovaks despised and often tried to escape, were the best ones of his life. Naturally, we asked him why.

Our entertainer had once served in the Soviet army that occupied our country for more than two decades from 1968. Even though Czechoslovaks disdained the presence of his comrades in the country, he could live enjoying peace, security, some authority, and allowances in a place much more developed than his homeland. Now we were visiting his country, and we loved it equally. This time, we seemed to have the geopolitical upper hand, but this encounter was about memories, cheerfulness, solidarity, and respect regardless of the past. It never crossed our minds that there was anything to forgive, just as he never thought there was anything to apologize for. He likely never knew the true reason for his stay in our country, which had been advertised back then as "brotherly help between two friendly nations".

We hired Samat's friend Bakil to drive us to Karakol in the eastern part of the country, with a detour to Song-Kul, where he didn't hesitate to ford rivers with his aged but cherished red Toyota to get us to our hosts, the nomadic shepherds spending the summer on the pastures of the plateau. Bakil spoke Kyrgyz and Russian. Just like with most others in the country, the few Russian words we remembered, together with the faint intersections between Slovak, Czech, Polish, and Russian, were our only means of communication. Our three-day hike to Lake Ala-Kul and back to Karakol started off well after we had rented a tent and cooking gear and left the town with its temperatures in the mid-thirties centigrade. We camped the first night a few hours walk from the lake at an altitude where vegetation was just about to disappear. The night was cool and dry. We reached the lake 3500 meters above sea level via the steep and challenging track in the afternoon on the second day. It was surrounded with breathtaking peaks covered in snow. We still had an elevation gain of a few hundred meters ahead of us. The only hikers we met during these three days were two Canadians, who warned us the day before that fresh snow had covered the track higher up and the pass was impassable. They turned back. We had to take a decision—attempt to reach the pass at 3800 meters or return the same way as we came. We agreed to continue our ascent on the track, the location of which we could only vaguely sense, and reevaluate our chances as we go along. The path on the steep side of the mountain covered with ten to fifteen centimeters of snow was narrow and dangerous. Rockfalls are frequent even under dry conditions, and a wrong step could make us tumble down towards the lake. It began to drizzle and snow, but we were determined to make it to the other side. The pass offered a stunning view of the endless chain of peaks everywhere we looked. It was spectacular.

After a few photos, we needed to get going and reach below the snow line before dark. But where to go? The snow on the other side of the ridge was much deeper, and no trail could be discerned. What we saw below us was scarily steep too. Even without snow, the trail could be muddy and very slippery at this time of the year, and every step would be sending gravel down the slope. There was only one thing we could do. Scramble down and hope that the deep snow would hide no surprises but offer its softness to our advantage.

We tremendously enjoyed stotting like gazelles down in the unknown. The snow slowly disappeared, and about an hour later we reached a beautiful green meadow, a perfect spot for our tent. We woke up to stunning scenery made even more impressive than the previous evening by the gorgeous morning sunshine. The walk through the Altyn-Arashan valley on the final day was a pure pleasure, despite the muscle pain in our legs barely able to carry us. The energy from the satisfaction with our success was our driving force. The valley's hot springs, a few rentable small concrete basins filled with unbearably hot water, each covered with a wooden shed, was all we needed to feel ready for our return to civilization. That return was realized by taking a local bus to Karakol from the village at the beginning of the valley. All seats on the ailing bus were occupied, mostly by elderly women. Their frequent glances at us, accompanied by smiles and loud laughter following a few sentences exchanged between each other, revealed that they liked the standing strangers with their weird outfits and huge backpacks. Next day was a rest day. Sitting on a carpet stretched out in a street restaurant while waiting with beer in our hands for freshly chargrilled *shashlik* was all we needed to feel in heaven. All we planned to do that day was to visit the animal bazaar, where horses being transported on open trailers behind decades-old Ladas stuffed with live sheep and goats were among the most natural things to see.

»«

One destination inspired me particularly deeply to develop appreciation for my past, for the place I've been born into, for my fortunes and misfortunes, for the smallest of privileges, the everyday blessings of life. My desire to understand the drivers of our destinies, impacts of our decisions, and the complexity of the world with its imbalances convinced me to join a volunteering program in Kenya. I could not see myself supporting volunteer programs advertised back home and run by Western facilitating companies, whose employees sit in expensive air-conditioned offices in European or American cities and earn relatively high salaries. I made a dedicated effort instead to find a reliable and devoted local institution. It was a challenge that required time, research, communication, and a gut feeling, but it was entirely worth it. The Kenya Voluntary and Community Development Project (KVCDP) was founded by a lovely and generous couple, Jackie and Albert. They were doing a fantastic job. Jackie ran KVCDP, while Albert was responsible for the Africa Home Adventure tour operator business. KVCDP entirely depended on volunteers. They could combine community work with safari at discounted rates, and a fixed percentage of the tourist business's profits went to support KVCDP. I joined the Shangilia daycare for orphans and children of underprivileged parents in a tiny village on the coast of Lake Victoria.

Jackie prepared me back in Nairobi for a potentially heart-breaking experience I might have upon arrival at the Luo village of Wagusu. Although I was given a tour of the world's largest slum in the capital, the overcrowded Kibera with its waste water filled streets, desolate houses, major railway running literally just a couple of steps from the houses on both sides (turning the rails into a street with people moving out of the way only when a train passes), and ironically a golf course just outside its borders, seeing the countryside was more distressing. After an extremely tremulous full-day bus ride to Bondo, I was told to board a motorcycle that would drive me on an unpaved road to my destination. We only fell once, when the bike's rear wheel slipped on the uneven, muddy surface of the road. When we arrived, I saw nothing but poverty. Desolate mud huts, cooking on open fire, children playing in the dirt, and women carrying sizeable buckets full of water (without ever spilling a single drop) on their head and their children on their back. Owning a donkey meant belonging to the upper few. The area was plagued with HIV/AIDS and malaria.

I was accommodated in a small concrete shack standing in the yard of the daycare. It had two rooms with bare concrete floors and walls, each furnished less than sparsely, with two bunk beds under mosquito nets and nothing else. One room was occupied by Joy the teacher and the occasional female volunteers, the other room was the male room accommodating Wilfred the project manager and now me. We lived without power. The phones could be charged for a tiny fee at one specific place in the village. Local women cooked for us incredibly delicious meals on fire. The fire was also our source of light and warmth and the center of our social life full of laughter and learning before the relatively early bedtime.

Clean water was scarce; limited amounts had to be carried from afar. The lake water carried the risk of bilharzia. Bottled water wasn't always available in the tiny local store, which was selling only the very basics in small amounts. The main goods were flour for *chapatti*, soap, beans, mobile phone top-up cards, and, of course, Coca-Cola. I took a shower occasionally; having a one-liter bottle filled with well water for this purpose felt like luxury.

In the mornings, Wilfred and I took the donkey with two large plastic canisters on its back for the fifteen-minute walk down to the lake to fetch water for washing hands, laundry, dishes, and to quench its thirst. By the time we and the donkey with its precious but heavy load arrived back at the facility with slow and careful steps across the rocky, hilly terrain, the children started to arrive for the day. I helped Wilfred and his local assistant Martin to carry out the daily health checks on the kids (mainly looking for fleas and lice, scars, and treating mosquito bites and rashes) and supervise their tooth brushing. Then I aided Joy with the reading, writing, and math classes and served the children porridge for lunch, which for many was the only meal of the day. In the afternoons, I cleaned the classroom, removed corn from the cob, and played with the kids until they were ready to go home. Some of them walked for an hour or more through the bush, often in the dark and always on their own. They had never heard of walkways, sidewalks, or streetlamps.

The children were marvelous. They needed little to play all day and stay content. Drawing in the dust with a wooden stick, chasing a car tire down the hill, or chitchatting with each other engaged them day after day. The kite that I brought with me was an unbeatable sensation, a bonding magic. They loved to be around *muzungu*, the white man. As soon as they glimpsed me, they shouted out loud the only English words they knew: "Muzungu, how are you, I am fine". Walking by my side was exciting, holding my hands was precious. When I lifted one child, all the others began to loudly chant "*tinga, tinga*", until I lifted one by one all thirty-something of them. They offered a smile, a happy face in return. They were clever, happy, and loving.

It was becoming clear that these children living in utter poverty were not unintelligent, nor worth less than other children in the world. Our children would struggle just like them if they were born into that world of trouble, and these lovely African children could be just as successful as our children if they were raised under identical conditions in our world. Most children in the daycare were talented, diligent, wanting to learn. And yet, the white man had a divine status in their eyes. Tradition, media, public perception, and colonialism made me into a symbol of wealth, wisdom, and power. The white men who fearlessly colonized the world for centuries, butchered and enslaved native peoples, chopped up and shared among themselves the African continent as if it was a loaf of bread, invaded and devastated foreign countries, generated wars to satisfy their own political and economic interests, they who after all this history dare to consider themselves most advanced on the planet, they received the highest respect. I felt a sense of confusion, unfairness, shame.

After the children went home, Joy and Wilfred made sure I got to know the area and learned about the community. We visited local families, health care centers, schools (usually with earthen floors, very many children in uniforms, very few benches, and no books), and other facilities in the region. On the first day, Wilfred took one of the children, the very ill Margaret, to a health center on a motorbike taxi for malaria treatment. Her father was also suffering from the disease, so we went to check up on the family a few days later. One of the days we visited a gold mine. It was a deep hole in the ground, with an entry about sixty centimeters in diameter, the size of a sewer cap. A man climbed down with a flashlight on his forehead and a rope around his waist. He brought up pieces of rock that were not unusual in any way. A woman then tirelessly pulverized one palm-sized rock at a time by hitting it with another, all day long, to find tiny traces of gold, a fraction of a millimeter in size, milligrams in weight. She was paid only if she found the miniscule shiny jewel. She seemed to be in her late fifties, but when we inquired about her age, we were told she was in her thirties. The mine owner was considered rich in the neighborhood. Little was there to bear witness to that though. A table, a few plastic chairs, framed pictures on the walls of the adobe house, and two dogs running around were the luxury excess. And perhaps the multiple huts, indicative of the fact that the man of the house had several wives, despite his Christian faith. Each wife was likely obtained against a generous dowry, sometimes equivalent of years of his income and often paid in post-marital installments of livestock, goods, or money.

Little Stanley was an emotional boy diagnosed with HIV. His mother became victim of the *Jaboya* system in which women engage in sexual relationships with fishermen around Lake Victoria to secure their supply of fish. The sex for fish practices heavily contribute to the high HIV prevalence. Stanley lived with his grandmother, a joyful, big-hearted woman. We walked home with him one afternoon and paid a short visit to his grandmother. She felt so honored that she came the next morning to the kindergarten to visit us. She carried a live hen under her arm. It was her present to us as a sign of appreciation for our visit on the previous day. A gift of infinite dimension in a place where survival was an everyday struggle. The heavy weight of indebtedness burdened my soul. She asked us about the day of our departure and promised to come again the day before to say goodbye.

Stanley's home was more than an hour walk from the kindergarten. He was four years old, and he made the journey alone every day, often while the morning was still dark. It was unsurprising when the sole of his old, ragged shoe finally got torn off one day. Stanley couldn't stop his tears over his only footwear. He went home barefoot. We walked down the hill to the only store in the village and bought him a pair of rubber sandals, the only ones available. He broke into jubilation when he tried them on the next morning. It was the day before we left Wagusu. His grandmother came by with a sack of delicious nuts, exactly as she had promised. I felt flabbergasted, greatly humbled, and embarrassed in a way. I was witnessing new meanings of words like love, respect, modesty, and generosity, dimensions perhaps unknown in the world I was coming from. Gratefulness had its own scale. People appreciated immensely not only every opportunity to have even a disproportionally low income but a good husband or a chance to learn anything that may prove useful one day.

Jacky also operated a small tailoring workshop on the premises of Shangilia. Caroline, the young, cheerful teacher with a lovely smile, taught a few young women of the village the art of sewing, the one my mother practiced with such perfectionism, with the hope that the vocation would keep them away from the sex for fish trade. I fell in love with the beautifully colored *kanga* and other garments worn by women in this country, always clean (despite the extremely dusty environment), always graceful. I asked Caroline if she would be willing to produce one two-piece dress for Gina and one for my mother before my departure. She happily accepted the challenge. I let her choose the fabric. She took the responsibility very seriously. She carefully considered the absent customers' age and estimated body shape and size when choosing the colors and patterns. I knew Gina and my mother would never wear the final products, but I also knew how much it meant for Caroline and her trainees to produce them. My mother converted the dress a few years later into something she truly loved and wore. The fabric never lost its charm.

The day before I left the kindergarten, I organized, with the help of Wilfred and Joy, a party for the children. We decorated the classroom, sang songs, danced, fooled around, and surprised the children with sweets and soft drinks bought at the local store. Especially the soft drinks received the appreciation like a rare Christmas present, making the day special even for the staff. It was a splendid afternoon for us all. I took a motorcycle taxi to the Luanda K'Otieno pier the next day and continued with the dangerously noisy, rusty ferry on Lake Victoria to Mbita and on to Rusinga Island. I headed to the unique community center Island of Hope established by the Czech organization Centrum Narovinu, which facilitated the distance adoption of the two children I shared with my long-time friend Zuzana. I was supposed to meet one of the center leaders and local coordinators, Joash Okongo, who would then arrange my meeting with the eight-year-old Yvonne. Joash was the man for the job. He enjoyed his authority, but he was a compassionate, generous caretaker of a great number of people in need. He drove me to the house where Yvonne used to live and informed me that her family had moved in the meantime to Nairobi. He assured me that I would meet her once I was back in the capital.

It was fabulous to see the well-organized Island of Hope, a true island of order, security, and relative prosperity. I was impressed by the difference in people's lives determination and effort of a few can make. I met the medical staff of the center's healthcare facility (mostly Czech and Slovak volunteers), the teachers at its school, which in fact had chairs, benches, and shelves, and the staff of its canteen and water treatment plant. And, of course, many happy and relatively well-fed children. Joash drove me to his squared brick house, a structure with plane mortar surfaces both inside and out, reflecting local modernity and status. He lived in it with his younger wife and several children. His older wife and the rest of the children lived in the hut across the yard. We were seated on a couch in the living room equipped with a television and a few light bulbs. What they called the kitchen was an open fireplace in the yard surrounded by a low wall and covered, just like the house, with metal roof sheets. Joash asked his elegant, tall wife to serve us lunch. She came in from another room in the house with a tray full of toast bread and sliced cheese. It very likely was a sign of well-being and respect towards the foreign guest, so it didn't matter that I stayed hungry after eating. Seeing the multitude of barefoot children running around the property, I only dared to take one or two slices of bread. I was generously offered to overnight in one of the rooms, about two-by-two meters in size and entirely filled with two bunk beds. I was hoping that no children were asked to sleep away from their beds to accommodate me. I was assured it wasn't the case.

I accompanied Joash on his business trip to rural

communities in the Homa Bay region in the afternoon, relatively near in European terms yet hours of driving on the poor and unpaved roads. He was inspecting numerous adoptees in schools far not as neat and equipped as the one in the community center. We talked with the school principals and the children, and I promised to forward a message and a few photos to those children's adoptive parents in the Czech Republic.

I went back to the center the next day. Joash's son Robert quickly became attached to me and escorted me everywhere I went. He was polite, respectful but especially curious and sincere. His questions revealed a desire to make friends and learn. He was fascinated by airplanes, and he wanted to know all kinds of details about them. How they look inside, what take-off feels like, can we eat in them. He walked with me to the nearby airstrip, a grass field where he often sat and waited for a light aircraft to occasionally appear. I remembered that I used to be equally excited about planes when I was a child. My first flight at the age of seven, when our parents treated Adrian and me to a special first trip to our then-capital Prague (although we were encouraged to save up and pay part of the flight tickets), meant the world to me for years to come. Almost a decade passed before I flew again. I never stopped appreciating every opportunity to fly, no matter how frequently with time I could (or had to) do it. Now I saw the same meaning of wings in Robert's eyes.

We distributed small gifts I brought with me from Denmark among some of the children at the center. They surrounded us and impatiently yelled over each other while reaching their hands out towards me: "I want!" "Me too!" Their compassion surfaced when we asked them who they thought should get the next item. They calmed down right away and agreed together on who should receive it, carefully looking for those who were not yet holding a present in their hands. Soon everyone had something to cherish. So did Robert. When we were waving goodbye that afternoon, he wept. I was wondering whether I would ever see this curious, tender-hearted boy again and whether he would have the chance one day to fly.

After exploring the life of the lake people, I thought I should take the opportunity to see the breathtaking Kenyan nature. Albert recommended a two-and-a-half-day safari in Amboseli National Park near Mount Kilimanjaro. I insisted on a budget version, staying in tents instead of luxury resorts. I was in a group with three others. A German man, an Irish woman, and, to my surprise and perhaps disappointment, a rather ignorant Dane. The presence of foreigners, especially unexpected tourists from one's own country and those whose native language one speaks, can spoil the authenticity of a travel experience. The following three days I could no longer consider part of my fascinating trip in Africa but rather repulsive tourism. They were my most awkward days in Kenya. With hindsight, it is possible that I would have had a different impression if I had started my stay in the country on a safari. But after all I had just seen, it felt kitschy.

It was like driving through a giant open-air zoo. The park was swarming with open-roof vans. I looked like a fool with my little compact camera, while everybody was decorated with lenses at least half a meter long. My travel companions talked only about birds and other animals they spotted or wished to spot. They were rather knowledgeable about them. They carried several very expensive cameras, and every moment they were prepared to take the picture of their lifetime. They often bragged about previous safari tours they undertook in various countries, in case of the German safari enthusiast nearly two dozen of them, some lasting months. The ignorant Dane with his encyclopedia of birds always at hand had no idea what he was about to do and where he was about to go the following day. When I asked him about his travel itinerary, he referred to the package tour he had purchased, the exact program of which he could no longer remember nor care about.

My recent travel experiences in Kenya seemed to them just as much a waste of time and money as their travel plans seemed to me. I tried to tell them some of my stories from the past weeks, but they showed no interest in hearing them. They diverted every conversation to the hyenas and servals they had spotted. They weren't interested in the country and its people, they had no understanding of its culture, its problems, and their causes. They had no idea how damaging their extensive tourism and hunt for good shots was to the environment and to the wildlife they so selfishly loved. I conversed instead with our driver, who coincidentally was a Luo just like almost everyone I had so far met in the country even though the Luo tribe forms only a little over ten percent of Kenya's population.

We stopped at a souvenir store on our way back to the camp. A group of little children ran to us. They shouted the usual: "Muzungu!" I knew they wanted to hold our hands. The Irish woman panicked and pulled her hands away while roughly ordering the kids not to touch her and go away. A tourist from an Asian group in the van parking next to ours stepped out already prepared for the scene; she pulled out a handful of candy from her pocket and threw it on the concrete floor few meters away. The children ran to pick up as many sweets as they could, like shoals of fish approaching the pieces of bread thrown into a pond. The group enjoyed the "fun" and considered the dog-like treatment the perfect scene for great photos and videos. I felt uncomfortable, ashamed to belong to the group of beastly white and yellow creatures. I felt the difference between a tourist, who pays for a luxury trip and takes pictures through the window of a vehicle frightened to directly face a poorer country's society and reality, and a traveler, explorer, who enjoys just that. I now appeared standing on the wrong side, where I never wanted to be.

After the two and a half days among wild animals and their even wilder spotters, I was ready to meet my two adopted children. Benson was fifteen and lived in Kibera. Centrum Narovinu's two local coordinators, Ben Ooko and Peter Otieno, arranged the meeting. I met Benson in his school. I noticed already during earlier school visits that the older children in higher grades behaved differently from the younger ones. They were reserved, they never smiled in the presence of adults. Schools had stringent discipline and strict teachers. Caning, although illegal, was practiced. When I asked one principal why I never see a child laughing, she answered that school is not about fun, laughter is not allowed.

Benson was no exception. He lacked self-esteem. The visit of someone he saw as a superior white man, one he was supposed to respect for his financial support, didn't make things easier. I tried to explain to him that I am no more worth than he is, and that I am his friend, an equal partner, someone who respects him just as much as he respects me. After a little effort, some monkeying and a couple of jokes, a smile finally appeared on his face.

He was very polite and kind. His teachers confirmed

that he was an ambitious student, who dreamed of becoming a doctor. I was wondering what chances a slum-dweller in an extremely corrupt society, where despite the relative riches of the country so many live in extreme poverty, might have to fulfil his dream. I could only remain hopeful that he may have a better future if we continued to support his education.

Benson walked with me to his two-room adobe house a few very narrow, muddy streets away from his school. There I met his brother and one of his several sisters. They lived together in a tiny house with an earthen floor, two beds (children often sleep on the floor), a shabby sofa, cookware, and a small television. His parents weren't home. His father was ill, lived elsewhere and came to visit a few times a week. His mother was illegally collecting and selling firewood, an arduous and dangerous activity in an urban area. I told Benson a little about myself, I showed him photos of my family, and I said a few words about Zuzana, whom he knew well. Zuzana was the primary adoptive parent who received his student transcripts and to whom he was asked to address his infrequent but mandatory letters. The conversation was awkward. Benson said very little; he only answered my questions, rarely making eye contact. I handed over some presents, and, after words of hope and encouragement, I was guided out of the slum of slums, labyrinth of poverty, a place of unique culture, art, and events, with a million inhabitants, many of whom are proud to call it home.

It was finally time to meet our eight-year-old girl Yvonne the next day. Two project coordinators, Joash's brother Ken Okongo and Elizabeth Olalo, helped to set up the visit. I was accompanied by Pablo Sigismondi, an older Argentinian traveler whom I had met few days earlier in the Nairobi International Youth Hostel. It was an incredibly simple place. The tiny room with a bunk bed and a little space next to it just enough to pass had a window without a pane. The bathrooms were shared. But in this hostel were the most wonderful guests one could meet. When I told Pablo about my plan for the day, he insisted on joining me. He lived for such spontaneous cultural adventures.

Yvonne's mother died just three days after Yvonne was born. True to Luo tradition, Yvonne was given the last name Ajwang, which means "left behind" or "survived despite neglect". Her father Ceasar, who was around fifty, married a much younger woman, Josephine. She referred to Yvonne as her daughter and Yvonne called her mother.

Yvonne wasn't comfortable with speaking English, but unlike Benson, she was cheerful, social, casual. We had a great time playing, joking, and laughing together. Yvonne had a special sense of humor; she was a lovely little teaser. And she performed impressively with the jump rope. We went for a walk to see her school, which she presented with great pride. She loved to go to school. We agreed with her teacher to meet her entire class the following day. On our way back, we stopped to buy meat, water, and flour for a couple of weeks. Josephine welcomed us with a delicious lunch, beef stew with *sukuma* and *ugali* (a dish made with collard greens and corn meal), which we ate with hands after washing them with water poured from a jug over a plastic wash basin that we passed around the table. It was relaxing to sit afterwards in the tiny but cool shack with walls painted blue, protected from the dazzling sun and sipping lukewarm Kericho tea. Pablo and I spent the next morning with Yvonne and her classmates. It was a joyful time filled with humor and playfulness. The children were blown away by seeing themselves on the display of our cameras while they enjoyed the lollipops we brought with us. We were Yvonne's peculiar guests, and she was the star of the class.

Ceasar came to the school to meet us. He said Yvonne was talking about me all evening after I had left the day before. He repeatedly thanked for our support through the Czech program, and he expressed how much it meant to his family. His gratefulness was coming from his heart. He deeply respected the program, and the only thing he asked from me was that I pass on his best wishes and thanks to Zuzana. He did so even after smartphones allowed us to be in closer contact a couple of years later. It was only ten years after we had met that he asked me out of desperation for help, when Josephine's ill-health that lasted for months was increasingly worrying him. He asked me to keep his request for cash to help cover Josephine's medical examinations (for which he provided photographs of receipts and examination reports) between the two of us. Josephine recovered within a few weeks.

It was time to say goodbye. Both Yvonne and I felt we were losing something precious. There was sadness in the air; the power of emotions was at work. What a deep bond few hours could generate between a European adult and an African child who had never met before and did not speak a common language.

The following day was my last in Kenya and I was filled with intense sentiment. In this land, where time has a different dimension, where things function with lower speed and questionable reliability, and where expectations of a traveler must be low in order to stay calm, everything worked like in a dream. Everybody I had met made an enormous effort to make me feel welcome and safe, and they provided much more than I could ask for. They didn't just ensure that I did what I came to do, but they were always on their mettle. They shared their home with me, they offered exciting adventures, they guided me through places they wanted me to see, and, most importantly, they blessed me with their honest friendship without expecting anything in return, without accepting anything I tried to extend as a sign of appreciation. They loved what they were doing, they loved the children above all. They worked tirelessly to improve their lives, and what they did for me was just a small part of the big picture. On this final day, Ken invited me for a drink in the afternoon and Jackie and Albert for dinner in a popular, very crowded one-of-a-kind grill restaurant. Then they drove me to the airport for my 2:50 AM flight.

I departed with my life changed. I wasn't only leaving full of memories; I was leaving something behind. A young man and a joyful little girl who grew to my heart but whom I might never see again. I remained hopeful that the program would help to make their dreams come true. They deserved it. They were pure, they were innocent just like the children in Wagusu and everywhere in the world. But innocence is insufficient. It is the history, the culture, the system that have been wounded for too long, and their legacy can hardly be escaped. I knew my days would soon go back to what they were before, days of modernity, security, and comfort of what I now saw as relative luxury, days of boundless dreaming. But their days would continue without change, in poverty, in struggle, in need, and with very different dreams, dreams of a better life they never knew, if they ever dared to dream them.

Benson dropped out of school and therefore the program in 2018 after he disappeared and could no longer be contacted. He may have gotten into trouble, perhaps he made a girl pregnant, or another reason simply forced him to start earning money. Yvonne, however, is at the time of writing eighteen years into the program, weeks away from finishing the first year of her college education. Our support for her education will not dry up. It is just a single soul out of so many in need, but it is one that proves that what a few young friends once began was meaningful and worth every penny. Yvonne is now not only our child but our friend too. When I told Ceasar that I would like to start to communicate with Yvonne directly, he replied that she had been longing to have her own phone, but his economy didn't allow him to buy her one. Sponsoring such presents is something Centrum Narovinu routinely helps to facilitate, and so, shortly after her eighteenth birthday, Yvonne received her first phone. We could finally reconnect and continue the laughter where we had left it off more than a decade earlier.

»«

Observing the rich and the poor, hearing the stories of the city and the countryside, talking with people from different walks of life made me see clearer the damaging nature of colonialism, the incompatibility of the white rule with tribal traditions, the devastation both can cause, and its exacerbation when a dysfunctional, corrupt pseudo-democracy arrives with independence. Sluggish traditions can feel especially destructive in our fast-moving times, which offer better alternatives. The contrast was massive between the struggling tribal countryside with its polygamy, female circumcision, days-long funerary celebrations and rituals, intricate marriage ceremonies involving payment of a bride price to the bride's mother and dowry to her father, obligation of women to take care of food and household while their often-unemployed men idle at home, and the cities with their relatively modern lifestyles. And yet, people didn't seem unhappier than in the idealized world I came from. Perhaps because they were not lonely, they were not locked up in their own little worlds, protected and unshared with others. As if they were perfectly accustomed to the life they were supposed to live.

When I later read Barack Obama's book *Dreams from My Father*, written before he entered the political scene, I found it encouraging that some of his earlier experiences and observations from Kenya resembled mine. (On a side note, the life of the man whose father came from a village near the one where I volunteered, made it all the way to Harvard and back to a senior position in the Kenyan Ministry of Finance before being destroyed by personal conflicts among the political elite, the life of the man who in fact never had a father but became, against all the odds, the American president of hope, reconciliation, and wide global popularity for his humaneness, wisdom, intelligence, wit, steep learning curve, and political elegance so wonderfully described in his book *A Promised Land*, has been a great source of inspiration to me. And to many regardless of political considerations).

I had to face the reality that I represented the part of the world which was partly responsible for what I had just witnessed in Africa. A region the wealth of which is unimaginable and so is its greed. Where politics has a goal to increase this wealth year after year, share it only symbolically with those in real need outside the borders, and never admit the consequences of all this for other parts of the world. I began to see my own world through very different lenses. I saw our lives back home being mostly out of balance. The amount of waste we generate seemed despicable. From food and clothing to vacations, nothing seemed to be enough to satisfy the ever-growing expectations and desires. I believed that even the most conscious who try to resist consumerism could find countless opportunities to cut back and pleasantly get by with fewer unnecessary privileges and less of what we consider basic everyday comfort I found it ridiculous, somewhat humiliating, when I saw toddlers having rooms filled with hundreds of toys or children for whom presents smaller than a television, computer, or telephone meant nothing. I could not understand how companies can spend a fortune on image but little on employee benefits, why the public sector spends foolishly at times just because funds must be spent by certain deadlines, why bakeries maintain their shelves full until closing time and empty them into the garbage container a minute after. I was more and more appalled by employers who don't pay their employees what they deserve but drive luxury cars and visit exotic destinations, where they ignore the local population, their culture, and their values but not their own hedonism.

After my return, it was difficult to find purpose in some aspects of my job. I did find the increasing concern about exposure to particulate and chemical pollutants in our environment and their health effects reasonable and worthy of my future scientific attention. But research that is supposed to improve the indoor climate of dwellings and office buildings in the world's most affluent, healthy, and comfortable countries appeared unreasonable. It seemed pathetic to talk about ventilation, odors, or tenths of degrees of temperature difference in order to increase the productivity of office workers by half percent, or advance the internet of things and automatize our homes with a truckload of sensors and technologies that don't help anyone, only to make us believe we save time in our unnecessarily hectic lives and we save the planet by conserving a bit of energy, while our lifestyle only keeps demanding more of it. I saw profit generation hiding even behind some science and technology meant to help people and move the world (but especially industry) forward.

My Kenyan experience motivated me to aim for research projects focusing on developing countries. (Household air pollution from burning solid fuels was and still is a major contributor to the global burden of disease.) I applied for an international development research grant of the Danish Ministry of Foreign Affairs. In collaboration with several Danish organizations and companies, we proposed to develop healthy, sustainable, and affordable houses in Ghana, using a promising technology that had the potential to generate jobs in rural areas. A Danish company had developed a simple pressing machine to produce cement-free, unfired, compressed earth bricks from local soil, and a small foundation began to develop the business model that would train and empower local rural communities. Since much of Ghana's soil is suitable for the application of the technique and the country was on the list of partner countries for Danish development projects, it was the ideal place to test the impact of the construction technique on the quality of buildings, indoor climate, health, and local economy. While working on the application, I visited our partners at the Kwame Nkrumah University of Science and Technology in Kumasi, the alma mater of its most prominent graduate, the seventh Secretary-General of the United Nations, Kofi Annan.

I was positively impressed by the Ghanaian

colleagues' international experience, attitude, and research capacities. To my surprise, Ghana's corruption perception index was identical with that of Slovakia (making me wonder if this meant that Slovakia was doing, relatively speaking, pretty bad or that Ghana was doing pretty good), which calmed my initial fear of economic challenges in case the project was granted. My Danish partners and I then travelled with our local contact around the country to meet other potential partners, leaders of vocational schools and cooperative societies, village chieftains, and villagers.

In Seketia, a remote village on the border with Ivory Coast, the village council gathered to honor our visit. The "castle" was a somewhat larger house among the many dilapidated and desolate adobe shacks. It had a room of about thirty square meters with tiled floor and about seventeen chairs forming a semi-circle along the wall. When we entered the room, the village king, the queen, and the rest of what the villagers called royalty were seated on their "thrones", wearing the fanciest of their celebratory garments. The meeting was rather ceremonial in nature; certain rules of the court had to be followed. The village was honored by a rare visit from Europe, and for that we were treated in a royal fashion. The potential collaboration was approved, our efforts were blessed.

My impressions formed in East Africa were reaffirmed in the western part of the continent. They were further vitalized by the fact that I was now on the Gold Coast, one of the major regions from which purchased and kidnapped Africans had been shipped to the Americas as part of the slave trade run largely by Western European countries.

The project proposal, which was seen among some colleagues (including the head of the department) as meaningless, was rejected in the final round with a ludicrous argument referring to the listed bibliography even though the reviewers judged it outstanding, crucially relevant, with no major recommendations for improvement. I continued working with the problems of the Western world, for which the chances of obtaining funding were higher. I tried to focus on issues that remain important regardless of location, economy, or culture. But since work looking at exposure to chemical and particulate pollutants in buildings and their effects on health does not leave space for product development or potential spin-off companies, and it "only" wants to improve people's lives, securing funding for such work at a technical university did not prove to be any easier. I soon had to accept working on projects in which public funding and corporate agendas walked hand in hand and fortunes were spent to help virtually nobody.

I was encouraged to execute a small experiment in my private life. Gina and I decided to minimize hardly noticeable and seemingly unnecessary expenses in our everyday lives for one year. We rarely bought what we didn't need even before, but now we sometimes skipped that one-last-drink when dining out, once in a while we cooked a delicious vegetarian stew when we felt for a steak, we refrained from taking a bottle of wine when visiting friends, and we minimized or entirely dropped a few birthday presents when we were invited to birthday parties outside the family. We gave instead a card with quotes and photos from Kenya and an explanation what we intended to do with the money we would otherwise have spent on the present. After a few months we could no longer hold out against the feeling of embarrassment and shame. Not everybody seemed to understand our little project, and I was slowly melting back into the society in which I was so deep-rooted.

We continued with the plan, restricting only ourselves. Though, we never felt restricted. The amount of money we put in the piggy bank every now and then was so small that we had to realize how much more we could sacrifice if we wanted to. After the twelve months had passed, the money box contained close to five hundred euros worth of Danish kroner. It was thirty-five percent more than the global daily per capita poverty line at that time for every day of one year. It could have taken one person out of poverty for one year or provided ten times the poverty line over nearly two months. We used the savings to donate badly needed medicine to an underprivileged child during our next visit to Bethlehem.

It crystallized in my mind that helping others is not a matter of being wealthy. Being charitable is a matter of the heart. We can't always get, but we can always give. Most adoptive parents in the distance adoption programs are middle-class citizens, and in the developing world the poor are often the most charitable towards their fellow citizens. How generous Stanley's grandmother was when she insisted that we eat her hen that evening. I had to realize how much I needed to work on myself. As Kahlil Gibran once said, "Generosity is giving more than you can, and pride is taking less than you need".

>×«

Travelling showed its power to teach, and it hid many lessons in its haversack. I had an experience of opposite nature when I attended a conference held in an all-inclusive hotel resort in Antalya, Turkey. It was one of the great many complexes stretching tens of kilometers along the coast, shallow replicas of famous cities, each accommodating thousands of tourists. Observing the ordinary guests made me speechless. Most of them never left this spurious place until they had to catch their flight home. They saw nothing of the beautiful country, they never met a local person, except perhaps the underpaid staff, who worked tirelessly to satisfy their wishes.

They never saw that the world outside the gates was not as glamorous as within but many times more appealing. They did not bother to support the wonderful little businesses, cozy stores, artists, family restaurants, or rental companies in town, which are genuinely visitor friendly, honest, and under increasing risk of going bust. They sponsored instead the extremely wealthy, the corrupt, who likely treat their employees unfairly and avoid paying their taxes justly. The hedonism among the guests was distasteful too. Some stuffed themselves with free food beyond imagination, others overloaded their plates to the extent that they soiled the floor as they walked to their tables, then ate a few bites and left the rest to decorate the garbage bin. Some went for a massage every day, others drank their minds to darkness early in the day, just not to miss out on excess available at no extra cost.

I knew I would never be able to go on such a holiday myself. The magic of traveling lies not in overindulgence but in learning and exploration, in understanding the flavors of a foreign country, in appreciating the warm-heartedness of the people and the faith with which they accept their destiny, in tasting the wonders of culture and nature, even the tiniest of its beauties. Traveling must be authentic and sustainable, it must be devoted to preserving and cherishing what a place has to offer, it must support those local individuals who need it and deserve it the most, it ought to exercise supreme respect toward local values and conserve the nature, even if it means restraint for the traveler.

I was deeply moved towards these realizations by Pablo, the impressive Argentinian traveler whom I had met in the down-at-heel hostel in Nairobi. The cheap, worn-down place concentrated fascinating people from around the world with an array of backgrounds and reasons for being there. They were mostly conscious travelers, who shared their well-grounded reflections on the most unexplored of places The Iranian Alireza, studying at the Harvard Kennedy School of Government, was regularly sent to some of the most unforgiving places to investigate the local social and political situation. The Portuguese João, then married and living in Ouarzazate in Morocco, had a degree in visual arts and could work and make his living from anywhere in the world, so that was what he did. By the time I met him, he had been exploring mainly Europe, North America, North Africa, and parts of the Middle East. Since then, however, he has been nearly continuously crisscrossing the planet, exquisitely documenting every place, person, adventure, accommodation, or vehicle on his journeys, and publishing on his website guides, recommendations, photo documentations, interviews, and reports on people, food, modes of transportation, and any other aspects of his nomadic life. He has visited about 130 of the 193 countries recognized by the United Nations and about 145 of what he calls the 266 UN+ countries. The list includes some of the most hostile places, and João has visited Antarctica in the company of Falcon Scott (grandson of the explorer Robert Falcon Scott) and Jonathan Shackleton (cousin of the Antarctic explorer Ernest Henry Shackleton, hero of the failed Imperial Trans-Antarctic expedition). The journeying and adventures so finely documented on João's website remains a source of motivation and learning.

But it was Pablo who was the most experienced globetrotter in our company. At the time, he had visited more than 150 countries, including some of the most dangerous places on the planet. He returned several times to places like Somalia, Iraq, and Afghanistan just during the past few war years. He had been continuously on the road most of his adult life, mostly with as budget a style as one can imagine. He slept in the most affordable places, where the most interesting people could be encountered. When he was young, he was asked to report on specific destinations. Now he had the freedom to choose wherever he wanted to go.

Pablo was a geographer, photographer, journalist, and academician. He chose a region, moved there for several months, and explored it in all its details, with a focus on its people, culture, environment, and geopolitics. He didn't just visit places, he lived in them. His impromptu program was steered by unexpected opportunities and the people he had met along the way. He then returned home, gave seminars, lectured at conferences and universities about the lessons from his voyage, published his findings and packed for the coming months to be spent in the next territory of his choice. "Family life wasn't invented for me," he once told me. He spent most of the year abroad. While at home in Cordoba, he stayed with his Syrian mother, and he strictly did not travel in Argentina or South America (not until the Covid-19 pandemic forced him to do so). It just wasn't challenging and exciting enough.

When I met him in Nairobi, he had arrived from South Africa and planned to stay in East Africa during the following five months. Kenya, Tanzania, Rwanda, Burundi, Democratic Republic of the Congo, Uganda, and especially South Sudan, the youngest nation in the world born just days before we met, made the list of planned destinations. His special goal was to visit the newly established refugee camps for the tens of thousands of mostly Somalis fleeing the 2011 East Africa drought. He was also determined to visit Mama Sarah, President Obama's step-grandmother (whom Obama called Granny) in Nyang'oma Kogelo, a stone's throw away from Wagusu.

Pablo's knowledge about the cultures hidden to the Western eye and about the environmental, social, and geopolitical problems of our times as seen from the perspective of the people who are impacted the most was extremely stimulating. I found it intriguing to hear a new view on the life of the Somali pirates and on the true reasons for their actions, and Pablo's reflections on the places on Earth he found most absorbing and on the evolution of his own travel preferences. He proudly climbed the Kilimanjaro a few years earlier, but he was now much more interested in slums, refugees, and impacts of political conflicts on people.

My own travel dreams were also rapidly evolving. I found more and more enlightening the places of recent conflicts and insufficiency, disputed regions, occupied territories, ghost towns, and enclaves. I became interested in places like Nagorno-Karabakh, South Ossetia, Kosovo, or Northern Cyprus. About the land of the Kurds, the "Sarajevos", the "Varoshas". When I actually visited Northern Cyprus as part of a family trip with Gina's parents and sisters to attend her sister Jessica's college graduation, I did enjoy visiting Kyrenia, St. Hilarion castle on the top of Kyrenia mountain range, the monastery of Saint Barnabas, the church ruins of Famagusta, or the Karpas peninsula, where nobody except Jonatan and Adnan was willing to leave the beach and join me in visiting the Apostolos Andreas Monastery at the north-easternmost point of the island. But I probably found more fascinating the decaying ghost town of Varosha, the once modern tourist area with apartment buildings and high-rise hotels suddenly abandoned during the Turkish invasion of Cyprus in 1974 and now still uninhabited, desolate, and blockaded.

I no longer saw much value in the kind of traveling I did a few years earlier in South America after my first year of full-time employment at DTU and two months before Gina and I got married. Vince and I had planned to meet at the airport in Santiago de Chile, visit Viña del Mar and Valparaiso on the Pacific coast, take the fabulous, unforgettable bus ride across the Andes with views of Aconcagua to Mendoza (where my camera would be eventually stolen, losing all photos from that magic bus tour), taste wine and steaks, fly to Buenos Aires, take a tango class, cross the Rio de la Plata for a daytrip to Colonia del Sacramento in Uruguay, fly to Iguaçu to witness one of the greatest natural marvels on the planet, the largest waterfall in the world with more than two hundred drops (we did it from boat, helicopter, and on foot on both sides of the Argentinian-Brazilian border), and finish with a few days in Rio on the Atlantic coast. Coast to coast, through four countries in fourteen days. When my parents heard about the plan, they insisted on joining, and I didn't mind that. We always enjoyed traveling together. But this kind of marathon travel now seemed overly superficial and faceless. And yet, one of the great memories of my life has its roots in South America.

During the last days of the trip, we stayed in the El Misti hostel a few streets from Copacabana. Here we met Karen and Annelies, two girls from Belgium, who were traveling across Brazil. Karen was struggling with a common cold, but she found our company enjoyable enough not to hurry to her room after dinner. The two of us continued talking even after our travel companions turned in. Our conversation became more and more personal and honest and continued for hours past midnight. We both felt we made an impression on each other, and we were truly looking forward to continuing our conversation the following evening, the final one before my departure. We went on to exchange further thoughts on life, values, relationships, and other matters over email during the next couple of months, but the communication eventually dwindled to a ritualistic happy birthday message the next year and a short Messenger conversation around Christmas seven years later.

Nearly twelve years after we had first (and last) met, I was going to a meeting in Lille, France. I remembered that Karen's hometown Kortrijk was in the south of Belgium. I looked at the map and realized the two were in each other's backyard, just across the border. I wrote to Karen, and she was right away just as excited to meet as I was, although later she did consult her still best friend Annelies and her mother about it. Annelies encouraged her, her mother was more cautious. We had not met for twelve years. The argument was that she didn't really know me, and who knows whom I had become. But Karen was determined even though she had to leave her two small children at home with their father.

We agreed to meet at the train station at 8 pm, the time of my arrival from Paris Charles de Gaulle airport. We did not specify anything else. I got off the train at Lille Europe station and went up to one of the two main halls connected with a long corridor under Avenue le Corbusier. I had virtually no idea where to look for

Karen. The hall wasn't crowded. I took the escalator up to street level, but I just turned around and went back down again. In that moment I noticed a girl about fifteen or twenty meters from me walking away. She walked slowly and did not have luggage with her. It seemed suspicious, as if she was looking for someone. But I did not have time for this thought exercise because in that very instant she suddenly turned around, looked me in the eyes, and we waived to each other. We approached each other and it felt as if we had met last time just the day before. The most awkward thing about our meeting was that it wasn't awkward at all.

Karen drove me to my hotel next to Saint Maurice church to check-in, I asked the receptionist to recommend a restaurant, and we walked to the very cozy Les Compagnons de la Grappe restaurant for an authentic dinner. Our conversation seemed to continue where we had left off in Rio. There were no secrets, no discomfiture. We enjoyed each other's company just like we did a decade earlier. It felt like we were having the most natural dinner with an old friend. After dinner, we walked the streets of Lille's old town for hours, often recognizing the same corners, which told us we were going in circles. It didn't matter. The old town was small, and we needed time to tell things. At one after midnight, it was time for Karen to drive home and for me to get ready for the next day's meeting. The evening was so incredibly pleasant that I was eager to share the latest of my top experiences with family and a few friends. All that was needed for it to happen was to remember an old travel story and suggest to its protagonist to meet. We promised not to let too much time go by before meeting again, and we regularly get in touch since then.

>«

I visited several faraway places during the years following my brief South American jaunt. I spent months preparing the relatively short visits. Preparation was half the fun. I studied the local geography, the road and city maps, the history and culture, I learned a few words in the local language, and sometimes I could even join a debate about the country's recent news or political developments. I was finding guesthouses and public transport connections, securing visas, communicating with local rental companies and occasionally with local guides and people I personally knew in the country of my destination. I met people from many countries through my work, and they made my trips all the more adventurous. What a wisdom hid in every place and every person I was able to connect with. A detailed travelogue would make up for another book, but a few stories can be enlightening.

In northern Vietnam, Jan and I hired a car, which came with a driver and a guide (traditional car rentals weren't available). Our guide was a Hmong girl named Ying. She was her mother's only daughter. Her mother didn't send her to school and didn't teach her to read or write. She didn't want her to leave the village; she wished to have her daughter by her side during her declining years. But Ying was fascinated by travelers passing her village as they hiked the trails of the Hoàng Liên Sơn Mountains. She went to the local library and taught herself literacy. She spoke perfect English and few words in several other languages. She knew modestly about the world, but she learned everything she needed to know to utilize her passion for the country's nature, move to Hanoi, and become a professional guide for an agency in the capital. It was a fascinating example of determination and self-education.

The hike in the hot and humid climate of the jungle was thermally the most strenuous I had ever tried, but resting on a seagrass rug over the bamboo floor at a local family, sipping tea, eating freshly roasted delicacies, and watching Vietnamese soap opera with the grandma of the house was worth every drop of sweat. Our host family around lake Ba Bể threw for us a goodbye party. Friends and relatives gathered around the tablecloth on the floor richly covered with the best the family kitchen could offer, from soup to meat, fish, rice, exotic vegetables, morning glory, and the family's best bottle of homemade rice wine. One rice wine shot followed the other with remarkable frequency. Jan and I thought the gathering was determined to get us drunk, but they were slowly falling victim to their own trap. One of the friendly guests was so excited about the country we came from (or just the fact that he had heard about it) that he proudly poured us a few extra drinks to celebrate. (When asked where we came from, we usually referred to our country as Czechoslovakia, which historically was a friendly communist nation, still much better known than its two individual, now independent parts). When late in the night he could barely stand on his feet, he announced that it was time for him to jump on his scooter and go to work. We asked him what the job that he would have to attend to at this late hour was. It turned out that he was the local policeman. We were in any case safe for the night in our hosts' forest house on stilts.

Henry from the eco-friendly Blue Swimmer agency was our company on the small but typical junk with battened lugsails, which we had to ourselves to sail for two days in the magnificent Ha Long Bay. The crew of three, a captain, a chef, and Henry, navigated us to the most fabulous and secluded limestone karsts and isles, floating fishing villages, caves, and bays to canoe and swim in. Henry hiked with us, told us about the life in the bay and in Vietnam in general, told us local history, and explained the young Vietnamese population's indifference to the Vietnam War, which was in deep contrast to the War's cult status in America. These were true travel highlights. Not that we didn't enjoy eating different versions of *phở* from street vendors in Hanoi or visiting the one and only Thang Long Water Puppet Theatre, the Imperial Citadel, the Ho Chi Minh museum with its proud photos of the National Congresses of the Communist Party of Vietnam, or the Military History Museum opposite the Lenin Park (we, of course, just like in Kyrgyzstan, posed imitatively for an ironic picture with Lenin's statue), where it became clear why the Americans could never win their war. We very much did so. But the personal encounters, like that with the cab driver taking us to the airport on our last day in Vietnam, whom we managed after a long effort to make understand that we wanted him to first take us to a restaurant serving *thit chó* (dog meat), where he would be our guest, just tended to have a slightly different weight.

But, of course, sights have the power to inspire too. They can do so while one prepares the details of an adventure, looks up places to visit, checks the security conditions, scrutinizes the map, searches for accommodation or rental services, reads about the rules and warnings. And travel adventures can especially motivate to further read about everything observed during a journey, eventually ripening all the new knowledge, experience and understanding of a foreign place and its people.

The Caucasian nations of Georgia and Armenia, the first ones to adopt Christianity as state religion, which they were able to preserve despite numerous setbacks since the fourth century, offered a unique set of intriguing escapades. Due to the local geopolitics, Georgia was in a conflict with Russia over South Ossetia, and Armenia was in their everlasting conflict with Turkey but also Azerbaijan. Afraid of the road conditions, we rented a behemoth, a Mitsubishi Montero, and it turned out to be a wise decision. The Georgian Military Highway from Tbilisi to the Russian border was partly unpaved, muddy, snowy, mostly lacking roadside barriers despite dangerously steep slopes, and its tunnels were narrow, low, and packed with lorries driving in the middle and still barely making it through, sometimes with just centimeters between them and the sides of the round or pointed arch tunnels. Overtaking was impossible, and those who tried often held up even more the already congested traffic. We took a turn into the valleys under the snow-covered, 5054 meters high Mount Kazbek to try the off-road capabilities of the Montero and climb up with it to the Gergeti Trinity Church at an elevation of 2170 meters.

After visiting the birthplace of Joseph Stalin in Gori and eating a plate of *khinkali* (Georgian stuffed dumplings) on Stalin Avenue, one of the very few remaining streets, if not the only one, to carry the name of the dictator, we drove out to the iron-age town of Uplistsikhe and tried to find a place to sleep. When we couldn't find a living being in all the town and the road came to a dead end at the parking place of the cave complex late in the evening, we decided to sleep in the spacious back of the Montero. We noticed light in the nearby house, so we went to ask if they had anything against our decision. The house happened to be a police station. The officers on duty kindly assured us that we would be very safe overnighting in the car, but they asked us to park on the lawn a little further away from the parking place. It was a small football field. We drove through its goal, parked in the middle of it and turned in.

The next day, we crossed to Armenia, drove around twenty kilometers, then turned around and went back to the border to purchase the mandatory car insurance, which we initially thought was included in the rental agreement. While driving away from the border crossing, Jan and I tried to figure out why everybody at the border was stopping by the insurance stands and whether we should have done the same. The rental company knew we would be driving into Armenia and emphasized that all paperwork was in order. They didn't mention that their insurance only covered Georgia. Eventually we decided that getting a coverage for the days in Armenia was the safest thing to do, and it turned out to be the only legally correct option.

We continued to Gyumri, where we found a modern pizzeria. Asking the waiter to recommend a place to sleep attracted the entire staff to gather around our table. The manager, a kind woman speaking decent English, began to make phone calls and debate with her staff the best way to help us. We received instructions on how to get to a worn-down Soviet-time hotel. We finished our dinner, thanked the staff, jumped in the car, and drove. We didn't get far before we were pulled over with sirens. The two policemen were calm and kind, and they explained to us (in Russian in response to our blend of Slavic languages) that we had made an illegal turn. Whether we committed the offence or were just unlucky to drive a car with foreign number plates was unclear. Looking for milking opportunities of this kind was a routine income generating activity, and this was not the last time we encountered it. But at least we did have the insurance in order. We paid the modest fine that the two policemen gladly negotiated with us, and even the reduced amount made them happy enough to escort us with flashing lights to our hotel.

The next morning, we walked the main street of the town and observed the daily business: meat being sold from the back of a Lada, bread from the trunk of a GAZ Volga, a few small grocery stores, and a few liquor stores. We continued our journey to the southern slopes of Mount Aragats, where due to deep snow on the road we didn't make it to the eleventh century Vahramashen Church near Amberd, the tenth century fortress located 2300 meters above sea level. The Montero ploughed its way in the deep tracks with ease, but eventually the narrow road was blocked. First a Lada got stuck in the snow. We helped to dig its wheels free and push it out of the worst to be able to continue. But a few hundred meters further up the road, an old truck with a trailer began to slide down the steep slope as it tried to drive around the worst of the snow and rocks that rolled down from the mountain and blocked most of the road. The driver stopped in time, but the truck was dangerously tilted, and its left rear wheel was nearly hanging in the air. Two men began to shovel the snow from the road and push the trailer back to safety. For us it was time to turn around and continue to Vagharshapat, where we visited the Echmiadzin Cathedral, the mother church of the Armenian Apostolic Church and possibly the oldest cathedral in the world.

The road from Yerevan to Goris near the border with Nagorno-Karabakh, passing Mount Ararat on the other side of the border with Turkey and various enclaves and exclaves of Azerbaijan (like the Nakhchivan Autonomous Republic), revealed great poverty, heavily deteriorating apartment buildings (with façades scattered with a profusion of satellite dishes), never completed houses, and terrible roads. After visiting Tatev, the ninth century Armenian Apostolic monastery near the border with Iran, which played a significant role in the history of the region as a center of economic, political, spiritual, and cultural activity and contributed to the advancement of science, religion, philosophy, arts and reproduction of books, we drove through Selim Pass with its desolate villages and well-preserved caravanserai built in 1332 at an altitude of 2410 meters above sea level. Armenia's silk road took us to Lake Sevan, where we stopped in the world's largest cemetery with *khachkars* in Noraduz.

Our last stop before reaching the Georgian border, with the Montero's wheels worryingly squeaking by now, was Sanahin, the home of a thousand-year-old monastery. We were completely alone during the whole time at this hard-to-find UNESCO World Heritage Site with no signs or official entrance, seemingly untouched for hundreds of years. Vegetation was growing out of its walls and roofs. The empty space between its stone walls, its vaults and domes, the tombs making up the floor, the crimson cloth, and a vase of flowers on its small stone altar, together with the drizzle on the other side of the open arches and the gravesites and *khachkars* scattered around it made us feel the presence of the bishops and chivalrous knights who once trod the floors of this important center of faith and education.

We walked the deserted streets of the remote, poor village, where houses were in disrepair and one small store offered the most basic goods to the villagers ensconced in their homes. The only living creatures we saw outside were a black sow with its piglets wandering the streets. Suddenly we noticed a fighter jet on display. Who would have thought that from this little Armenian community rose to fame the two Mikoyan brothers, sons of a carpenter and a rug weaver. Artem was the designer of many MiG military aircraft. His brother Anastas became the longest serving high ranking politician in the very volatile Soviet system, the only one to remain at the highest levels of power from the days of Lenin in the 1920s till those of Brezhnev in the 1960s. An achievement virtually impossible in a regime in which a shift in power, an act of the past, or an undesirable opinion could carry the risk of imprisonment or death.

We returned to Tbilisi, parked the car in front of our hostel, thanked it for its endurance and service, and we understood that it was time for it to give up. Its right rear wheel would not make another turn. We called the rental company and asked them to pick it up. Our contact person arrived, jumped in the Montero, and forced the poor four-wheel drive to move on three rotating wheels amidst fearful uproar. We went to our favorite restaurant for a plate of *khinkali*, a wonderful *kachapuri adjaruli*, a boat-shaped hot bread filled with cheese and decorated with a piece of butter and an egg yolk in the middle, and a glass of Khvanchkara wine.

»«

The eye-opener in Kosovo was the life in this partially recognized, disputed state and the memories of the recent war in which many lost everything. My father and I were splendidly hosted by Mustafë Muhaxheri, the gentle and generous professor whom I had met in Denmark during his guest professorship a couple of years earlier. He met us in Pristina, where he worked. He drove with us to his family house in Peja. He showed us the thirteenth century Serbian Orthodox Patriarchal Monastery, the Rugova canyon, several traditional Ottoman tower houses called *kulla*, and the local market, where we tried *kaymak* and other local dairy products. Joined by his sons, we dined at his favorite places in town. He then asked one of his sons to join us on our journey to Prizren, with a stop at the medieval Serbian Orthodox Visoki Dečani Monastery.

Mustafë's fair account of the daunting recent Kosovar history and his recollections of the days of war were striking. Airstrikes began when he was visiting his family during his sabbatical year in Denmark in 1999. When someone rang the doorbell one night, an inner voice told him not to open the door. He then sneaked to the window and witnessed as the paramilitary walked from home to home, rang the bells, and shot everyone who opened for them. Mustafë and his family fled to Montenegro via a dangerous route over the mountains. With support from a journalist whom they briefly met at the mountain pass, they miraculously obtained visas at the Italian embassy the next day and boarded a cargo ship bound for Italy, from where the trip to Denmark, in possession of a valid work permit, was relatively straightforward. The family returned after the war to find their house looted and burned down. Undismayed, Mustafa rebuilt the house, rebuilt his life, his career, his business, but he remained saddened about never being able to reconnect with the woman at the Kula Pass and thank her for saving his family's life.

However, Mustafa had a copy of a Vanity Fair article in which his benefactor described their encounter. As I was writing this paragraph, I remembered that Mustafa gave me a copy of the article. I looked it up and read it again. I noticed the author's name: Janine di Giovanni. After a little research, I found the article republished on the website of the magazine years later. Plenty of information was available on the web about Janine, who in the meantime became a highly respected, internationally acclaimed war reporter, editor, and author. I forwarded the link to her website to Mustafa. He wrote to me the next day that he had heard back from Janine, and nearly two decades after those dreadful days, they had established contact. He could now tell her about his successful second life that began with her phone call to the Italian Embassy.

But how many couldn't rebuild their lives, and how many have not returned? Kosovars living all over Western Europe return every summer to visit relatives. Life in the cities revives, businesses flourish, weddings multiply. The country inflates with luxury cars with German and Swiss number plates mostly rented by the expats to flash with the lives they have built abroad. Or with the lives they want their friends and relatives to believe. My father and I drove our oldest, shabbiest car to visit Kosovo because we wanted to avoid undesired events. We had no idea how extremely pitiable we were going to look after crossing the Serbia-Kosovo border. The superficiality continued to haunt us until we crossed the Hungarian-Serbian border on the way home, where we had to queue for four hours along with the former Yugoslavs, all of whom seemed to be returning on the same day from their ostensible vacations into their real lives in the West.

But what about the truth of the other side? Dusan Licina was a child in Belgrade during those troubling years. With his interest in history and the objectivity of a scientist, his views on the NATO bombing of his city were as fascinating as Mustafa's story. Dusan studied in Singapore, was a guest doctoral student at DTU, continued to work at the University of California at Berkeley, became a tenure track professor at the Swiss Federal Institute of Technology in Lausanne (EPFL) in Switzerland, and within a very few years built up an impressive research group and a lab of his own. Dusan always impressed me with his humility, dedication, steep learning curve, and his continued confidence in my often-unnecessary advice on a range of issues over years of both scientific collaboration and friendship. When he asked me to review his 140-page document he had compiled for his promotion to associate professor, which contained his scientific, educational, managerial, and administrative achievements over the preceding six years and his academic career plan and vision for the future, I realized that he, being younger than me, had achieved more than I in shorter time and without the helping hands of more senior colleagues, like those I had the fortune to be guided by. A few years back, Dusan had asked me, who never had to have a job interview, to help him prepare for his intense multi-day interview for the tenure track position. It was now fabulous to see that EPFL could hardly have selected a better candidate.

»«

Iran was undoubtedly one of the most enthralling places, where the unparalleled hospitality leaves no space for discontent. It is the inverse of what one would expect when judging from the political masquerade exacerbated by mainstream media. Because of the strict sanctions on Iran imposed by Western countries, the usual preparation for the trip turned out partially unfeasible. Western companies did not operate in Iran, bank transfers were not permitted, online booking was impossible. Jan and I needed an invitation letter or a reservation for an organized tour to obtain our visas. I shared our travel plans with Taha, an Iranian student enrolled in Sweden and spending a few months at my department at DTU. He immediately mobilized his connections; his mother went to the relevant ministry to ask about approvals of invitation letters, and his friends shared their limited experience with inviting foreign friends.

We finally decided to find on the internet a couple of Iranian travel agencies that could help us obtain the visas. After a long correspondence with several of them, we selected the one that our gut feeling judged to be the kindest, fairest, and reliable. They were willing to book for us accommodation and arrange some of the local transfers as well. Taha, like a personal counsellor, gladly burdened himself with the unnecessary responsibility for the success of our trip. In an effort not to allow anything to go wrong, he checked the agency's price offers, the quality of the suggested hotels, and the feasibility of our proposed itinerary.

But there was a catch-22. The travel agency required a nonrefundable deposit for its services but offered no alternative to cash payment in person. We could not get into the country without their help, but we couldn't get their help without entering the country. I told Taha about the obstacle we were facing. He remained calm. The next day I received an e-mail from a person called Mostafa in Teheran. He wanted to know how much cash he should deliver and where. Mostafa was Taha's best friend. I was puzzled. Why would he go to an unknown agency and deliver four hundred dollars, a substantial amount for most people anywhere, let alone in Iran, on behalf of two guys he had not heard about before or might never meet?

There was no guarantee that the visas would be granted or that no unexpected event could force us to cancel the trip. Even if we made it to Iran, it would take months before he would receive his money back. He didn't mind all that. Taha's friends were his friends, and there was nothing we could do about it. It was our first taste of the supreme Iranian hospitality.

When we met Mostafa in Teheran and handed him the crunchy American dollars, he said with a clear surprise, disinterest, and the friendliest smile on his face that he never expected to get the money back. He drove us to his modern home in a new apartment building in the northern part of Teheran. He had recently moved in, and the place wasn't yet fully furnished. A few days before we reached Teheran, he called me and asked me how tall I was. I didn't understand what he was driving at. But everything became crystal clear when we entered his home and he began to unpack a brand-new bed in the guest room. That evening he invited us to taste fabulous culinary delights and smoke *ghaliyan* (water pipe) on the rug of a traditional restaurant, drove us back to his home, filled the fridge with food, unpacked the newly purchased breakfast table and four chairs, handed over his keys, wished us good night, and, to our astonishment, he left to sleep at his father's place. These were the first few hours after we had just met for the very first time.

This was the spirit that prevailed throughout the trip across Iran. There was no sign of tardiness, confusion, misinformation, mistrust, or begging for baksheesh, which we somewhat expected based on our earlier experiences from the Middle East despite the known differences between the Persian and the Arab world. Sara from the travel agency met us at Teheran's Mehrabad airport after our arranged transfer from Imam Khomeini

International Airport, where we had arrived. We were hoping to quickly lighten the burden of the hundreds of dollars of cash in our pockets right at the beginning, but Sara didn't want any money. She handed us our tickets for the domestic flight to Shiraz, and she said we would pay at the end, perhaps, if we were satisfied with Iran.

We were more than satisfied. We were blown away by the country's beauty, its cultural richness, millennia-old history reflected in the well-preserved, breathtaking architectural wonders, the religious diversity, literary excellence, and the mouth-watering cuisine. But most of all by its sophisticated, warm-hearted, most hospitable, and understandably proud Persian people. The cab driver who drove us from the international to the domestic airport after we had arrived in the middle of the night refrained from taking us to his place to sleep a few hours before our next flight only because he and his wife had a newborn baby. He wasn't comfortable with leaving us at the airport on our own, so he was determined to wait with us until the morning and insisted that we sleep in his car. We convinced him to go home to his family. Since his services were arranged for us by Sara, he never asked for any money.

In fact, nobody ever asked us for a single *rial* in return for kindness. People on the streets often approached us. They wanted to show us their city, invite us for tea, practice their English, or just ask who we were, where we came from, why we were in Iran, and whether we liked it.

We were picked up at the airport in Shiraz by Shahin. She worked as a tour guide and was hired by Sara to look after us while we were in town. We could ask her to help us out with anything we wanted to do or see, from buying a prepaid SIM card or finding a traditional restaurant to getting to places and visiting specific sights. She was available the next three days, and she suggested a program, but she was also flexible and gave us the freedom to plan our days. It was perfect. It was like traveling with a local friend. She gave us a wonderful tour of Shiraz, the home of two of the greatest medieval masters of Persian poetry and mysticism, Saadi and Hafez. We visited the Tomb of Hafez, the monumental Shāh Chérāgh, the elegant nineteenths century upper-class house and garden of Narenjestan-e Ghavam, the Eram Garden, the picturesque stained glasses and their colorful reflections on the walls and floors in the Nasir al-Mulk Mosque, the museum complex and palace in the Afif-Abad Garden but also the surroundings including the magnificent Persepolis, the necropolis of Naqsh-e Rostam, and the ancient Achaemenid capital of Pasargadae. Shahin drove us to the university where she worked as a computer scientist, and she told us about her children studying in Europe, her divorce, personal independence, and her decision to become a tour guide in her beloved city, the magic of which she wanted to share with foreigners. We invited her for dinner, where she let us try the sheep brain soup and *ghormeh sabzi* (herb stew).

Shahin introduced us to her English teacher, a comic Iranian American in his sixties, who guided us through the Vakil Bazaar and the Karim Khan castle while sarcastically criticizing the regime, the fanatics, the radicals, and the Americans. In return, we taught Shahin something as well. While she was driving us from Shiraz to Isfahan, the engine noise became unbearable on the highway. She never dared to use the fifth gear of her Peugeot 206, that is, if she knew it existed. Finally, we convinced her to put the car into fifth. After a few reminders, she became an accomplished fifth gear user. She repeatedly thanked us for helping raise her self-confidence, and she promised to drive back to Shiraz in fifth gear.

The next few days we visited the Vank Cathedral, a Zoroastrian fire temple, the Palace of Eight Heavens (Hasht Behesht), the Palace of Forty Columns (Chehel Sotoun), the numerous fine Safavid era arch bridges spanning the dry riverbed of the Zayandeh and used as recreational gathering places, and the breathtaking Jāmeh Mosque of Isfahān, which reached its current grandeur over the past thirteen centuries. We were absorbing the majestic splendor of Naqsh-e Jahan square with its Shah Mosque, Ali Qapu Palace, Sheikh Lotf Allah Mosque, its surrounding Safavid era buildings with bazaars and its lawns, fountains and strolling crowds, when two girls approached us. They both studied at the renowned Sharif University in Teheran and went out to catch up on things while visiting their hometown. They wanted to hear about our jobs, our country, and our opinion about Iran. We were captivated by the deep respect they expressed towards Westerners. We enjoyed hearing their views on the disconcerting political situation, the culture that they felt was being forced upon them, and the two types of everyday life in Iran, one lived on the façade and one that existed under the surface.

Niloofar was proud to wear the *rousari*, while Saeedeh, as so many Iranian women, was vehemently against its mandatory use. She repeatedly let it slide down on the back of her head, so low that it was legally questionable, and Niloofar or someone among the passersby soon asked her to pull it back up where it belonged. After half an hour of powwowing, they invited us for ice cream and a drink. We wanted to make sure they would not get into trouble for going out with two foreign men. We didn't want problems for ourselves either. Before we could say anything, they were already on their phones, spoke for a few minutes, then turned to us and said that their fathers agreed and wished them a good time. They drove us to their favorite place and stubbornly insisted on paying the bill.

During our drive back to Teheran, we stopped at the traditional red village of Abyaneh and in Kashan's Fin Garden and Borujerdi House. We met Sara and her boss on the final day of the trip. They gave us a tour of the modern Ab-o-Atash Park with its planetarium, pedestrian bridges, and various elegant facilities situated in a beautiful, green area, and they showed us the three-hundred-hectare Sa'dabad complex built by the Qajar and Pahlavi monarchs and used by the last shah of Iran. They finally drove us into the mountains north of Teheran to eat an authentic *dizi* (mutton stew) on the carpeted floor of the restaurant they thought served the best one. Sara then invited us to a café, asked us whether we liked the country and whether we were satisfied with our trip, and only then, minutes before saying goodbye, she accepted the exact amount we had agreed to pay for the generous services we received from the agency she worked for. A cab arranged by her picked us up that night and drove us to the airport. The driver was a very kind man speaking perfect English. He was a teacher, but he secured himself extra income in the taxi business. He asked us what we were doing for a living. When he learned that we were civil engineers specialized in building services, he explained to us the history and principle of *bâdgir*s, traditional windcatchers (wind towers) used already in the Achaemenid architecture, most notably in the city of Yazd, to create natural ventilation and passive cooling in buildings. Receiving these professional insights during the last drive in Iran perfectly ornamented our final moments in this fascinating country.

»«

I arrived on my second visit to the United Arab Emirates (UAE) with the same reservations as in the past, with a sort of uncertainty regarding to why we need an unsustainable, superficial, show-off place such as this one, which has limited respect for some of the values we hold dear in the West. But is such a judgment fair or does it reflect a worldview equally biased as the ones we rarely like to encounter, let alone accept, when they approach the borders of our homeland from the outside?

Our worldview reflects our history and our psychology. Our cultural evolution. But to judge the world fairly we must see it through a range of philosophies and cultures. Shortly before I travelled, and during my stay in the UAE, I was reading Joseph Henrich's book *The WEIRDest People in the World*. In Henrich's work, WEIRD stands for Western, Educated, Industrialized, Rich, Democratic. Henrich explains at length why the culture in Europe took a different turn in history and became individualistic, self-reliant, free-spirited, and thus different from the rest of the world. It occurred largely due to the Catholic Church's efforts through what he calls the Marriage and Family Program, which ended cousin marriages, polygyny, and kin-based social structures. Western psychology embraced individual independence, fairness, trust, analytic thinking, and it moved away from conformity and obedience. This had giant consequences for the future evolution of social structures. Western culture, which we tried and still so often try to impose on the rest of the world in our belief that it is the only right culture and that it is the only one that can bring peace and prosperity, is indeed weird and unusual in the world. Its various characteristics constitute a minority among world cultures.

My trip turned gradually more and more enlightening not because of successful meetings at Ajman University, a well-received lecture I gave to staff and students, or because of my visit to the impressive Expo 2020. It remains special because of the people I met and the time I spent on my own, which gave me the opportunity to reflect on everything I observed and place it into my world, my always-limited world that continues to expand with every experience and adventure.

After spending a week talking to academicians, Western and Eastern expats, and visiting numerous pavilions at the Expo, I had to admit that there is something about the UAE few in the West understand, and it deserves some respect. The UAE provides opportunities for millions. I asked most people I had met, with a sense of my own reservation and prejudice about the place that, I thought, cannot provide a life any average European could ever want, whether they liked the country. I have not met a single person who disliked it. They found the country beautiful, the nature amazing, personal safety unparalleled in the world. I managed to meet with an old friend from my high-school in Bratislava, whom I had not seen for two decades. She and her Italian husband, a vet who just opened his private veterinary clinic, have been living in the Middle East (Qatar, Abu Dhabi, and Dubai) over the past ten years and did not intend to leave it. They, and their Western circle of friends, found the mountains in the Eastern part of the country breathtaking, frequent camping in the desert a favorite weekend activity, closeness to wonders like Oman and the wider region as well as the multinational flavor something certainly worth staying for. They considered the weather unbearable only in the three to four summer months, when most expats leave for extended vacations anyway. Lebanese colleagues at Ajman University found the hospitality in the country to be second to none because 90 percent of the population of UAE is immigrant, looking after each other, helping and supporting each other. Criminality is virtually non-existent, racial or ethnic discrimination is unknown.

The leaders of the seven emirates decided in the 1970s to unite and run the country differently from what has been the norm in the region of differences and conflicts. They were determined to provide unparalleled unity, security, and comfort for their citizens. Can we blame them for it? Can we blame them for unconditionally providing great wealth to their citizens and letting foreigners do most of the work for them? For long I thought we could. But I began to see it in a different light. Many of the expats enjoy a life they could not have in their home countries. The extensive Asian communities, mostly from India, Pakistan, and other Middle Eastern and Asian nations, live peacefully together despite their cultural and religious differences. Some come for a few years to earn and save up money for their families or to start a business, others decide to stay longer. Many Westerners settle down in the UAE despite the limited social security, lack of unemployment support, time limited residence permit, some of the highest prices of health insurance and schooling in the world, elevated prices of these services for expats compared to locals (a hidden tax in the otherwise nearly tax-free country), and the associated uncertainties.

It is a place of dreams for many. It is welcoming, open, prosperous, and safe. The young Pakistani cab driver who drove me from the airport to my hotel in Ajman worked twelve to fifteen hours a day, seven days a week. He got a month off after a year to go home, and he earned a modest income and accommodation in a room shared with three others in an apartment shared by twelve. His dream was to expand his dairy farm in southern Pakistan, which he started with his brother, and which had at the time thirty-six cows. His goal was to have 150. While he was saving up, he was in a country that is as developed, clean, and safe as a country can be. It is relatively free as well. If one obeys the basic rules of decent behavior, there is plenty of freedom for everyone to enjoy.

Ajman University's professors originally from Syria, Iraq, Lebanon, but also from African and Western countries, mostly with degrees, years of professional experience, and even citizenships from the West, found little to complain about, except for the high school prices, which can limit their ability to save up a pension. To anyone from a Nordic welfare state it may seem like a huge setback, but not to those who find it hard to believe in the future of pension plans, and this routinely occurs in many corrupt and unstable European and other Western countries. The truth is in the eye of the beholder.

We often judge places and peoples based on outdated information, based on beliefs that got us stuck in time. I had to admit that the UAE dreams big and makes things happen. Only a very few percent of Dubai's economy come from oil. Technology, infrastructure, groundbreaking solutions that Europe dreams about or advocates for often move faster in places we tend to ignore. From mobile payments to transportation solutions, applications, and steps towards greater sustainability and improved ecology can happen faster in countries we don't talk about because we consider them poor, backward, dangerous, or just too weird to match the values we believe should be universal. For example, in the recently opened Museum of the Future in Dubai, I witnessed a tribute to human ingenuity and its future fruits that are under development, partly thanks to UAE initiatives. The museum is allegedly also the prettiest building in the world.

The size, design, and organization of the World Expo 2020 was so impressive that its description could occupy many pages. Hundreds of buildings and structures, many of them architectural marvels, have been erected for the six-months celebration of cultures, diversity, development, sustainability, mobility, and world unity. There wasn't a country representation that wouldn't brag about whatever it finds progressive from its own perspective, and there wasn't one that exhibited its challenges or problems. Even the poorest African countries boastingly displayed images of doctors and hospitals, mobile communication infrastructures, and national parks. They showed with pride images of the power plants or solar farms they had built, or the few thousand kilometers of road network they possess, happily emphasizing that 30 percent is now paved, up from 20 percent over the last decade. Really? A few new roads and a new operating room? Is that pathetic, or something rightly to be proud of? Again, it depends on the observer's point of departure. But no doubt it is encouraging to see how much good, how much beauty and progress can be found across the world, and every single country contributes to that positive net sum of global hope. There is rightly much pride, positivism, and aspiration on display, even though some Western countries, famously including Denmark, showed underwhelming exhibitions. The other side of the coin is that the financial means invested in the Expo could probably eradicate much of poverty in the world or provide healthcare or schooling to large fractions of the most vulnerable populations.

Enlightening was to visit the pavilion of Ukraine, the walls of which, just weeks after the war with Russia began, were completely covered with messages of support written on thousands and thousands of colorful sticky notes. Young Ukrainians left to showcase the advances of their country when there was still peace at home, but they did not know where to go once the Expo came to an end a few days later. One young staff member's family was now in Poland, and he said he would likely visit his relatives there before moving on. But where should he go then? Ilona, a charming young woman who began to speak fluent Czech when she learned I was from Slovakia, told me with endless humility how thankful she was for everything my country was doing for her people. She made me feel for the first time compelled to be proud of my country for helping others. I had mixed feelings. Does my country deserve that acknowledgment? I also met Syrians. One of them was Riad, the dean who invited me to Ajman University and treated me like a brother. He never let me take a cab or public transport from the hotel, he invited me for wonderful lunches, and told me stories about Syria, about the plunder of his father's factory during the war, and his own road to academia and US citizenship, despite which he prefers to live in the UAE. I could only remain silent when he brought up the war; my country and Europe's reaction to the wave of refugees from his country a few years before that from Ukraine could only be described as refusal, rejection, humiliation, fear. Perhaps dislike or even hatred towards those with darker skin and a different religion. Perhaps racism. During my visit, I was informed from Denmark that the ongoing debate on television was about the differential treatment of arriving refugees fleeing war. Some in the political arena were too vocal about the justified differentiation between refugees from geographically near areas and those from farther away. But the definition of near area was likely concealing something very different. Ilona was unable to tell what would happen to her in the coming days. Her parents did not speak English, they were afraid to leave Ukraine, and she was afraid to leave them on their own for much longer. I gave her my contact in case she decided to go westward.

While I was waiting to enter the Palestinian pavilion, I met a group of young people who spoke to each other in a blend of Arabic and English. I asked them why they mixed those languages if they all understood both. They turned out to be students from Ajman University's College of Medicine. They were exuberant when I told them that I had met their dean a few days earlier and that we were considering inviting them to hear my talk. They were from Syria and Iraq, although they lived most of their lives in the UAE and could not imagine going back to their countries. They expressed their desire to continue studying and working in Europe, not because they wanted a better life (they loved their lives in the UAE), but because they thought Europe was where medicine was at the highest level, and they wanted to continue learning. They were very polite, kind, engaged, motivated, bright young people. And they were indeed cheerful when I said a few words in Arabic.

I stood in line at the crowded Palestinian food stand called Mana'esh next to the pavilion when Bashir, a man with German roots living in the UAE, and his wife Heba, of Yemeni and Somali background, began to talk to me about the meals offered at the stand. We ended up ordering and eating together, and I learned that Bashir was a retired pilot and pilot instructor for Lufthansa and Emirates. He showed great interest in my field of expertise and demonstrated a relatively good understanding of the importance and technical challenges of a good indoor climate. Bashir had a company providing consulting services in operation and logistics for airlines and the military, but he now spent much of his time volunteering and organizing volunteer activities with young people, mainly in the field of sustainability. He also worked as a volunteer stem cell courier traveling across the globe. Two girls from Sudan were waiting next to us for their meals. Both were extraordinarily attractive, kind, smiling, and talkative. One of them lived in Dubai, the other came to visit her but wanted to stay and find work. They were pleasant company, as self-confident and well-informed as one would expect any Westerner to be. But they were not from the West, not from a country with developed economy and advanced society. I realized that young people from such unforgiving countries as Sudan, no matter how open minded, honest, or educated they might be, would hardly ever be able to enter Europe unless as refugees, but the UAE was open for them, providing attractive opportunities, security, and perhaps a future likely not very different from that in Europe, at least in their eyes. They were, no doubt, appreciative of this.

As I was watching the plans for the future of the Expo 2020 site after the end of the exhibition, Michael from Nigeria stood next to me and could not comprehend that most of the buildings were planned to be demolished, and a new city was about to be built at the Expo site. He asked me if he understood this correctly. We began to chat about the true sustainability of the

Expo, which was built for just a few months with a large part of it furnished with the theme vehemently advocating global sustainability. It sounded ironic. Michael finished high school ten years earlier, and he took courses in graphic design. He did not have a degree though. He came to the UAE very recently to work and save up for further education. His plan was to study in Europe. When he asked me about my work and learned that I was an academician, he became even more humble than before and began to call me "mister". He wanted to hear about the European higher education system, studying possibilities, tuition fees, and language barriers. We exchanged contacts and wished each other good night.

An Expo visitor can rapidly realize the immense diversity in the world and that there should be no place for such things as European or American (or any other) exceptionalism. People outside the Western regions do not seem to care much about what *we* consider right or wrong. Just as we are rarely interested in hearing what they consider high culture, or a standard legal system, religion, or social structure. We all belong to the human species, but we tend to be very different in many ways across regions and cultures defined by our histories and psychologies. Diversity should be our strength. Yet, we often wrongly wish, or even demand, that everyone follows what we consider right. No doubt, the peculiar Western history and psychology did achieve great prosperity, equality, fairness, and well-being. But democracy, as we imagine it, and Western social structure and values may not work for everyone or fit every society the same way. True, democracy feeds on people's well-being, dictatorship on their struggle. However, not all non-democracies are dictatorships. There is a whole range of political and societal structures and their unique local adaptations (some functioning better, some worse) between the two. It should be also remembered that corrupt and failing democracies do exist, and those can make people in relatively successful non-democracies (whatever success in this context means) only shake their heads in amusement and pride.

It was close to midnight when I said goodbye to Michael on my last day before flying back to Denmark. I could not stop wondering about how much this place means to so many people. They have such a different view of the world and their lives – a view I naturally do not share by default. It may simply be because of my ignorance and the limitations of my inherited culture. I had to realize there was still a lot to be learned. No matter how open-minded and well-travelled I was, the world was still largely unexplored to me, and it is highly likely it will always remain so. But every little step forward, like this week in the UAE or finishing Herrich's book, brings me a tiny bit closer to a better understanding of humanity. I feel that I need it more than most people. I am indeed WEIRD.

»×«

The encounters during my journeys described above are only examples of moments that perhaps have not radically changed my life but made me ponder, reevaluate my own existence, my role in the world and in the society I live in, my mission in life, and my values. Many more pages could be written about the stories heard, people met, lessons learned, and knowledge obtained during my travels to foreign places. The numerous visits to the various corners of Hungary (for example, to show Budapest or the Puszta to friends or to taste wine with DTU colleagues under the guidance of my father and his horticulturist acquaintances), to the Czech Republic with its immense number of castles, to the gorges and waterfalls of the Slovak Paradise, or to the top of the 2501 meters high Mount Rysy, all have the power to inspire. I was fascinated by the remains of the Wolf's Lair, Hitler's mostly destroyed Eastern Front military headquarter in Poland, by the war-bombed iconic national library and countless bullet holes in building façades in Sarajevo but also by the grandiose treatment I received from colleagues in Japan, who, after our work was done, spent days showing me the wonders of the unique Japanese culture in the country's cities and mountains and treated me with a stay at an elegant *ryokan* with *tatami*-matted rooms and *onsen* (hot springs with bathing facilities). The regular work visits to Kaunas in Lithuania were as special an experience as the wedding in the spectacular, historical Valetta and its yacht marina in Malta, which Gina's friend invited us to attend, when Dalia was a few months old. I enjoyed conversations with cab drivers, the company of the friendly, poor man who joined us on our walk through the *medina* of Tetouan in Morocco, or the children in Tangier doing the same just to earn a little change for guiding us through the labyrinth of narrow streets (and carrying two-year-old Jonatan in their arms to help) during a two-day visit from southern Spain. The chat with the sympathetic host and her children at the exotic *riad* (a mini palace with an inner courtyard of columns and arches decorated with traditional Moroccan craftsmanship) where we stayed and the late-night debates with the little weird but kind flat-earther hostel keeper in Skopje, Macedonia (now more correctly North Macedonia) continue to bring back lovely memories.

I have visited more than seventy countries, some of

them for a few days, others for extended periods, occasionally with somewhat understandable reservation and caution but always with open eyes, open heart, and respect for everything that was there to be found. They have colossally enriched my life. Their memories continue to ignite new inspirations both in me and in those who they are shared with. The true gift of exploring the world lies in the realization of the beauty that comes with our differences and in the appreciation of our similarities.

Globetrotting, meaning responsible and sustainable explorations much beyond resorts, city breaks, and skiing or beach holidays teaches us to treasure and respect other cultures and peoples as we respect our own. Our culture may mean the most to us. We grew up with it, it is dear to us. But all cultures mean the most to someone, all have something unique and rich to offer, and therefore they deserve respect, even if we disagree with some of their elements. The right to own culture, just like the right to peace, love, freedom, health, or religion, is a universal right. Generalization is the evil, not cultures, religions, and beliefs different from ours. Diversity, however much we have benefited from it over the course of history, is often seen to be threatening because the different, the unknown is hard to appreciate but easy to misinterpret when we see it with *our* eyes and never with *theirs*. Muslims or Hindus, Buddhists or Christians, Shinto or Jews, Easterners or Westerners, Africans, Middle Easterners, or North Americans, all of them are rich in values, generous in love. Contrary to what we are often told, Muslims may be among the most generous of them all. But it seems comfortable to demonize refugees and people of different faiths without ever speaking to one, to vilify entire countries never visited, and commend the loud voices that do so without questioning the truthfulness of their own claims.

We should not let political rhetoric, mainstream media, and superficially informed individuals form our views without digging deep to get closer to the truth. War, violence, backwardness, and poverty are not caused by those who fall victim to them, while the ones responsible try to project alternative truths. Peoples and nations are not to be judged from fragmented news and cursory impressions about them. How much, if any, of what we are told in our everyday lives lived in our "perfect" world, where the flow of information is often controlled by higher interests, is true and complete to the extent that it does not allow misinterpretation? Taking the courage to suppress our pride and accept both our ignorance and the views and beliefs of different peoples lifts us to a new level of understanding of the world, provides us with fresh appreciation and brings us a higher standard of humanity. All this is possible to achieve without exploring the wonders of foreign lands and their populaces, but there is hardly a more enjoyable, effective, and authentic way to do so than first-hand exposure.

Traveling also raises a sound awareness of ourselves, our limitations, and our good fortune. It helps us to appreciate what we have and perhaps realize that we have much more than we need. But it also helps us to see that no matter how developed the society we live in is and how wealthy we are, our virtues may be far from the top. We often hear that we should be proud of our Christian heritage and values, but isn't it only a cliché used to support a certain direction some want our society to follow—the direction of our own wealth and well-being, our economic growth and ours alone, unshared with anyone who is different from us? There are certainly important societal values to praise and cherish, but, looking at our own individual values and those in other parts of the world, we may realize that there are much more "Christian" people out there, many of whom might not even be Christian. With a little self-criticism, which we are rarely willing to practice, we may realize that in the way we treat each other in the everyday life, in the way we exercise respect, love, solidarity, and tolerance, our values, which we like to call Christian, may be rather flimsy. Material values have conquered them, and there is much to be learned from simpler, poorer societies.

Exploratory travel driven by curiosity makes us notice that we can always find others who are better, more advanced, more sophisticated at what we think we are great at and even more so in things we don't find particularly interesting in ourselves. There is in everybody something hiding to be discovered and learned. Even those living in poverty on the other side of the world can enrich us. Traditions or recipes, skills or memories, virtues of the heart or teachings of life from another point of view, everybody possesses something that deserves our attention. The greater diversity we are exposed to, the more authentic, complete, and unbiased we become.

Diversity is a wise tutor both on the road and at home. So much was there to be learned from the generations of Palestinian refugees, from the victims of the Yugoslav wars, from a friend working with the victims of the 2010 Kyrgyz ethnic clashes just weeks before our visit to the country, or from every refugee I had met as a volunteer for a Red Cross asylum center and as a mentor in my employer's integration program. It was enlightening to listen to the tortured and imprisoned Iranian mother who after fleeing her country has not seen her son for thirty years (she is still working on it), the Kurdish elderly who recalled being forced to fight eight years in the Iraq-Iran war, the young couple that survived the treacherous boat trip through the Mediterranean with their dream to live (and a hope that it would be a better life than before), the young Syrian engineer who, while passing between Denmark and Sweden on the Lebanese cargo ship he worked on, jumped into the sea to put an end to his unbearable maltreatment and swim to freedom, or the once successful sixty-year-old Yazidi businessman who knew well what freedom, comfort, and security tastes like because he had travelled the world with his family, but, after being deprived by war of everything he had ever possessed, he had to flee and live on humiliatingly low state support despite all his efforts to work in the wealthy country that made him feel unwanted.

My travel adventures also taught me to appreciate that I had never experienced problems from belonging to an ethnic minority. I enjoyed equal opportunities and perhaps some benefits of being different, which often come in the form of a little extra motivation and determination. I took liberty and equality for granted, but seeing the world gave my secure past a new facet. Witnessing the results of oppression, poverty, and conflicts gave a new dimension to my sense of global inequalities and our potential indirect contributions to them, which we prefer to leave unnoticed. It challenged my perception of our luxury problems and our "unthreatened" peace and freedom. The peace and freedom that is more vulnerable than we may think and that we happily exploit, while we rarely realize that it wasn't us who have paid with lives to secure it in the first place. Because nothing comes without a price, nothing lasts forever, and therefore nothing should be taken with indifference.

But where is the limit to the sense of pride in one's country and to the gratitude to a society, and how does better knowledge of the world shape the wobbly balance between pride and shame, which is so subjective and dependent on one's reference point? Not long ago, Adrian and I found ourselves in an unwanted, fierce battle of opinions against our father. Dad had been critical of communism for a long time, especially after its end in 1989. Following the Velvet Revolution, I heard for years the blame for all the new hardship the country was facing being put on the old regime. But as that new era continued to fail to bring the expected progress and intensified instead corruption, uncertainty, deterioration of social and economic conditions, and moral decline, dad's critique turned against the very capitalism that made him freer and richer than he could ever imagine during the first forty years of his life. Yet, he reached a point in his early seventies when he realized that his ultimate security, success, and comfort were rooted in the conditions and opportunities his country had provided, especially the more stable, social, and equitable society of his younger years, and, despite its many flaws, it now deserved his respect big time. We sensed patriotism at last, something that had never occurred in our family before. And given our background, happy childhood, education, and significant parental help over the years, dad thought we should share his gratitude for the country.

Adrian and I partly disagreed. We thought dad, with his ingenuity, determination, and perseverance, would have achieved his success probably in any society. We knew that progress between the 1950s and the 2000s was nearly inevitable in all parts of Europe and in most parts of the world, almost irrespective of politics or ideology. We also believed that dad had underestimated the scale of struggle under communism compared to the more recent capitalism in Slovakia. Indeed, we tend to idealize the past, although it wouldn't be surprising if, purely statistically, dad had been correct about general happiness under the two political systems. But we can't directly compare one system in the past with another in the present without considering how the old system would have changed with time and how the new system had worked elsewhere before it arrived to us, or how it would have worked for us in the past if it had been given a chance. Anyway, the subjective case dad was making wasn't representative of the two eras in the country's history and certainly not of the general population in the given country. We were not swayed by his arguments.

After having lived nearly two decades in a society more developed and fairer in almost every way, should I really close my eyes and downplay the flaws of my homeland? Should I praise the opportunities of those who succeed (and are destined, perhaps more so genetically, to succeed under most circumstances) and ignore the many who struggle to make ends meet mainly due to poor governance? How thankful should I be to a country for a safe childhood and a basic education, which are human rights and the provision of which should be, at least in developed countries, in the utmost interest of the state, if not its outright obligation? Does Denmark owe to Slovakia, as my father once suggested, for a scientist it has obtained in me without the financial investment into my basic education, or should in fact Slovakia thank to Denmark for what the latter made of me beyond the basics the former could not surpass?

Should the numerous expats, including great many Nobel laureates, scientists, thinkers, artists, or sportsmen, who could succeed (and often survive) only away from home feel forever indebted to the land of their childhood? How thankful should I be to a country that allowed me to leave but did nothing to attract me back and appreciate what I was ready to offer?

And yet, grateful to (Czecho)Slovakia I am and proud of many of its elements I can be. But seeing the world with open eyes and an open mind facilitates not only our appreciation of the homeland but its critical assessment too, which gives a better understanding of ourselves and our place in the world.

6

UNDRAINABLE WELL

"I thank you for this teaching with all my heart and lift my glass to human solidarity, to the ultimate victory of knowledge, peace, good-will and understanding."

–Albert Szent-Györgyi

The number of potential inspirations that target us all the time is enormous. Some of them are results of deliberate search, others inadvertently try to strike. Ones work with us, and we don't even know they do, others might need our help to unfold and complete their purpose. For it to happen, we need to slow down, appreciate their workings, let them guide us, contemplate their effects. It has been the purpose of this book to look back and try to identify some of the key moments that might have helped to make me who I am.

Not only did my professional inspirations gain intensity with the years, but so did those more important ones that determine a person in his greater completeness. They are the ones that make us ponder, reflect, evaluate, and evolve. They form our personality, our principles, perhaps they make us behave in a certain way. And they are those that most easily suffer from negligence, they are often replaced by wrong inspirations. Although some of them may be seemingly unimportant or overly generic, familiar in nature to every reader, a few examples deserve to be mentioned. I believe they have made an impact on me and may therefore be worthy of your attention.

My own little immediate family is a daily source of spiritual stimulation. The beautiful moments of family life generate more such instants, while arguments make me want to find solutions and discern my weaknesses in a spiritual mirror. Conflicts are uncomfortable, but they are powerful when they make us want to be better towards others and ourselves.

Observing successful, empathetic, and educated children and young people makes me want to be a better parent. Like a proud colleague's young daughter, so passionate about pediatric surgery, emotionally attached to the patients, and enthusiastic about the heartfelt appreciation she receives from them that on her first day in a new job her boss, a renowned chief physician, entrusted her with a long and complicated surgery under his supervision. "You take the lead today, you have firmer hands," he said to her. Trust, respect, and empowerment bridging the abyss of hierarchy can indeed be a long-lasting, heart-warming stimulant.

Manifestations of love and righteousness in the name of faith regardless of its form and the name of its god or its holy book have again and again strengthened hope, peace, and empathy in me. Personal stories, not gossip, are central to the development of empathy. Stories of unconditional forgiveness in the hearts of those who have so much more reason for abomination than most of us will ever have. Stories of success through hardship and hardship without success. Memories, my own or those of others, good ones and bad ones. They help me place my life in the context of history and history in the context of my own life. Like my father's childhood memories of swimming in the lakes near his village while tending the cattle. There wasn't anywhere else to swim in the scorching summer, so they used the old gravel pit lake even though the kids always came out of the water with dozens of leeches feeding on them. How ironic it sounds with the gigantic water parks, swimming pools, and perfect beaches where I can take my family on any day.

Or the story of the private who asked his corporal, my father, for permission to leave the barracks and go home nearly every weekend during his compulsory service in the Czechoslovak army. When questioned why he needed to go home so often, he answered that his father, an aggressive alcoholic, who had been beating his wife and children and never expressed love, was living on his own, ill and in need of care. When dad asked him why he was so attentive towards a man he described as a monster, he said, "He is my father, no matter what. I must respect him". Even those intimate stories that my father's friends often shared with him (which he would confidentially discuss with me so I could learn from them), interpreted perhaps with bias but still illustrative of the convoluted impacts of love, hate, envy, adultery, pretention, greed, or exploitation, were moving and teaching. First-hand accounts of family tragedies, bankruptcies, financial challenges, emotional rollercoasters (like those of the generous and kind old friend who struggled with failing romantic relationships throughout his life and whose much younger girlfriend he finally found and loved suddenly admitted her long-lasting lesbian affair that went on all those years while he was gifting her with love, money, employment, property, and globetrotting) were reflecting the hardships of life, the cross we all have to carry, the ultimate equality of us all in our fate we are most often unable to control.

I have been fascinated by the tales of individuals

whose nomadic lives were guided by destiny and history. For example, Sabu is a friend of Indian descent, who was born in British Somaliland when much of the world was a British colony. His father, a humble man who helped great many people and was decorated by the Queen of England and the Indian government, worked as an accountant for the British government and was soon moved with his family to Aden in today's Yemen. The family then moved to India, a relatively safe place during World War II. Sabu studied later in London, married a Dane, and lived in Denmark for the next six decades. The rare opportunities to hear what influenced the values of such people throughout their long lives and what wisdom they can share are never to be missed.

There was a lot to be learned from the friend who was raised to have tarnished self-confidence but succeeded in getting a good education and making an impressive career, until stress and poor health convinced him to seek more spiritual values in life. Another person close to my heart faced tremendous challenges after moving to a foreign country. She felt lonesome, entangled in a sense of desperation and purposelessness, which eventually made her want to mature, integrate, and learn to appreciate little things in life. But my own past mistakes, weaknesses, and vulnerabilities are equally, if not more, powerful to inspire. Causing others unintended emotional struggle or disappointment can be a loud teacher. And so can unnecessarily missed opportunities.

András, my second cousin, grandson of my grandfather's sister Vinci in Budapest, began to fight cancer when he was in his mid-twenties. He was a smart, well-raised, kind person, who enrolled in a school of economics after a short detour to become a car mechanic. Our parents stayed in a very close relationship over their entire lives, but András was several years older than I, and we didn't have the chance to meet very often. One summer day, when I was studying for an exam in our summerhouse in Bacsfa, András, who was feeling better after several surgeries and challenging years with his illness, was visiting my grandparents, and I was told he would come over sometime during the day before driving back to Budapest. I hadn't seen him for years, and I was glad he made the brief solo trip. Yet, I took the message lightly, and to take a break from my studies, I went on a brief afternoon bike trip with the girl I was very fond of, who was living in the village and was preparing for the same exam. I thought I was back in good time to see András, but when I arrived, my aunt, who lived next door, told me that he had been looking for me and that he already had to leave for Budapest. He passed away a few months later and I could never forgive myself the carelessness that prevented me from seeing him one last time.

And what was the end of the story about the Kuchta estate, where my great-grandparents served in the 1920s and 1930s before the property was confiscated by the communists and turned into a nursing home? The post-communist era in the 1990s returned it in restitution to the last descendant of the family that originally owned it. A common jobholder became one day a wealthy man, an owner of vast property and a castle in a desolate condition. He was wealthy but not wealthy or experienced enough to carry the burden. He attempted to painstakingly blow a new soul into the estate, but he became its victim and a victim of brutal modern-day power games of financial speculators. The man of noble roots lost ownership of the family heritage and became again a jobholder in what used to be his new little kingdom. Being observant and reflective on the troubles of others brings out the power of empathy and learning, compassion and appreciation. They might be even more influential than achievements and successes, or the moments leading to them, which many of us think of in the first place when we are asked about those who have influenced us.

In the world of information overflow, powerful, inspirational stories are always at hand. They can be found in news, documentaries, films, on the television, in the newspaper, online, or in the endless world of books. I don't turn everyone whose story moves me into my hero, I don't try to ignore their faults, I don't want to be like them. But I look up to humbling achievements, and I appreciate the grueling work behind them. These stories are not only about the Albert Einsteins, the Bill Gateses, and the Elon Musks. They are everywhere where our curiosity takes us, in the past and the present, from our neighborhood to the global scene, from the world of business, science, activism, politics, to arts, spirituality, or just everyday survival. I don't remain unimpressed with all the training that earned Michael Phelps twenty-eight Olympic medals (twenty-three gold), with the seventeen-year-old Kwase Enin, who was accepted to all eight Ivy League universities (he chose Yale), with the creation of the engineering wonder, the Boeing 747, by Joe Sutter, who managed the team that developed the Queen of the Skies in twenty-eight months from the drawing board to takeoff, or with W. Edwards Deming, who inspired Japan's post-war economic miracle and its reputation for innovative quality products and who began to win recognition back in his native country, the United States, nearly half a century after being honored in Japan. Such tales can arouse reflection and dedication.

So can Padre Pio, the Capuchin friar beloved around the world, whose incredible life continues to strengthen the hopes of many; Nicholas Winton, the organizer of the Czechoslovak *Kindertransport* and savior of more than six-hundred children on the eve of World War II, who let his achievement go unnoticed for half a century; Gail Halvorsen, the Chocolate Flier, who dropped candy from the sky for poor children during the Berlin airlift in 1948 and advocated for candy drops around the world since; Nick Vujicic, who despite being born without legs and arms overcame his disability to live a fulfilling and inspiring life; or the Austrian writer Martin Pollack. His father was a devout Nazi and gestapo staff. His family wanted him to study Germanic studies, but as an act of defiance, Pollack picked Slavic studies and Eastern European history, a career honoring the ethnic groups considered by the Nazis, including his father, impure, inferior, and subhuman.

And there are the many creative young individuals committed to turn the world into a better place through passion and determination. For example, the Dutch designer Dave Hakkens endeavors to minimize waste, protect the environment, care for communities, and raise awareness. Together with his dedicated friends around the globe, he constructs simple stuff in a simple way with the potential to create a better future on the planet. There are endlessly many such passionate men and women out there, whom most of us have never heard about. Living with curiosity and an open mind will make us continuously come across such people or at least their stories. Embracing their efforts can do incredible things to us.

It is likely clear by now that in the vast world of books, which constitutes probably the greatest of all sources of inspirations, it is especially historical and biographical literature (and, of course, popular science literature, which often also relies on history) that I find most intriguing. The more diverse culture and world geography it represents, the more fascinating I find it. Literary fiction can be very powerful, but I seek inspiration especially in the written records of defining moments, game changing events, major steps forward in our understanding of the world and our development, and of those standing behind these, like inventors and their inventions, major findings and their finders, but also the horrendous and heroic stories of the world wars and other conflicts and the hardships and perseverance of those we now consider famous, influential, heroic, or perhaps just lucky. The figures we look up to and whom we try to partly emulate did not reach their achievements without tremendous effort and substantial costs. But books do not only bring stories of the few to whom history assigned key roles but also those of the everyday men, women, and children in different places and eras. Life in most parts of the world has never been as good as it is now, and that needs to be understood in a detailed historical and global context, which then helps us not to take our condition for granted but to appreciate and cherish it, no matter how hard it may look sometimes.

»×«

I wouldn't be honest if I claimed that celebrities cannot inspire me. True global stars within sports, arts, entertainment, politics, science, or any other field can utilize their achievements and celebrity status to mobilize millions for good causes and principles worth fighting for. But only if celebrities and their efforts are examined with care will their impact on us match that of our most cherished personal encounters and experiences. Without deliberate and selective effort, very little of the omnipresent but superficial celebrity culture of mostly poor quality can sway us in the right direction. It is not the wealth, sensational lifestyle, and empty statements in the tabloid press that should make anyone admire celebrities.

The power of artists and entertainers lies not in the deplorable affairs, gossip, and other useless elements of the private lives of otherwise ordinary people but in their ability to create the wonders of art and in the art that they create. Art to me isn't about its own shine but about its ability to touch my soul, make me seek the story behind its creation, awaken my desire to learn, form opinion, and take a stand. Its value is reflected in my keenness to share it. All arts can encourage rumination. But it is music that has had the strongest influence on me. Much of what comes out of the recording studios today is nothing more than detritus often filled with vulgarity and noise that serves commercial interests and satisfies lust for fame or teenagers' desire to party. But there are musicians, some of advanced age, others hiding from the masses, whose works can elicit thoughts that caress the soul.

The music, lyrics, powerful and very visual live shows, and activism (especially strong anti-war and pro-Palestinian activism) of Roger Waters, and his own inspiration by the fact that he had lost his father to a war when he was just a few months old, have substantially contributed to my pacifist conviction. His works with Pink Floyd like *The Wall*, songs like *The Gunner's Dream*, *The Fletcher Memorial Home*, *Two Suns in the Sunset*, and later solo songs such as *Perfect Sense* or the more recent *Déjà Vu*, *The Last Refugee*, and the fabulous adaptation of the poem *Wait for Her* written by the Palestinian poet Mahmoud Darwish have strongly shaped my worldview and values. So did Bob Dylan with his unparalleled *With God on Our Side* and endless other songs, Leonard Cohen, and the Hungarian Zorán with their remarkable poems and melodious stories.

Photographers like JR or Steve Bloom awoke my attachment to many inanimate and living wonders of our planet, including the human race with its beautiful diversity. Documentaries about nature, science, history, and world cultures continue to keep my curiosity awake. Awe-inspiring visualizations of natural history, evolution, astronomy, and cosmology help me to comprehend our humbling smallness and insignificance within the complexity of the vast universe and its past of four and a half billion years. One presenter stands out. No matter how knowledgeable or unconcerned one is about nature, David Attenborough's films and narrations are astonishing. They strengthen my devotion, they awaken the child in me.

Of all arts it is theater that has a special place in my heart. My first visit to the Hungarian National Theater in Győr together with Adrian and our parents was followed by about a decade of regular visits with yearly season-tickets, which usually included seven or eight performances, a blend of comedy, drama, opera, musical, operetta, and other genres. I might have been in my early teens when I was obsessed with the recordings and shows of Hungarian comedians. I learned their jokes and parts of their shows, and I occasionally entertained my family with plagiarized live performances. Whether genuinely or out of compassion, my parents always laughed. I carved a string-free mini guitar-like thing out of a plank and sang my mother's favorite song from Julio Iglesias on her birthday. I learned the Spanish lyrics after I played back the song dozens of times to write it down phonetically, without understanding a single word. Naturally, the gig ended with applause. And so, perhaps encouraged by my early successes in the living room, later in adulthood I wrote, choreographed, and staged with great pleasure my own rather primitive but much appreciated short comedy shows and stand-up performances for family and colleagues at various events, trying to bring moments of joy into the hearts of audiences made up of those nearest and dearest to me.

I certainly developed a closer relation to theater than to sports fandom (which never meant much to me). On the eleventh of May in 2002, I borrowed my parents' car, picked up a friend and headed to see Chekhov's *Uncle Vanya* in theater Astorka on SNP Square in Bratislava (named after the Slovak National Uprising of 1944). We parked the car and walked to the square, only to find it crowded with thousands of ice hockey fans staring at a huge screen. The final game of the World Championship was about to start at 19:00, the same time as the performance we had tickets to. Slovakia, where ice hockey is the national sport, played for gold only the second time since its independence, just two years after its first appearance in the final, which it had lost to the brotherly Czech Republic. Now it was taking on the mighty Russia, and Slovakia was heading towards its first and so far only World Championship title. Dressed in suits, we fought our way through the horde of cheering fans. When we arrived at the theater, its barred outer door was locked, and an employee was sitting in the lobby on the other side. We innocently asked why the performance had been cancelled, but he just silently pointed at the crowd behind us. We didn't think it was a good enough reason. Was everybody supposed to watch the game? Have they never considered that some people might prefer culture over a bunch of skaters chasing a black rubber disc? The theater employee didn't sympathize with our disappointment. We left the square without giving any thought to watching the game amid the throng. (Two years later, I did end up watching a football game on Copenhagen's City Hall Square with friends, when Czech Republic played Denmark in the quarterfinals of the 2004 UEFA European Football Championship. Our presence did not last long though. With the Czechs scoring towards their 3–0 victory, our small group of Czechs, Slovaks, and Poles wedged in the middle of the Danish crowd had to soon flee and seek protection from the angry mob and flying glasses and bottles.)

Nobel laureates belong to a special group of celebrities. They rarely exhibit superficiality, especially within their field of expertise. Although they are often expected to make judgments in areas they know little about (mostly society and politics), they are worth listening to. They are interesting, experienced, and highly educated, even if it is primarily perseverance and frustration-tolerance in one concrete field, not necessarily general wisdom, what is needed to win the prize. A bit of luck helps too. In the case of Tim Hunt, the recipient of the 2001 Nobel Prize in Physiology or Medicine, it was an overnight fire that destroyed the entire lab where he and his colleagues worked. He said during a public lecture I once attended that it was the best thing that could have happened. The group was temporarily relocated to another building, where the tea-room became the room of inspiration. It was filled with Hunt's childhood heroes, Nobel laureates, amazing scientists with whom he could now mingle during lunchtime. Who would have said that with time most of his colleagues and himself would end up being Nobel laureates. There is often some benefit in a loss.

A few years ago, I began to attend the regular Nobel Laureate Lectures hosted by the Royal Danish Academy of Sciences and Letters. The more I became interested in such individuals and their achievements, and the more I exploited the growing opportunities to watch mind-boggling TED videos and startling talks by renowned experts, thinkers, pioneers, from Jacqueline Novogratz or Hans Rosling to Noam Chomsky or Pope Francis, the more I realized how little I knew and how little I was. My awareness of the vastness of knowledge and of my intellectual limitations with which I (and everybody) must face it makes me continuously seek out those who can enrich me with their accomplishment, wisdom, and experience. From war correspondents, champion interviewers (like CNN's Christiane Amanpour or BBC's Stephen Sackur and many of the guests on their programs), investigative journalists, and activists to Nobel Peace Prize winners, people who risk their lives to tell the truth or represent and help the most vulnerable, and everybody who tirelessly endeavors to advance the world and the well-being of all, but also historians, philosophers, travelers, authors of various genres, and others. It is the aggregate effect of numerous such people and their works what is indispensable to develop and satisfy a breadth of interest on our journey to authenticity. Fortunately, the sources where they can be found have now become undrainable.

It would be unfair not to mention the positive influence some wealthy individuals can have on me. They include those who have built their wealth with hard and honest work over decades, who understand that human dignity is an asset too and engage in philanthropy to give away for charitable causes most of what they have accumulated. They run not only progressive companies but especially foundations and other institutions devoted to giving rather than gaining.

Political decisions alone never moved me as much as the stories of their making and makers, their history, the personal struggle endured, and the weight of the decisions carried by those taking responsibility for them, but also the lives of those decision makers described in so many fine biographies, their journeys towards the acts that remain in history books and perhaps in our memories. The contemporary politician who has influenced me most with his life story, humility, intelligence, compassion, success despite his seemingly unfavorable background, his tireless work to address the needs of ordinary people, his honest writing, and his captivating and refined speeches is Barack Obama.

But many others have, I believe, profoundly influenced my worldview and developed my appreciation for the difficulties honest parts of politics have to face and for the determination their champions demonstrate. They include, for example, Winston Churchill with his brilliance during World War II (not his imperialist views though) and Alexander Dubček with his heroic courage to attempt (and fail) to transform communism in my country (and thus Europe) when it was not yet transformable, giving hope to millions including my parents. They also include the many who have used their power to make peace and facilitate reconciliation, numerous of whom have been awarded the Nobel Peace Prize. Among them is Mikhail Gorbachev, the powerful leader of the feared country, whom I vividly remember seeing daily on television when I was a child. The smiling man with his port-wine stain birthmark on his forehead gave me the impression of a cordial, affectionate, and accommodating person. Regardless of whether he was such or not in reality, he will remain the man who had laid the foundation that ultimately allowed me and millions of others to live the lives we live today, instead of sinking in what my parents' and grandparents' generations had to endure.

Some politicians can indeed shape our principles. Honest politicians devoted to their job that can be extremely difficult do exist. Former U.S. presidential candidate and Massachusetts governor Michael Dukakis, who rode the subway on the way to his office every day and picked up trash along the way, once said in an interview that the overwhelming majority of public servants is honest and willing to live moderately. They enter politics because they care for people and society, even if we happen to disagree with their political standpoints. They can inspire with their personality, skills, speeches, or achievements, and sometimes with views that are opposite to our convictions and evoke our resistance. (I have discussed this line of thought in greater detail in my book *Reflections on the World of Human Inspirations: In Search of Authenticity.*)

The personal inspirations of various nature described in this chapter are naturally only a few examples among the multitude of moments, elements, and sources that provoke my curiosity. Perhaps some of them awakened your interest and made you read or contemplate. If we pay attention, we can encounter inspirational sources very frequently. Apart from seeking them, we can learn to recognize them around us, and, instead of treating them as pieces of information that come and go without an effect, we can give them a brief thought and turn them into impulses that can enrich us, even if only momentarily. Life is made up of countless short moments. The more of them are made remarkable, the more memorable lives we live.

EPILOGUE

Most of us have a few memories that mean to us a little more than others. We remember examples of persons, events, places, or things that have left a mark on us. We may remember the moment that has railed us into the arms of a passion. We think we know who (or what) to thank for doing the job we are doing and for other visible elements of who we are. For being an opera singer, a doctor, a gardener, for our interest in pottery, wine, or sports, for restarting a hobby, or for wanting to gain a new skill. But we rarely appreciate the multitudinous instants that shape us into who we really are or want to be deep inside. In this book, I tried to identify some of the major sources of both concrete and more abstract, spiritual influences on me.

Every now and then we experience the power of personal stories, but we rarely realize that we have such stories too. They often remain untold. Every person's account of his life's stimulating moments can be fascinating. Mine isn't perhaps particularly unique. My story is just a story of a once Eastern European boy who, like so many others, had opportunities in the West, traveled the world and kept his eyes open. It isn't one filled with fear, war, and poverty. My parents weren't persecuted, imprisoned, or in any way marked for life by the communist regime. My hardships can hardly be called hardships next to those who have tasted true suffering. And yet, maybe ordinariness is what makes my recollections appreciable for those who would love to live a more unique life but, perhaps fortunately for them, they don't.

I had a happy childhood with no understanding of the war of ideologies in the middle of which I was growing up. I had no idea that some of my elementary school teachers might be secret agents lurking to catch words about some of the parents that should be reported to the secret police. I did not question why we were shortly after 1989 suddenly told not to read certain sections of our schoolbooks, especially in history class and in class called *homeland study (vlastiveda)*.

My childhood was comfortable, but it was not pampered by a society where everything was allowed and available. School was about discipline (besides the usual subjects, we got grades for behavior), and technology was lagging. Our black-and-white television was just replaced with a color TV with four channels, and natural gas replaced coal for heating our house. We got our first landline telephone at about the same time, and Adrian and I received our first computer for gaming (Commodore 64, named so for its "breathtaking" 64 kilobyte RAM) even later, when we were teenagers. We could not fly to France or Canada for skiing holidays or to Thailand to escape the bone-chilling winter. Bananas and oranges were available on the market only around Christmas, and automatic doors and escalators were rare wonders entertaining every child who sporadically came across one in the country's capital, when they were already commonplace to the west of the Iron Curtain. The few available Western goods could be purchased in limited numbers, often after weeks of waiting, against vouchers in special stores called *Tuzex*. And yet, we had our material needs fulfilled. Because it was a world of simplicity, economic equality, low expectations, and considerateness, a world that showed how to enjoy while having less. There was a feeling of general security, free health care and education, job certainty, often free vacations, and plenty of time and means for family togetherness, friendships, and frequent joyous events.

Had the communist/socialist system continued into my adulthood, I would have perhaps become its opponent in disguise, like so many, including my father, who quietly disagreed with the system but agreed to party membership as payment for a better life, when there was no hope for a change anyway. Or like my friend in China who, well in her adulthood in the 2000's, was determined to join the Communist Party of China after finishing her studies because "people just do it and life is easier that way". But I could have also turned into an outspoken critic of the system, risking everything. However, the system collapsed days before I turned ten. Maybe exactly for that reason I appreciate having experienced it. Not because I agree with it in any way, but because it constitutes a significant part of history. It was an era that taught me, while it did not harm me.

After that so-called democracy appeared overnight, it was again my parents' generation, not mine, who carried the burden of uncertainty. When I was in high school and I was considering studying at a university, my uncle said, "If they find out your father was a party member, you'll never get into college." Such an attitude was reminiscent of the preceding forty years. But now it was different. It turned out to be the easiest thing to be admitted to college. It rarely occurred to me that some members of the university leadership and the more senior professors may have had communist pasts without which they would likely not have achieved the academic titles they carried. Nobody cared about the past anymore. Some quietly wished it would come back, others were happy it was gone. And some at the highest levels adapted to the new conditions or fell into oblivion without being persecuted for their past. With hindsight, it is perhaps growing up with the sense of certainty in the times of intense uncertainty that I find worthy of appreciation and sharing.

Besides the feeling of security, I see two things having been crucially important on my journey, especially in its early stage: parental guidance and opportunities. The two are intertwined because the right guidance generates opportunities and facilitates their recognition. True, I may be blessed with genes of an autotelic person (likely inherited from my dad). An autotelic person does not need material possessions, power, fame, entertainment, or comfort because she is internally driven by a sense of purpose, curiosity, and persistence. Such a person experiences frequent *flow* in everyday activities; it is the complete absorption in a given task, which elicits an energized focus and provides enjoyment and reward in itself. An autotelic personality may be an asset, but guidance and a diversity of opportunities in which that personality can assert itself are still crucial, especially at a younger age. I might also be lucky with the possession of some useful emotional intelligence, an ingredient critically important to self-awareness, communication, social skills, and overall contentment, well-being, and success. It can be learned and developed, and thus it also, to a great degree, starts with good parenting.

Mom and dad made me understand that hard work was the price of everything of true value, they provoked my curiosity in a myriad of directions, they opened my eyes to everything they thought was worthy of attention, they shared fascinating thoughts, they were untiring advocates of education and reason. They were visionary enough to realize very early on the need to teach me Western languages when Russian was still the only one taught in all schools. I was seven or eight years old when I was sent on my little green bike for the first time to visit Mrs. Janek in her apartment on Hlavná street, receive her private German lesson, and pay her in cash. I continued doing so twice a week for a few years. It gave me a significant head start by the time I reached fifth class in which foreign language began to be taught. By that time, German had replaced Russian.

I also enjoyed a major advantage in English class in high school (and repeatedly in life) after I had spent a year as an exchange student in the United States. More importantly though, mom and dad supported every opportunity I chose to pursue to grow in education and values. Especially the ones they never had, even if those moved me far away from them. And they helped me fall in love with the world, its nature, cultures, and peoples, its diversity, which serves as one of the strongest inspirations. Although dad did have tendencies towards material values as well, they basically helped to pave my way to the understanding of what the Czech folk singer Jaromír Nohavica sings in his song *To Nechte Být* (Leave It Alone) (loosely translated, but you get the point):

To take my car and my house, my bed and the air you can
tighten the rope, poison the spring, cut the thread
to deprive me of everything if you want you can
but what I have in me, you'll never get
leave it alone, leave it alone, leave it alone

All the wonders I ever knew I have in me
dizzying love and contents of books and people I see

to deprive me of everything if you want you can
but what's inside of me, you'll never get
I won't give it to you, I won't give it to you

Garment and bread, light and honor, take it all
if I were a beggar, you wouldn't tell, but I would have more
to deprive me of everything if you want you can
but what I have in me, you'll never get
that's only mine, that's only mine, that's only mine.

As I matured, I was more and more fascinated by knowledge, wisdom, and people who possess these. The possession of knowledge, once considered a quality of the most knowledgeable, wisest role models, may no longer be an asset. It may soon be totally unneeded. With all the knowledge of the world being accessible any time anywhere through our mobile phones, accruing knowledge may soon no longer be something we need to strive for. We may also come to an age of the disappearance of wisdom, as Simon Winchester argues in his fascinating history of knowledge transmission *Knowing What We Know*. But I do believe that wisdom will remain a quality still much appreciated for a while. Wisdom is the capacity to judge rightly and act accordingly, with good sense and prudence, employing cognitive and emotional skills, and it is driven by experience. Knowledge is an indispensable contributor to wisdom. And it is these, useful or not in the expanding world of smart machines and artificial intelligence, that will forever remain the only things nobody can take from us.

»«

I realized a few years ago that I had reached the age my parents had at the time of my first memories of them.

Later I also realized that my son had reached the age I had at the time my earliest memories can recall. I could now tell him what we all heard our parents say, "When I was your age…" These moments help us to see the true effects of time. A generation achieves maturity, and the next one begins its journey to it. This made me also realize (or convince myself) that I might have something to share, something to inspire with. It was time to not only receive but consciously spread inspiration as well.

Any attempt to reflect on our capacity to positively influence lives through stimulation and encouragement will likely result in a report modest in examples but rich in hopes. We hardly realize how frequently and deeply we may inspire others. And it can begin rather early. When I was in elementary school, the head teacher told my parents that I had a positive influence on my pal with whom I shared the school bench over several years. Apparently, he tried to equal my grades and achievements, which wasn't always an easy task. That kid was my cousin Peter, so there was naturally a sense of healthy rivalry, which continued throughout our studies at the same university after a break during the high school years.

I was told that I had that pulling effect on my long-time bench mate in high school too. And when I asked Jan, my frequent travel companion and former office mate during our doctoral studies, who or what inspired him most in life, I found, to my surprise, myself on his list. He said he continued to benefit from the determination, perseverance, order, and efficiency he had learned from me. It was an unanticipated answer. But I was equally strongly inspired by his calmness, kindheartedness, modesty, and his deep faith harmoniously combined with pragmatism. We continue to stimulate each other when we meet (or travel together) through deep discussions about all possible aspects of life and the world, built on absolute trust and considerateness.

The opportunities to encourage students and motivate audiences through lectures have a special meaning to me. I remain hopeful that some see in me what I saw in my mentors and professional role models when I entered the science arena. I do not mean scholastic stardom but the respect for knowledge and the satisfaction that comes with diligent academic work. I wish to inspire perhaps even more on a personal level. To become for younger colleagues the person that Dušan, Geo, or Charlie were for me, someone more than a colleague, someone who cares. Because that is what I received, and the baton must be passed on. It is just as important to discuss with younger colleagues the challenges life places in our path, the happiness we strive for, the ethical elements of our existence, the books we read, or the lessons to be learned from lives of others, as the tools they need to use or the literature they are supposed to read during their studies. I'm delighted when they approach me not with a professional question but with a request for an opinion.

After my first invited plenary talk at a large international conference (Indoor Air 2016 in Ghent, Belgium), Geo came down from the audience, gave me an unanticipated hug and said that he felt like father watching his son excel in front of hundreds of people. My father thanked him for something in this sense nine years earlier, right after my doctoral defense. He thanked him for the fatherly care I had received while working on my future in a foreign country. That notion likely culminated during my keynote, when my performance inspired Geo in a unique way. It may have surfaced clearer than ever before that the way my career (and I) was developing was worth the years of support and the effort he invested in me.

The demonstration of his pride after my talk meant the world to me. It symbolized the compensation I very much owe him for everything he has done for my professional and personal development. It was also a source of renewed inspiration to offer others what I had received, to share what was shared with me, and to comprehend that the true meaning of academic career lies in giving others the opportunities that were given to us by those giants whose shoulders we stand on.

For a few years, I used to regularly pay a visit as a guest lecturer to my alma mater, the Slovak University of Technology. I lectured on topics not covered in the local curriculum. Future civil engineers, who were used to attending lectures on building design and construction, could now hear about the science of exposure to particles and chemicals in the built environment and their impact on health. Some of the students demonstrated excitement, they were enthused, they approached me after the lecture and wanted to know more. Others, naturally, showed no interest whatsoever, and I could only try harder to raise their attention next time.

I was often told that many of the doctoral students were disengaged, uninterested in science, sometimes reluctant to finalize their studies. Academic career was of no value to them, knowledge beyond what was needed to find a job seemed worthless. "Please tell them something. They need it," Dušan usually said when we were planning the program of my visit. I was supposed to hold inspirational talks, be a source of encouragement, and disprove their viewpoint by demonstrating that to be interested in the workings of the world can turn out to be great fun and bring opportunities and success. I was to be the example of someone who had once been in their place at the very same school and was now an "internationally recognized, award-winning scientist" (as Dušan liked to introduce me, to my embarrassment, because I never thought I was). Sowing the seeds of attraction is not always happening on a downhill road because what moves one leaves another untouched. But the smallest step forward is worth the effort.

During one of my visits Dušan introduced me to Veronika, a girl who seemed to be just as passionate about learning and trying a new experience abroad as I was a decade earlier. An opportunity emerged to repeat history, but this time I was the host, not the guest. There I was with the chance to offer Veronika everything I had received from people I looked up to. She became my first doctoral student. Like me earlier, she was enrolled in Slovakia and co-supervised from Denmark, where she spent much of the four years of her doctoral studies. During this time, she travelled the world and became known in the indoor air circles. She continued as a postdoc at the University of California at Berkeley, moved on to the WELL Building Institute in New York and finally to the Swiss Federal Institute of Technology in Lausanne (EPFL). It is invigorating when we can help someone to emulate our own success story.

The similarities do not end there. Coincidentally, Veronika is also a Hungarian, and she grew up not far from my own hometown of Šamorín. We happen to have similar backgrounds, we had a similar upbringing, we share a history. It turned out that we even had mutual acquaintances. And when she was performing her field measurements in apartment buildings in Šamorín, she noticed that several of the residents had recognized my name on the letter of invitation to participate. "Your father has quite a reputation in town," Veronika said.

I feel fortunate to have a job that has the potential to make a long-lasting impact on others. It is in itself an inspiration, which helps me continue the work and evolve through seeking answers and sharing knowledge. It inspires me to give and to inspire others. But such inspiration is surely not confined to academic environment nor to career in general. Knowledge, experience, and ultimately wisdom can be shared always and everywhere. It is not only the recipient who benefits from it. Telling moving stories makes us relive them, understand them better, and feel their power again and again. Sharing our personal history helps us to value what we have gained from experience in the past. Sharing the latest piece of information that we found fascinating, the content of the book, documentary, or artwork that has just awed us, or our enlightening reflections on it, sharing what makes us wonderstruck multiplies its positive effect. But most importantly, we need self-exploration to recognize the human virtues and values we have inherited and those we have developed under the impulsions of the environment as well as those we have not yet obtained, and we need to share the results of our critical self-assessment so that we and our listeners can exploit their empowering potential. This was the primary purpose of this book. We have this responsibility especially towards our children. They are the ones to receive our inspirations in the first place, so we'd better polish them. For that we need to know ourselves.

»×«

Knowing oneself comes in handy especially when some of life's most difficult challenges present themselves. And sometimes those challenges appear as a result of the growing understanding of ourselves. When I was working on an early version of this book, I had no idea that before it was finished I would go through one of the hardest periods of my life. Hardest but immensely inspirational. Challenging but, in a way, exciting and strangely fulfilling. My inspirations would not be complete without a few words about the recent life-changing events, and without it I would not be true to my own advocacy of the responsibility to share our self-observations. But the full story will have to be told in a future book, once its full extent becomes known. New events in life are continuously happening, and a line must be drawn for a book to reach completion. My line was somewhere around the age of forty, just before these events began to unfold.

To be more accurate, they have been slowly unfolding for years. My marriage to Gina always had its challenges. It may well be that our differences motivated me in the first place to write this book. I may even have hoped that the book would help Gina to understand me better and help me to understand myself sufficiently enough to make the necessary changes needed to preserve the relationship. The early version of the book did not fulfill this role, and the current one comes too late. The marriage failed, disintegrated, vanished. We are picking up the pieces to get the best out of it, to rebuild our lives, our friendship, to keep the children emotionally safe, healthy, and happy. This is where inspiration works big time as it covers both the past and the future.

I spent the past two years trying to understand the reasons for our failure and its impacts on everyone in the family and to work out a contingency plan, a roadmap for how to move forward with the family structure, our parental responsibilities and collaboration, and eventually with my own life too. It has been an incredible journey, presumably one of the most intense periods of my life in terms of inspiration, self-development, and learning. Learning of a different kind.

The path to understanding the problems in our marriage and its ultimate failure took me on a tour through the psychology and neuroscience of emotions. First there were a lot of accusations to be heard, pain to be witnessed, but besides tears and fights there were things to be discovered, realizations to be made, realities to be faced. There were dives into our childhoods and into our memories of the past fifteen years, revealing deep scars and their long-term effects. And there were many fascinating, life-changing books. From Daniel Goleman's *Emotional Intelligence* and Lisa Feldman Barrett's *How Emotions Are Made: The Secret Life of the Brain*, to Gabor Maté's *When the Body Says No* and *Hold On to Your Kids* (with Gordon Neufeld), and some more. I read the books about adults with my children also in mind and the books about children with my own and Gina's childhood in mind.

The newly acquired knowledge and understanding helped me to get over the turmoil relatively quickly, focus on the children, provide an emotionally safe and secure home environment, and develop the attachment between us, which is so crucial for the development of emotional competencies, for a happy childhood, and eventually for a happy adulthood. This became priority number one. The increased responsibilities that came with single parenting were outweighed by the joy of being in this role relatively undisturbed, with better control and predictability and more stable conditions (including moods and feelings) under which I could operate. Parenting, under the given circumstances (because nothing can be better for children and their parents than a functional, harmonious, complete family), became greater fun with better effects.

But the golden link in this chain of events was my former scientific collaborator at the Norwegian Institute of Public Health, Anette Kocbach Bølling. She is a perfectly organized first-class scientist with whom working together remotely was always productive and pleasant. We met in person for the first time a couple of years after we began working on a scientific article. Our conversations were soon marked with openness and trust as if we had been friends for decades. We did not maintain contact when her marriage disintegrated after two hard decades. But when mine began to crumble about half a year later, she provided some of the most insightful advice on how to try to save it and the most rational guidance towards seeing my painful situation clearly and navigating in it.

The parallels between the difficulties of our two marriages and between their main actors were striking. But seeing them was not the true source of Anette's wisdom. It was her organized, rational, solution-oriented mind combined with empathy, tenderness, care, and love. It was her profound understanding of the vast and complex world of emotions and their physical manifestations. It was her self-awareness, her understanding of the connections between her past, present, and future. It was her self-molding, her continuous willful maturation, defying some effects of her past and making herself the kind of person she wanted to be. She was a prime example of the power of observation combined with the will to act on it in some of the most hidden domains of the human character. All this I only learned later.

As I was realizing the key elements in my past, Gina's past, and our marriage, I had to realize that some things are irreparable because some scars are too deep to heal, they were caused too long ago, their fixes are treacherous, and easy fixes only postpone the true trouble when two people have grown apart. My conversations with Anette helped me to put in a much better perspective some of the fascinating literature I was reading on my path to understanding my past fifteen years. But there was much more than that. There was she, the bravest I had ever met, who never gave up facing her own past scars. After twenty years of doing so through constant learning and through writing and drawing hundreds of pages of self-analysis, she was just becoming ready for the most difficult step in addressing those scars. Because for the first time she felt there was someone she could share with, and entrust to, her deepest secrets untold for decades. With time, we became friends, soulmates, each other's source of hope and light, and eventually everything one can dream of in a relationship. She may well be my most important source of inspiration, a true hero.

Her judgment is always accurate because it is built on knowledge turned into wisdom through her values. It is especially her knowledge of herself and others, of thought, feeling, and behavior, of the world, and of me that leads us to powerful realizations about ourselves, our past, and our lives. We learn together to be ourselves again and to let go of some of the inner barriers we might have developed over the years. Being who we really are, being authentic, seems to be the only precondition to the other one's perception of our perfection.

This is possible because we feel the utmost emotional safety and openness in each other's presence. Trust and respect, but also loving and being loved, gained a new dimension, one we could never imagine. And when perfect selections of words of two analytical minds match corresponding thoughts and feelings, misunderstanding has very little space. What it brings is that nothing is wrong to say, nothing elicits unpredictability, nothing remains unheard. We can think, feel, and say what we want, we are able to compromise, take decisions, behave as we never could. This situation feels unnatural and accepting it must be newly learned. But through it, Anette always pushes me in the right direction, at the right moment, shaping me into a better person and a better father. And even a better scientist, as her vast knowledge combined with her unrelenting faith in me nudges me to drop the hesitancy and enter unchartered territories, those dealing with the role of emotions in the indoor air and exposure sciences. She also completes my family with her love towards the children and with her motherly wisdom. And she makes me proud of her many times more than she can ever be proud of herself.

Throughout our lives, we constantly change. And we change ourselves. Often unconsciously but sometimes consciously. Perhaps looking for the roots of the problems and for their solutions exposes them even more. Perhaps searching and finding ourselves, when unmatched in extent by the two sides in a relationship, can do some harm to it. When a person faces profound realizations about his own self, his past, and his true needs, when he works his way to a more robust self with a bigger self-esteem, a deeper self-respect, and a more mature self-awareness, and when such development is not equaled by one's partner despite an obvious need for it, the two become estranged. Perhaps living my adult life in a foreign country, in a chosen environment away from the default influences set by birth, and writing this book and the one I wrote before about human inspirations, both being largely a work of complex self-searching, contributed substantially to making me into a different person over the years and to my evolving authenticity. On the other hand, when two people think, feel, observe and self-observe, learn, weigh, judge, take decision, value, listen and communicate, and love almost identically the connection and everything it brings, even occasional differences and their consequences, become life's biggest and most enjoyable adventure. It is the match in emotional competences, rather than in education, religion, nationality, or anything else, that is the key to a functional, happy, harmonious relationship and a long marriage.

Sometimes, under a given blend of circumstances, the price of a perfect relationship may be living for a few years in a poor one. And maybe not even a perfect relationship can fully compensate for all the potential downsides of a failed family constellation. But it is a magnificent source of spiraling inspiration. What happens with it next is the story of the future.

CREDITS

The quote on p. 1 is by Franklin D. Roosevelt, address at University of Pennsylvania, September 20, 1940, available at www.presidency.ucsb.edu, accessed 25 September 2024.

The quote on p. 92 is by Albert Schweitzer, interview published under the title *God's Own Man*, United Nations World magazine, New York, 1952.

The quote on p. 140 is from *Hours in a Library* by Virginia Woolf, Harcourt, 1957. Reprinted with permission of publisher.

The quote on p. 175 is from *The Innocents Abroad, or The New Pilgrim's Progress* by Mark Twain, American Publishing Company, 1869.

The quote on p. 205 is from *Sand and Foam: A Book of Aphorisms* by Kahlil Gibran, Alfred A. Knopf, Random House, copyright © 1926 by Kahlil Gibran, copyright renewed 1954 by Administrators C.T.A. of Kahlil Gibran Estate and Mary G. Gibran. Reprinted with permission of publisher.

The quote on p. 248 is by Albert Szent-Györgyi, speech at the Nobel Banquet in Stockholm, 10 December 1937, copyright © The Nobel Foundation. Reprinted with permission of The Nobel Foundation.

Every effort has been made to contact the copyright holders; in the event of an inadvertent omission or error, please notify the publisher.